TWO GREAT MEN

TWO GREAT MEN

WHO CHANGED OUR WORLD FOREVER

*To Joanne
with much love*

Jenny

Jenny Hovsepian

Mal 9:20

Unless otherwise stated, Scripture taken from KJV or author's paraphrase.

This is a work of fiction. Names, characters, places and incidents either are the product of the author's imagination or are used fictitiously, and any resemblance to any actual persons, living or dead, events, or locales is entirely coincidental.

To order additional copies of this book, contact:
Xlibris
1-888-795-4274
www.Xlibris.com
Orders@Xlibris.com
754514

CONTENTS

Dedicated

to the twenty Christian Egyptian men, and to Matthew Ayairga,
who were tortured by ISIS
and then were beheaded as they were singing to Jesus
(February 15, 2015, Sirte, Libya)

Hani Abdel Messihah, Yousef Shoukry, Towadros Yousef, Maged Suleiman
Shahata, Milad Makeen Zaky, Abanub Ayad Atiya, Kirollos Shokry Fawzy,
Bishoy Astafanus Kamel, Malak Ibrahim Sinweet, Girgis Milad Sinweet,
Mina Fayez Aziz, Samuel Alham Wilson, Samuel Astafanus Kamel, Ezat
Bishri Naseef, Loqa Nagaty Anees, Munir Gaber Adly, Esam Badir Samir,
Malak Farag Abram, Sameh Salah, Girgis Sameer Maglee, and Matthew
Ayairga from Chad. Matthew, watching the bravery of the twenty
Egyptians, professed Jesus moments before his beheading, saying, "Their
God is my God."

Preface

This book is about two great men without whom the great religions of Islam and Christianity would never have come into being. This book compares the story of their birth, life goals, attitudes, teachings, and the way each chose to accomplish his goals. It also details the end of their lives and the legacy they left to their followers and to the world.

The sources of information for this book are predominantly the sacred writings of each religion.

For Muhammad, the author of the religion of Islam, the two sources cited are the Qur'an, the holy book of Islam, and the Hadith, the sayings of the prophet Muhammad. When relevant, recognized Islamic theologians and historians are quoted for explanation and development of ideas.

For Jesus, the Author of Christianity, we relied on the books of the New Testament as records of His life and teachings, as well as additional references from the Old Testament, the Jewish Scriptures, for prophetic witness.

Chapter One

Muhammad's Early Life

Before the time of Muhammad, Arabia, now Saudi Arabia and neighboring countries, consisted of pagan tribes who worshiped idols. The Kaaba, a granite cubic building in Mecca, was the center of their worship of 360 gods. People came there from the surrounding areas to worship their own god. The worship of Allah, however, was known before the beginning of Islam. We know this because Muhammad would later say about the pagans who refused to believe him that they swore by Allah.

> And they swear their strongest oaths by Allah that if a
> sign come to them they would certainly believe in it.
> (Qur'an 6:109)

There were also Jewish and Christian tribes living in Arabia, especially to the north and northeast, and it appears that the knowledge of Allah as one supreme being arose out of contact with them. Today, Arabic-speaking Christians still use the word "Allah," which means "Al Elah (the God)" in reference to Yahweh (Jehovah), the God of the Bible.

Before Muhammad, all religions in Arabia, including paganism, enjoyed the freedom to worship in their own way. Women also enjoyed many freedoms. They ran their own businesses and were free to choose their husbands.

The Birth of Muhammad

In the year AD 569, in the Arabian Peninsula in Mecca, a young couple of the Quraysh tribe by the name of Abdullah (slave of Allah) and Amina were married. Soon after they were married, the newlywed Amina became pregnant. Could they predict that they would have a son? A great son? Sadly, young Abdullah died before he would ever find out; and the young widow, Amina, was the only parent to welcome their son, Muhammad, in the year AD 570. Did Amina know that her baby, Muhammad, would impact the world and forever change history?

The Early Life of Muhammad

Amina decided to send the baby away to be nursed by Halima, a woman from one of the local nomadic tribes of the Hawazin. She was to breastfeed Muhammad along with her own son for two years and then return him to his mother. But after the two years, Muhammad's mother asked Halima to keep him longer because she did not think the climate of Mecca was good for him.

One day, Muhammad was playing with Halima's children close to their settlement when he suddenly had an unusual fit and went into an apparent trance. Halima and her husband were greatly troubled because it was commonly believed that such behavior was a sign of the influence of an evil spirit. They tried to return him to his mother, Amina, but she talked them into keeping him a while longer.

When Muhammad was four years old, he went to live with his mother; but unfortunately, after two years, she died when he was only six years old. Orphaned by both parents, Muhammad was taken to live with his paternal grandfather, Abdul Muttalib. Abdul Muttalib had established himself as an influential leader of the Quraysh tribe in Mecca, and he took care of their holy sanctuary, the Kaaba.

Grandpa loved Muhammad very much and even favored him over his own children, letting him sleep in bed with him. But this too did not last very long because after only two years, Grandpa Abdul Muttalib also died, so Muhammad went to live with his uncle Abu Talib.

Muhammad's childhood was sad, lonely, and difficult. He suffered from depression and a possible neurological problem that stayed with him all his life. His uncle was not well-off, and to help, Muhammad was sent to tend sheep.

Muhammad as a Young Man

As Muhammad grew older, his uncle took him on trading caravans across Arabia and north to Syria. During his caravan trips, Muhammad saw idols being made and sold and transported to the Kaaba, where people bowed down to them. He must have reasoned, "How could one bow to an idol he made himself?" He vowed that when he grew up, he would never bow to idols even though his tribe, the Quraysh, benefited financially from the trade of idols. Kaaba, being the center of worship, brought in much business to Mecca and the Quraysh. Today, the Kaaba and the black stone still exist in Mecca, where Muslims go for their annual pilgrimage. The hajj is one of the five pillars (practices) of Islam.

Muhammad and Khadija

When Muhammad grew up, he made his living by going on caravans. He was hardworking and honest. He acquired the name Al-Amin (the faithful one) because of his integrity. One day, he was hired by a man named Maysara, who led the caravans of a very wealthy lady named Khadija. She was a very successful Quraysh businesswoman whose caravans were the largest. Upon their return from the caravan, Khadija asked Maysara about Muhammad, and she got a very good report about his character and ability. Khadija was forty years old and had been married and divorced twice but was now single, having turned down many suitors. Muhammad was twenty-five years old and poor, but Khadija wanted to marry him! The Quraysh lady had fallen in love with Muhammad!

Muhammad's Marriage to Khadija

Khadija sent her trusted maid, Nafissa, to propose marriage to Muhammad on her behalf, which he readily accepted. This marriage transformed his life from poverty to great wealth. It is interesting to note that the Qur'an does not mention Muhammad's marriage to Khadija by name nor to any of his other wives. However, it refers to his marriage to Khadija in a verse that says,

And we found you poor and made you rich. (Sura 93:8)

While married to Khadija, Muhammad did not marry other wives. He did not want to risk the wealth and prestige he enjoyed as the husband of a prominent businesswoman. Khadija was also compassionate and gave him the attention and love he had missed in a mother. It could also be that because Khadija was Ebionite, their marriage was an Ebionite marriage, which did not allow polygamy. Probably for these reasons, Muhammad chose not to marry another during her lifetime.

Khadija's cousin Waraqa Ibn Naufal was an Ebionite priest who helped perform the wedding. The Ebionites were a Christian cult that believed in the sacred writings of Moses and the virgin birth of Jesus Christ but denied the crucifixion. The priest Waraqa Ibn Naufal, Khadija's cousin, was knowledgeable of Christianity; and it is said that he studied the

Bible under Jews and Christians and read an Arabic translation of the New Testament.[1]

Waraqa took great interest in Muhammad, teaching him a lot of the religion of the Ebionites.

Muhammad's marriage to Khadija lasted twenty years. They had four daughters and two sons. The sons died in infancy. The daughters survived; but only one daughter, Fatima, outlived her father by six months. Muhammad also adopted a slave boy by the name of Zaid, who was given to him by his first wife, Khadija.

Muhammad and the Black Stone

The Kaaba had been damaged by a flood, and the people were afraid to fix it for fear of the gods. Al Walid ibn al-Mughira volunteered for the task. He picked up an axe with which he demolished a part of the building, pleading with Allah continuously to recognize that the act was not sacrilegious, but necessary to improve the shrine. When people saw he was unharmed, they joined in till the work was completed.

Now when they needed to replace the special black cornerstone (which fell from heaven) on the wall of the Kaaba, the various tribes began to argue about who was to have the privilege of taking the black stone and sealing it again in the wall. When the dissension became very serious, the people agreed that the next person who came into the precincts would be chosen to have the honor of replacing the black stone.

[1.] Bukhari 4:55:605. Bukhari was a Persian scholar that compiled the most authentic traditions about Muhammad. He finished his multivolume work in AD 832. There are over seven thousand Hadith in his works, grouped into ninety-seven collections by topic. "Sahih" means authentic, and Bukhari is notable for collecting the chain of transmission in the various sayings. After the Qur'an, his work is considered the most authoritative.

Muhammad was thirty-five years old and respected among his people. By chance, he was the first person to enter through the gate. When the people saw him, they said, "This is Al-Amin (the trusted). We agree to what we have decided." Then they informed him of the affair. Muhammad took his mantle and spread it on the earth, then put the black stone on it. He then said, "Let a person from every quarter of the Quraysh come . . . and let every one of you hold a corner of the cloth." Then all of them raised it, and Muhammad put the black stone in its place with his own hand.[2]

Besides the wisdom Muhammad displayed in solving the problem of placing the black stone, he also liked to reflect and meditate, spending a lot of time at the Cave of Hira by himself. There, at the age of forty, Muhammad had his first revelation.

Muhammad's Experience at the Cave: Call to Be a Prophet

Quoting from the Hadith of Bukhari, volume 9, book 87, Hadith 111
Narrated by Aisha[3]
The commencement of the Divine Inspiration to Allah's Apostle was in the form of good righteous dreams in his sleep . . . He used to go in seclusion to the cave of Hira where he used to worship Allah . . . He used to take with him food for the journey and then come back to his wife Khadija to take his food again for another period to stay, till suddenly the Truth descended upon him while he was in the cave of Hira. The angel came to him in it and asked him to read. The Prophet replied, "I do not know how to read." The Prophet added, "The angel caught me forcefully and pressed me so hard that I could not bear it anymore. He then released me and again asked me to read, and I replied, "I do not know how to read." Whereupon he caught me again and pressed me a second time till I could not bear it anymore. He then

---

2. Ibn Sa'd Kitab al-Tabaqat al-Kabir, vol. 1, p. 166.
3. Muhammad's favorite wife, whom he later married at age nine.

released me and asked me again to read, but I replied, "I do not know how to read (or what shall I read?)." Thereupon he caught me for the third time and pressed me and then released me and said:

"Read in the name of your Lord, Who has created man from a clot . . . who taught man what he knew not." (Qur'an 96:1–5)

Then Allah's Apostle returned with the Inspiration, his neck muscles twitching with terror till he entered upon his wife Khadija and said, "Cover me! Cover me!" They covered him till his fear was over and then he said, "O Khadija, what is wrong with me?" Then he told her everything that had happened and said, "I fear that something may happen to me" (meaning that he would die). Khadija said, "Never, Allah will never disgrace you, but have the glad tidings . . ."

Khadija then accompanied Muhammad to her cousin Waraqa Bin Naufal . . . who during the Pre-Islamic Period had become a Christian . . . (He would copy from the Gospel in the Hebrew language.) Khadija said to Waraqa, "Listen to the story of your nephew, O my cousin!" Waraqa asked, "O my nephew what have you seen?" God's Apostle described what he had seen. Waraqa said, "This was the one who keeps the secrets, whom Allah sent to Moses (the angel Gabriel) . . . and if I should remain alive till the day when you will be turned out then I would support you strongly." (He was referring to the day when his people would kick him out.) But after a few days Waraqa died and the divine Inspiration was also stopped for a while and the prophet became so sad as we have heard that he intended several times to throw himself from the tops of high mountains and every time he went up the top of a mountain in order to throw himself down, Gabriel would appear before him and say, "O Muhammad! You are indeed Allah's apostle in truth." Whereupon his heart would become quiet and would return home.

Muhammad's suicidal intentions were repeated several times; but again, he was comforted by his wife, Khadija. Eventually, he started telling his contemporaries about his call to be a prophet.

The Challenge

Muhammad's contemporaries did not believe in him. They ridiculed him, challenging him to perform a miracle so they could believe his claim to be a prophet. Muhammad's answer came through these Qur'an verses:

> And they say we will by no means believe in thee till thou cause a spring to gush from the earth . . . or have a garden of palms . . . or a house of gold. Or thou ascend to heaven . . . bring down to us a book we can read . . . Say Glory to my Lord am I ought but a mortal messenger? (Qur'an 17:90–93)

The majority of the people in Mecca did not believe Muhammad's message. They mocked and persecuted him and his followers, saying,

> O thou to whom the Reminder is revealed, (Allah reveals) thou art indeed mad. (Qur'an 15:6)

Other verses called him "bewitched," "forger," and "possessed poet." Because Muhammad was unable to perform any miracle, the people made fun of him and rejected him.

This rejection, however, became very serious when Muhammad denounced idol worship in Mecca and started his new religion, Islam, stating that there was no God but Allah. Denouncing idol worship would mean serious financial loss to the Meccans, who benefited greatly when pilgrims came to their city to perform their yearly pilgrimage. This angered the Meccans and especially the Quraysh tribe, who benefited the most from the idol trade and the pilgrims' visits. In addition, Muhammad claimed that all those who had not accepted Islam before their death were now suffering in hell. Arab society revered their ancestors, who had established and stood for virtuous behavior. So to hear someone say they were in hell was very grievous indeed and caused ill feeling to escalate. Muhammad had also attracted a few young converts, who left their clans and families to follow him. This generated further animosity and hatred from their families toward him.[4]

Rejection, Ridicule, and Hatred

Because Muhammad was rejected, ridiculed, and hated by his own people, he was not able to declare himself a prophet and start an Islamic state. To escape assassination, Muhammad fled Mecca, taking with him some of his followers. Muhammad and his company migrated about 210 miles north to Al-Medina, which was then called Yathrib. He was fifty-two years old. His wife, Khadija, had already died at the age of sixty-five. This migration, known as the Hijra, occurred in the year AD 622, and marks the beginning of the Islamic calendar. The year 2017 corresponds to the Islamic year 1395 H. Muslim countries go by the Hijri calendar.

The people of Al-Medina welcomed Muhammad. But we cannot say that he and his followers lived happily ever after because Muhammad never forgot the rejection of his people. Sadly, this led to many years of fighting and bloodshed. In chapter 3, we will continue the story of Muhammad's revenge toward the Meccans. In the next chapter, we will begin the story of the Other Great Man: Jesus.

[4.] The history of al-Tabari, a Persian scholar, historian, and commentator who explains Muhammad's sayings. He died in AD 923. (http://kalamullah.com/tabari.html)

Chapter Two

Jesus' Early Life

The Birth of Jesus

Less than eight hundred miles from Mecca, where Muhammad was born, the story of our Other Great Man took place. Fourteen hundred years before Muhammad's birth, a virgin girl called Mary lived in the city of Nazareth. Nazareth was part of the Roman Empire at that time and is now in northern Israel. She was engaged to be married to a man named Joseph, a descendant of King David. The angel Gabriel was sent by God to Mary. He greeted her by saying, "Hail, favored one! The Lord is with you." Mary was afraid and wondered what kind of salutation that was. The angel said to her, "Be not afraid, Mary, for you have found favor with God. You will conceive in your womb and bear a Son, and you shall name Him Jesus. He will be great and will be called the Son of the Most High, and He will reign over the house of Jacob forever and His kingdom will have no end." Mary answered, "How can this be since I am a virgin?" The angel said to her, "The Holy Spirit will come upon you and the power of the Most High will overshadow you; and for that reason the Holy offspring shall be called 'the Son of God.'" Mary answered, "Behold, I am the bond slave of the Lord. Be it done to me according to your word" (Luke 1:26–38).

Joseph: Mary's Husband

Mary's husband was a good man and wanted to divorce her quietly when she appeared to be pregnant because they had not yet come together.[5] But the angel of the Lord appeared to him in a dream and said, "Joseph, do not be afraid to take Mary for your wife, for that which has been conceived of her is of the Holy Spirit. And she will bear a Son and you shall call His name Jesus, for it is He who will save His people from their sins." So Joseph took Mary for his wife but kept her a virgin until she gave birth to her Son, and he called Him Jesus (Matthew 1:18–25).

Joseph and Mary Go to Bethlehem

Before the baby was born, a decree went out from the Roman emperor, Caesar Augustus, that a census should be taken. Everyone had to register in his own city. So Joseph went with Mary to Bethlehem, their ancestral city, because he was of the house of David. While they were there, Mary gave birth to Jesus in a stable because there was no room in the city due to the census (Luke 2:1–7).

An Angel Appears to Shepherds

In the same region, there were shepherds watching over their flocks during the night. Suddenly, an angel of the Lord stood before them, and the glory of the Lord shone around them, and they were afraid. The angel said, "Do not be afraid, for behold, I bring you good news of a great joy which shall be for all the people. For today, in the city of David, a Child was born to you who is Christ the Lord." Suddenly, a multitude of the heavenly host appeared, praising God and saying, "Glory to God in the highest, and on earth peace among men." The

---

[5.] Betrothal made a couple husband and wife, but the consummation of marriage happened at a different date. This is still true in Islam.

shepherds went straight to Bethlehem and saw Mary and Joseph and Jesus wrapped in cloths, lying in a manger. And when they saw that, they started telling what they had seen (Luke 2:8–20).
The angel announced the fulfillment of God's promise by the mouth of his prophet Micah about seven hundred years before.

> But as for you, Bethlehem Ephrata, too little to be among the clans of Judah, from you One will go forth for Me to be ruler of Israel. His goings forth are from long ago, from the days of eternity. (Micah 5:2) NASB

The shepherds were the first to hear of the Child whom the prophet Isaiah prophesied about seven hundred years before.

> For a child will be born to us, a Son will be given to us; and the government will rest on His shoulders; and His name will be called Wonderful Counselor, Mighty God, Eternal Father, Prince of Peace. (Isaiah 9:6) NASB

The Child that was born would be a Man of sorrows and acquainted with grief as noted by the prophet Isaiah.

> Surely our griefs He Himself bore, and our sorrows He carried . . . He was pierced through for our transgressions, He was crushed for our iniquities, the chastening for our well-being fell upon Him, and by His scourging we are healed. (Isaiah 53:4–5) NASB

Filled with awe, the shepherds went straight to Bethlehem to see the newborn baby! As for baby Jesus, before He had done anything, someone great in power wanted Him dead. Why?

Baby Jesus Visited by Wise Men

After the birth of Jesus in Bethlehem, wise men (magi) from the east arrived in Jerusalem, asking, "Where is He who has been born King of the Jews? For we saw His star in the east and have come to worship Him." Now when King Herod heard this, he was troubled, and he called together the chief priests and scribes of the Jews and asked them where the Messiah was supposed to be born. When he was told "in Bethlehem," he called the magi and inquired of them as to when they had seen the star. Herod, the king, told the wise men the baby was to be born in Bethlehem; and he asked them to go and carefully search for the child and when they had found him, to report back to him so he too might go and "worship." After hearing the king, the wise men went on their way, and the star that they had seen in the east went on before them until it came to the house where Jesus was. They came into the house where Mary was; and when they saw the Child, they fell down and worshipped Him, offering gifts of gold, frankincense, and myrrh (Matthew 2:1–11).

Warned by a Dream

The magi did not go back to inform King Herod about the whereabouts of the Child because they were warned by a dream not to return to him. An angel of the Lord appeared to Joseph in a dream and told him to take the Child and His mother and go to Egypt because Herod was going to search for the Child to destroy Him. Joseph fled to Egypt with Mary and baby Jesus and lived there until the death of Herod (Matthew 2:12–15).

Herod Orders Children Killed

When King Herod found out that he had been tricked by the wise men, he became enraged and sent soldiers to kill all the male children two years old and below in the area of Bethlehem. Herod wanted to ensure the death of the child Jesus, but God protected Him because He had a plan for His life.

The killing of these children had been predicted by the prophet Jeremiah when he said, "A voice was heard in Ramah, weeping and great mourning, Rachel[6] weeping for her children; and she refused to be comforted because they were no more" (Matthew 2:16–18, quoting Jeremiah 31:15) NASB.

Jesus Back in Israel

After the death of Herod, Joseph was told by an angel to take Mary and Jesus and to go back to Israel because the one who wanted the child killed was dead. When Joseph heard that Herod's son was reigning over Judea, he was afraid to go there; instead, he took his family north to Nazareth (Matthew 2:19–23).

Jesus the Nazarene

Jesus grew up in Nazareth with His mother, Mary, and her husband, Joseph; therefore, He was called the Nazarene. It is interesting to mention that today, Arab Muslims refer to Christians as Nazarenes (Nosrani). The word "Nosrani" (نصراني) is used in a derogatory sense. When I was growing up in Egypt, some people would refer to an undesirable creature as "Nosrani." We did not think much of it when my sister's maid rushed to tell her that she saw a Nosrani snake in the garden (meaning it was a poisonous snake).

The Arabic letter ن has been used by the Islamic State (ISIS) to mark homes and businesses owned by Christians. The letter ن (pronounced "noon"), the twenty-fifth letter of the Arabic alphabet and the equivalent to the Roman letter N, is painted on their property before confiscation.

---

6. Stands for Jewish mothers

The ن stands for "Nosrani" or "Nazarene," a pejorative Arabic word for a Christian.

Jesus at Age Twelve

When Jesus was twelve years old, He went with his mother and Joseph to Jerusalem for the feast of Passover. On the return trip, Jesus lagged behind; and when his parents missed Him, they went back looking for Him. After three days, they found Him in the temple sitting in the midst of the teachers, both listening and asking them questions. All who heard Him were amazed at His understanding and His answers. His mother then said to Him, "Son, why have you treated us this way? Your father and I have been anxiously looking for you." Jesus said to them, "Why is it that you were looking for Me? Did you not know that I had to be in My Father's house?" (Luke 2:41–52).

Jesus from Age Twelve to Thirty

After this, we are told that He lived with Mary and Joseph in Nazareth and that He worked with Joseph as a carpenter. By the next time the Bible talks about Jesus again, He was thirty years old. Joseph had probably died by then because we do not hear about him anymore.

Jesus Begins His Ministry

Jesus was about thirty years of age when He began His ministry. Before He actively engaged in the work he had to accomplish, a few important things took place. He was baptized by John, He was tempted by the devil, He chose His disciples, and then He performed His first miracle.

Jesus Baptized by John the Baptist

John the Baptist was a prophet sent by God to announce the coming of Jesus to the people of Israel. He was preaching to the people and telling them to repent and turn away from their sins. The people of Jerusalem and all of Judea and all the districts around the Jordan River were going out to him, and they were being baptized by him in the Jordan River as they confessed their sins. John was saying to them, "As for me, I baptize you with water for repentance, but He who comes after me is mightier than I, and I am not fit to remove His sandals; He will baptize you with the Holy Spirit and fire." Then Jesus came to be baptized by John. But John tried to prevent Him, saying, "I have need to be baptized by You, and You come to Me?" Jesus answered, "Permit it at this time, for in this way it is fitting for us to fulfill all righteousness." After being baptized by John, Jesus went out immediately from the water. The heavens were opened, and He saw the Spirit of God descending as a dove and coming upon Him. Then a voice out of heaven said, "This is my beloved Son, in Whom I am well pleased" (Matthew 3:1–17).

John the Baptist was preaching to the people, asking them to leave their sins behind, to repent, and to get ready for the Messiah they had been waiting for. He was saying, "Repent, for the kingdom of heaven is at hand." Being baptized by John demonstrated a recognition of one's sin, a desire for spiritual cleansing, and a commitment to follow God's law in anticipation of the Messiah's arrival. Aware that Jesus was sinless, John the Baptist tried to prevent Him from being baptized. Yet Jesus knew that it was for this reason that He had come to the world: to identify with the human race and its sinfulness in order to save humanity from sin.

Jesus Tempted by the Devil

We are told that after His baptism, the Holy Spirit led Jesus to the wilderness "to be tempted by the devil." Jesus fasted forty days and forty nights, and He became hungry. The devil knew that Jesus was vulnerable at this point, so he came to Him and said, "If You are the Son of God, command that these stones become bread." Jesus answered, "It is written, Man shall not live on bread alone, but on every word that proceeds out of the mouth of God." The devil then took him to the pinnacle of the temple and said to Him, "If you are the Son of God, throw Yourself down, for it is written, 'He will give His angels charge concerning You.'" Jesus said to him, "You shall not put the Lord your God to the test."

Satan wanted the Man Jesus dead because he knew that He had come to earth to free mankind and save them from his evil destructive dominion. But Jesus knew the plan His Father had for Him, and willingly, He was going to accomplish it.

The third time Satan came to tempt Jesus, he went all out, showing Him all the kingdoms of the world; and he said to Him, "All these things I will give You, if You fall down and worship me." Then Jesus said to him, "Be gone, Satan! For it is written, 'You shall worship the Lord your God, and serve Him only.'" The devil then left Him (Matthew 4:1–11).

Jesus Chooses His Disciples

John the Baptist was standing with two of his disciples when he saw Jesus walking and said, "Behold, the Lamb of God."[7] One of the two who heard John speak and subsequently followed Jesus was Andrew, Simon Peter's brother. He found his brother Simon and said to him, "We have found the Messiah." He brought his brother to Jesus. Jesus looked at him and said, "You are Simon the son of John; you shall be called Peter (rock)." The next day, Jesus found Philip and said to him, "Follow Me."

[7.] The lamb had been offered as a sacrifice for the forgiveness of sins. At the Passover feast, the blood of the lamb saved the firstborn from death (Exodus 12:1–14).

Philip found his friend Nathanael and said to him, "We have found Him of whom Moses and the prophets wrote, Jesus of Nazareth." Nathanael said to him, "Can any good thing come out of Nazareth?"[8] Philip said, "Come and see." Jesus saw Nathanael come to Him and said, "Behold an Israelite indeed in whom there is no guile." Nathanael said to Him, "How do You know Me?" Jesus answered, "Before Philip called you, when you were under the fig tree, I saw you." Nathanael answered Him, "Rabbi, You are the Son of God, You are the King of Israel." Jesus chose twelve disciples, who became close to Him. They spent a lot of time with Him, learning from Him (John 1:35–51).

Jesus at a Wedding in Cana

Jesus was about thirty years of age and had not yet declared Himself to be the Messiah. He was invited to a wedding in Cana, along with His mother and His disciples. Before the wedding party was over, the wine at the wedding ran out. Mary, the mother of Jesus, did not want the hosts to be embarrassed; so she went to Jesus and said to Him, "They have no wine." It was obvious that Mary, His mother, knew that her Son could do something about it. Jesus answered His mother, "Woman, what do I have to do with you? My hour has not yet come." "Woman," meaning "lady," was a word of respect. But when Jesus answered, "What do I have to do with you?" He was actually making a distinction between His relation to her as a human son and as the Son of God. He did not love her less, but now He must work under the direction of His heavenly Father. His answer did not deter Mary, for she directed the servants to do whatever Jesus told them to do.

Jesus said to them, "Fill the water pots with water." They filled them to the brim. He said to them, "Draw some out now and take it to the headwaiter." And they took it to him. When the headwaiter tasted the water, which had become wine, and did not know where it came from,

---

8. Nazareth was a small insignificant town.

he called the bridegroom and said to him, "Every man serves the good wine first, and when men have drunk freely, then that which is poorer; you have kept the good wine until now."

Changing water to wine was the first miracle that Jesus performed (John 2:1–11).

Chapter Three

Beginning Ministry of Muhammad in Medina

After Muhammad and the first converts to Islam were forced to leave Mecca, they fled to Medina some 210 miles north, where there were Jewish tribes as well as some Arab tribes. The Jewish tribes had been there for many centuries and were well established.[9] To please them, Muhammad commanded his followers to pray facing the destroyed Jewish temple in Jerusalem. Both Arab and Jewish tribes received Muhammad and his followers very well. The Jewish and Arab tribes of Medina had a lot in common: culture, dress, and even customs. However, when it came to religion, the Jews followed their own traditions and worshiped their God, Yahweh. The Arabs, on the other hand, had been worshiping multiple gods.

Medina before the Arrival of Muhammad

The city of Medina, earlier known as Yathrib, had originally been settled by Jewish tribes from the north, especially the Banu (sons of) Nadir and the Banu Qurayza.[10]

---

9. http://www.jewishencyclopedia.com/articles/10545-medina
10. https://en.wikipedia.org/wiki/Banu_Qurayza

The Banu Qurayza were ethnically Jewish or Arab converts to Judaism. Just like the other Jews of Medina, they claimed to be of Israelite descent and observed the commandments of Judaism but also adopted many Arab customs and intermarried with Arabs.[11] They were dubbed the priestly tribe. Ibn Ishaq, the author of the traditional Muslim biography of Muhammad, traces their genealogy to Aaron and even further to Abraham.[12]

Al-Wakidi wrote that the Banu Qurayza were people of high lineage and properties, "whereas we were but an Arab tribe who did not possess any palm trees nor vineyards; being people of only sheep and camels."[13]

Arab Tribes in Medina

Two Arab tribes, the Banu Aws and the Banu Khazraj, arrived from Yemen. At first, these tribes were friends of the Jews; but toward the end of the fifth century, they revolted and became independent.[14] Eventually, the Arab tribes, the Aws and the Khazraj, became hostile to each other. Two Jewish tribes, the Banu Nadir and the Banu Qurayza, were allied with the Aws while a third Jewish tribe, Banu Qaynuka, was allied with the Khazraj.

After coming to Medina, Muhammad was invited to mediate disputes as a result of the constant tribal skirmishes between the two Jewish and Arab alliances, the Aws and the Khazraj.[15]

[11] 11. https://wikiislam.net/wiki/The_Genocide_of_Banu_Qurayza
[12] Gillaume: The Life of Muhammad. A translation of Ibn Ishak's Sirar Rasul Allah, pp. 7–9.
[13] Al Wakidi, Muhammad and the Origins of Islam, p. 192f.
[14] Watt, Encyclopedia of Islam, Al Medina.
[15] W. Montgomery, Watt, The Cambridge History of Islam, vol. 1A, p. 49.

Arrival of Muhammad in Medina

After his arrival, Muhammad established a compact, the Constitution of Medina, which committed the Jewish and Muslim tribes to mutual cooperation.[16]

In spite of the many later disagreements about the Constitution of Medina, the Jews were bound by a general agreement and by their alliance to the two Arab tribes not to support an enemy against Muhammad.[17] Muhammad would have preferred the tribes to fight with him against the Quraysh tribe of Mecca, but at the very least, they had to agree not to ally themselves with the Quraysh.

The Jews of the Banu Qurayza called on Muhammad as arbitrator between them and another Jewish tribe called the Nadir because the blood money[18] paid for killing a man of Qurayza was only half of the blood money[19] required for killing a man of the Nadir. Muhammad judged that the Nadir and the Qurayza should be treated alike and raised the assessment of the Qurayza to the full amount of the blood money. Muhammad also delivered the following Qur'an verses:

> Devourers of forbidden things, so if they come to you judge between them or turn them away . . . and how do they make thee a judge and they have the Torah wherein is Allah's judgment? Yet they turn away after that! And these are not believers. (Qur'an 5:42–43)

---

16. The nature of this document is disputed among modern historians.
17. Watt, Encyclopedia of Islam, Kurayza, Banu.
18. Blood money is money paid to the family of the one murdered to avoid prosecution. This is still done in Yemen and other Arab countries.
19. Nomani, Sirrat al-Nab, p. 382; Guillaume, p. 363; Stillman p. 122; Ibn Kathir p. 2.

The *Ummah* (Nation)
Muhammad's Followers in Medina

In Medina, Muhammad had two groups who supported him: the Muhajirun (Immigrants), who migrated with him from Mecca, and Al-Ansar (the Helpers), who converted to Islam and joined him in Medina. Muhammad united these two groups and established the first religious Islamic *ummah* (nation). However, he did not limit this nation to a single tribe or religious affiliation. The Constitution of Medina ensured that the ummah was protected from tribal warfare. The ummah was made the highest authority. Tribes were no more to be governed by kinship or blood relations.[20] At the time of Muhammad, before the conception of the ummah, Arab communities were typically governed by kinship. In other words, the political identity of the Arabs centered around tribal affiliations and blood-relational ties.[21]

The Word *Ummah* Takes a Different Meaning

As Muhammad and the Muslims became stronger during their residence in Medina, the Arab ummah became exclusively for Muslims, excluding all other existing tribes who were living in Medina at the time. Muhammad also changed the direction of prayer. Whereas he previously had asked people to pray facing Jerusalem, he now ordered them to pray facing Mecca. Eventually, the word "ummah" became *Ummah Wahidah* (one nation), which referred only to the Muslim community.

During the beginning of Muhammad's call to Islam in Mecca and early on in Medina, Muhammad was all-inclusive, actually trying to unite many people with peaceful Qur'an verses given by Allah. Chapter (sura) titles in the Qur'an are identified either as written in Mecca or Medina.

[20.] Goitein, S.D. 1968. Studies in Islamic History and Institutions. Leide, Netherlands: E. J. Brill.
[21.] Watt, W. Montgomery, Muhammad at Medina. Oxford: Clarendon Press.

24

A close look at the Qur'an will reveal that the Meccan verses were friendly to other religions, while those revealed later in Medina were strong and often harsh toward non-Muslims. Furthermore, the final verses that refer to the ummah in the Qur'an refer to the Muslims as "the best community" and accordingly are an exclusive reference to Islam.[22]

In Qur'an 3:110,[23] which was delivered in Medina, Muhammad tells his followers, "You are the best nation (ummah) raised up for men: you enjoin good and forbid evil and you believe in Allah . . ."

Muhammad told his followers to love Muslims, but not unbelievers.

The Qur'an says that Allah loves people who believe in him and obey his prophet but has no love for infidel sinners.

> But as for those who believed and did righteous deeds, He will give them in full their rewards, and Allah does not like the wrongdoers. (Qur'an 3:57)[24]

> Surely Allah loves those who fight in His way in ranks, as if they were a solid wall. (Qur'an 61:4)

> Fight those who believe not in Allah . . . nor forbid that which Allah and his messenger have forbidden . . . (Qur'an 9:29)

---

[22] Denny, Frederick Matthewson. The meaning of "Ummah" in the Qur'an. History of religions. The University of Chicago Press, 15 (1): 34–70 10. 1086/462733.

[23] The chapters in the Qur'an are organized by length (longest to shortest) and not by chronological order. The Qur'an has 114 suras, or chapters, which are given named titles. The Shia have one additional sura.

[24] Qur'an 3:57: Allah does not love the unjust. The Qur'an specifies Christians because they deified Jesus.

Fight them, Allah will chastise them at your hands and
bring them to disgrace, and assist you against them and
relieve the hearts of a believing people. (Qur'an 9:14)

To become a member in the ummah, one had to declare his allegiance and
to take the oath that there is only one god, Allah, and that Muhammad is
his prophet. Thus, the ummah was the first Arab nation based on religion,
following Allah's command rather than Arab kinship. The Muslim
allegiance became subject to Muhammad rather than Arab tradition.
Muslims today refer to the ummah as "the whole community of Muslims
bound together by the ties of Islam regardless of clan or geographic location."

Muhammad taught his followers to pray. The first chapter (sura) of the
Qur'an is called Al-Fatiha (The Opening). Muslims are required to
recite it every time they pray, or their prayer is not valid.[25] Also, this is
recited before marriage contracts and business deals are drawn.

Muhammad's Prayer: Al-Fatiha

In the name of Allah, the Beneficent, the Merciful.

1. Praise be to Allah, the Lord of the worlds,
2. The Beneficent, the Merciful,
3. Master of the day of Requital.
4. Thee do we serve and thee do we beseech for help.
5. Guide us on the right path,
6. The path of those upon whom Thou hast bestowed favors,
7. Not those upon whom wrath is brought down, nor those who
   go astray.[26]

[25.] Muhammad's Hadith recorded by Al-Bukhari: 001.012.723 (and others).
[26.] The Holy Qur'an 1:1–7: "wrath is brought down" refers to the Jews, and the
Christians are "those who have gone astray." Commentary by Maulana
Muhammad Ali in his translation of the Qur'an.

In Medina, Muhammad had no source of income to support himself, his family, and all his followers. Muhammad knew a lot about caravans. To make a living, he now resorted to raiding caravans that were transporting goods from Mecca to Syria and back, a practice that was not uncommon at the time. Muhammad had led caravans before and knew they carried valuable goods. He also knew the routes the caravans travelled and set forth to raid and plunder them. After six unsuccessful caravan raids, the Muslims succeeded. Muhammad had been ill-treated in Mecca by his Quraysh clan, and now it was time for the revenge that would also supply his financial needs!

Nakhla (Palm Tree) Raid[27]

The Nakhla Raid was the seventh, but the first successful caravan raid against the Meccans. It took place in January of 624. Muhammad sent Abdullah ibn Jahsh in the month of Rajab[28] with twelve followers on a fact-finding operation. Muhammad gave Abdullah a letter not to be read until he had travelled for two days and then to do what he was instructed to do in the letter without putting pressure on his companions. Abdullah travelled for two days and then opened the letter, which told him to proceed to Nakhla and lie in wait for the Quraysh and observe what they were doing. Abdullah, sensing an opportunity to attack, gave his companions a choice: whoever chose martyrdom was free to join him, and whoever did not could go back. The companions all followed him.

At Nakhla, the caravan passed, carrying loads of grapes, foodstuffs, and other commodities. After much deliberation, the group did not want this rich caravan to escape. Abdullah told them if they allowed the caravan to leave safely, it would reach Mecca the following day and

---

27. *Wikipedia*, January, 18, 2016, https://en.wikipedia.org/wiki/Nakhla_raid
28. The month of Rajab was considered by Arabs a holy month in which fighting was not allowed.

would be out of their reach because they were not allowed in Mecca. On the other hand, if they killed them today, it would be in the holy month of Rajab, when killing is forbidden. They decided to attack and take the booty. In the short battle that took place, the leader of the Quraysh caravan, Amr ibn Hadrami, was killed; and two other men were taken captive. The Muslims returned to Medina, planning to give one-fifth of the booty to Muhammad. The Quraysh spread the news of the raid and the killing by the Muslims in the sacred month. When Muhammad heard it, he was furious and told his followers, "I did not instruct you to fight in the sacred month." This made his companions deflated until at last they were relieved when Muhammad revealed a new Qur'an verse regarding fighting in the sacred month:

> They ask you concerning fighting in the sacred months. Say, "Fighting therein is a great transgression but greater transgression with Allah is to prevent mankind from following the way of Allah, to disbelieve in Him . . . and Al-Fitnah (believing in other than Allah)[29] is worse than killing." (Qur'an 2:217)

This verse brought relief and justification to the Muslims, and Muhammad then accepted his share of the booty. In this verse, Muhammad acknowledged the transgression of fighting during the month in which fighting was not allowed; but by not fighting, they were allowing people to continue in their polytheism, which would be worse than killing in the sacred month.

This Qur'an verse emphasized that the ummah was subject to Allah and not to national laws or Arab traditions. This is now the pattern followed by ISIS.

A couple of months later, Muhammad also succeeded in his first battle against the Quraysh tribe.

[29.] According to Ibn Qayyim, he said most of the scholars have explained the word *fitnah* here as meaning "shirk" (believing in other than Allah).

The Battle of Badr (Full Moon)

Abu Sufyan, a Meccan noble, led some caravans to Syria. Since he was chased on the way there by Muhammad, he expected trouble on the way back. After he sent a messenger to Mecca explaining their caravan was at risk, the Qurayshi nobles organized an army to protect their goods. They outnumbered the Muslims three to one but were not particularly enthusiastic about fighting. On the way back, Abu Sufyan took the long way around to Mecca to avoid the Muslims. He sent word to the army that the caravan had returned to Mecca safely. Several clans turned back; but Abu Jahl, another Quraysh noble, urged the rest onwards to the wells of Badr. After the warfare, there he planned to enjoy feasting, wine, and minstrel singing regarding their bravery for three days. After Muhammad's forward spies captured a Qurayshi man and learned of the coming army, he held a council to discover if the Ansar would support him in an offensive action. (Previously, they had pledged only to defend him.) Muhammad conducted a forced march to Badr and occupied the wells there before the Qurayshi arrived. On the day of battle, after three Muslim champions killed their Qurayshi counterparts, the battle began with archery, then swords. It was over after only part of a day. Most of the Qurayshi fled, and some seventy were killed, and another seventy taken prisoner. A few of the ringleader prisoners were killed, but most were ransomed, some by promising to teach ten people how to read.[30]

The Battle of Badr was the first key battle (not just raid) in the early days of Islam and a turning point for Muhammad's success over those who opposed him from the Quraysh nobles of Mecca. The nobles expected an easy victory and did not strategize very well, unlike Muhammad.

Muhammad claimed that Allah had promised him victory against the Quraysh when he was still living in Mecca. He says, "Behold Allah

---

[30.] https://www.al-islam.org/the-message-ayatullah-jafar-subhani/chapter-30-battle-badr

promised me that He would definitely help me. I'm taking an oath by Allah's excellent name. 'Here will be the grave of Abu Jahl, and there will lay Utbah ibn Rabiah (his enemies).'"[31] He also mentioned fourteen different names of unbelievers he wanted dead and assigned graves for their bodies—even before engaging in the battle. Muhammad was looking forward to the defeat and death of his enemies, and his prediction came true, for he did win the Battle of Badr. The Battle of Badr marked the beginning of Muhammad's success. It was won on 17 Ramadan in the year AH 2 of the Islamic calendar (March 13, AD 624).

The Sword and Revenge

Now that he had won his first big battle and killed the chiefs, it was time for revenge! First, Muhammad ordered the corpses of the Quraysh leaders to be thrown in a dirty dry well. The following was narrated by many Arab sources:

> On the day of Badr, the prophet ordered that the corpses of twenty-four leaders of Quraysh should be thrown into one of the dirty wells of Badr. It was the habit of the prophet that whenever he conquered some people, he used to stay at the battle-field for three nights. So on the third day of the battle of Badr, he ordered that his she-camel be saddled, then he set out and his companions followed him saying among themselves, "Definitely he (i.e., the Prophet) is proceeding for some great purpose." When he halted at the edge of the well, he addressed the corpses of the Quraysh infidels by their names and their fathers' names, "O so–and-so, son of so-and-so! Would it have pleased you if you had obeyed Allah and his Apostle? We have found true what our Lord promised us. Have you too found true what our lord promised

31. Muhammad-Sahih Muslim (Hadith), sayings of Muhammad.

you?" Umar (one of his followers) said, "O Allah's apostle! You are speaking to bodies that have no souls!" Allah's apostle said, "By Him in whose hands Muhammad's soul is,[32] you do not hear what I say better than they do." Qatada (one of his followers) said, "Allah brought them back to life again to let them hear him, to reprimand them and slight them and take revenge over them and caused them to feel remorseful and regretful . . ."[33]

Muhammad was not expected to win this battle against the nobles of Quraysh, but unexpected rainfall worked to his advantage. Allah gave him this verse after the battle was won:

When thy Lord revealed to the angels: I am with you, so make firm those who believe. I will cast terror into the hearts of those who disbelieve. So smite them above the necks and smite every fingertip of them. This is because they opposed Allah and his messenger. And whoever opposes Allah and his messenger—then surely Allah is severe in punishing. (Qur'an 8:12–13)

We sometimes wonder why it is that some Muslims feel they have the right and maybe the obligation to kill those who do not believe like they do. Well, perhaps they believe that it is Allah's and Muhammad's command to cut off the necks with the sword. This is what devout fanatic Muslims are carrying out to this day. To soothe their conscience, Muhammad also gave them the following verse: "You slew them not but Allah slew them" (Qur'an 8:17). That is why devout Muslims shout, "Allahu Akbar!" (God is great!) when they kill the infidel or non-Muslim. Allah is taking moral responsibility for the action that they are committing.

[32.] That is, by God
[33.] Vol. 5, book 59, #314, Religious- texts/hadith/bukhary/059-sbt-php/ Center for Muslim-Jewish Engagement, January 7, 2016.

After his conquest of Badr, Muhammad decided to go back to Medina. On his way back, he wanted to establish a way to distribute the war booty, so Allah gave him this verse: "So know whatever you acquire in war, a fifth of it is for Allah and for his messenger . . ." (Qur'an 8:41).

Muhammad became rich by the booty, and his popularity grew—and so did his desire for more battles, more revenge, and more wealth.

The Muslim victory also signaled to the other tribes that a new power had arisen in Arabia and strengthened Muhammad's position as leader in the often fractious community in Medina.[34]

Actually, the victory of Badr proved that Muhammad was not only a powerful religious leader, but also a state leader as well as a great war general.

Operation Badr

Muslims, especially those in the Middle East, have named many of their battles Badr, referring to Muhammad's first conquest. In fact, a year before the Arab–Israeli War on October 6, 1973, Egypt's president Anwar El-Sadat met with his Supreme Council of the Armed Forces and secretly declared his intention to attack Israel. The plan to attack Israel in concert with Syria was code-named Operation Badr,[35] referring to the first victory of Muhammad, the prophet of Islam, in the Arabian Peninsula more than thirteen hundred years earlier!

Egypt's war against Israel in 1973 (Operation Badr) was successful. It is commemorated in a special Egyptian museum, the 6th of October Panorama in Cairo and Damascus.

[34.] Dr. Iftikhar-ul-Haq and Maulvi Jahangir Mahmud. O Islamiyat (endorsed by CIE, Bookland Publishers, 2008), p. 74. Pakistani educator and producer of educational books for schools, Cambridge O Level.

[35.] Several military operations in the last fifty years were named after this battle.

In spite of this victory, President Anwar-El Sadat later changed his mind about pursuing wars and tried to begin peace negotiations with Israel. He was quoted to have said "I cannot fight the United States" in reference to the US support of Israel. He must have thought of the proverb that says, "If you can't beat them, join them."

When Sadat expressed his willingness to go to the end of the world for peace, President Menachem Begin extended him an invitation to Israel. Sadat accepted and made his historic visit to Israel, becoming the first and only Arab president to go to Israel.

Sadat was very well received in Israel and was given a fabulous welcome dinner party. The following day, he was invited to address Israel's president and political dignitaries at the Knesset on November 20, 1977. In reference to peace, during his speech, Sadat said the following, "Ladies and gentlemen, there are moments in the life of nations and peoples when it is incumbent on those known for their wisdom and clarity of vision to overlook the past, with all its complexities and weighing memories, in a bold drive towards new horizons."

Former prime minister Golda Meir, to show appreciation for the Egyptian president's visit, asked Sadat, "What took you so long?" She also told the president, "I can't wait till I do my shopping in Cairo." Golda Meir gave the president a gift for his baby granddaughter, saying, "From a grandmother to a grandfather." Sadat also gave her a gift for her grandchild. They both vowed to work together toward giving their children and grandchildren a more peaceful future. Forgiveness brings forth the best in humans, including politicians!

As I watched this unfolding on TV, I could only hope and pray that this peaceful debut would cause both sides to genuinely work together at achieving lasting peace.

Both Sadat and Begin were awarded the Nobel Peace Prize in 1978. The peace treaty that was signed at Camp David on March 26, 1979, was a promising start.

Unfortunately, this peacemaking attempt cost President Sadat his life. He was assassinated by radical Muslims in Cairo, Egypt, on October 6, 1981; and the peace treaty between the Arabs and the Israelis remains long frozen. It is the opinion of the author that the Arab–Israeli conflict did not start in this century. Revenge in the Middle East is much stronger and goes wider and deeper than people in the West can begin to comprehend!

Chapter Four

Beginning Ministry of Jesus

In the previous chapter, we read that Muhammad started his ministry inviting people to join him in Islam. To fulfill his goal, he fought against the nonbelievers in Mecca. Allah told Muhammad,

> I will cast terror in the hearts of those who disbelieve. So smite above the necks and smite every finger-tip of them. (Qur'an 8:12)

Jesus also started His ministry by teaching. We read in the gospel of Matthew that after choosing His twelve disciples, Jesus was going about in all Galilee, teaching in their synagogues and proclaiming the good news of the kingdom of God. Along with His preaching, we read that Jesus was also healing every kind of disease and every kind of sickness among the people. His fame went out into all Syria. The people brought to Him epileptics, paralytics, and those possessed by demons; and He healed them (Matthew 4:23–25).

The Sermon on the Mount (Matthew 5–7)

When Jesus saw the multitude, He went up on the mountain and began teaching them a message of repentance:

Blessed are the poor in spirit, for theirs is the kingdom of heaven.

Blessed are those who mourn, for they shall be comforted.

Blessed are the gentle for they shall inherit the earth.

Blessed are those who hunger and thirst for righteousness for they shall be satisfied.

Blessed are the merciful for they shall obtain mercy.

Blessed are the pure in heart for they shall see God.

Blessed are the peacemakers, for they shall be called sons of God.

Blessed are those who have been persecuted for the sake of righteousness, for theirs is the kingdom of heaven.

Blessed are you when men cast insults at you and persecute you and say all kinds of evil against you falsely, on account of Me, rejoice and be glad, for your reward in heaven is great, for so they persecuted the prophets who were before you.

You are the light of the world, let your light shine before men in such a way, that they may see your good works, and glorify your Father who is in heaven.

Jesus and the Law

Jesus assured the Jewish people that he did not come to change God's law given to them through Moses and the prophets; rather, He came to fulfill it. In fact, He told the people, "Until heaven and earth pass away, not the smallest letter or stroke shall pass away from the Law until all is accomplished." He taught that sin encompasses your thoughts as well as your actions. For instance, malice is on one end of a continuum of which murder is the worst example. Both are sins that God will judge.

Jesus and the Law of Murder

You have heard that the ancients were told, "You shall not commit murder, but I say to you that everyone who is angry with his brother . . . will be guilty enough to go into the fiery hell." Jesus, therefore, tells Christians that they are not allowed to hold a grudge. If they are bringing a gift to God and recall that someone has a reason to be angry with them, they are to leave their gift at the altar, go reconcile with their brother, and then come back to God. If they are angry with someone, they cannot make up for it or appear before the Lord until they have reconciled with their opponent.

Jesus Teaches on Adultery

You have heard that it was said you shall not commit adultery, but I say to you that everyone who looks on a woman to lust for her has committed adultery with her in his heart. (Matthew 5:27-28)

Jesus brought the standard of righteousness to a very high level, encompassing not only external actions, but also internal thoughts and attitudes. He instructs Christians to flee temptations by saying, "If your eye or your hand stumble you, tear them off" (Matthew 18:8–9). Avoid looking at evil.

Teaching on Divorce

It was said: "Whoever divorces his wife let him give her a certificate of dismissal," but I say to you that everyone who divorces his wife, except for the cause of adultery, makes her commit adultery; and whoever marries a divorced woman, commits adultery. (Matthew 5:31–32)

Teaching on Vows

You have heard that the ancients were told, "You shall not make false vows, but shall fulfill your vows to the Lord," but I say to you make no oath at all, either by heaven, for it is the throne of God, or by the earth, nor by your head, because you cannot make one hair white or black. But let your statement be yes, yes, or no, no, and anything beyond these is of the evil. (Matthew 5:33–37)

Teaching on Nonresistance

You have heard that it was said, "An eye for an eye, and a tooth for a tooth." But I say to you, do not resist him who is evil; but whoever slaps you on your right cheek, turn to him the other also. (Matthew 5:38–42)

Jesus did not only say these words, but He also lived by them. As we continue the study of these two great men, we shall see that the message Jesus brought to the world was about total forgiveness no matter how hurtful the offense is. Jesus forgave His enemies unconditionally!

Teaching on Love

You have heard that it was said, "You shall love your neighbor, and hate your enemy." But I say to you, love your enemies, do good to them that despise you and pray for those who persecute you in order that you may be sons of your Father who is in heaven; for He causes His sun to rise on the evil and the good . . . For if you love those who love you, what reward have you? Do not even the tax-gatherers do the same? (Matthew 5:43–48)

Jesus commands us to love everyone, including our enemies—no exclusions!

Teaching on Almsgiving

Beware of practicing your righteousness before men . . . when you give alms do not let your left hand know what your right hand is doing. Your Father who sees in secret will repay you. (Matthew 6:1–4)

Teaching on Prayer

And when you pray, you are not to be like the hypocrites; for they love to stand and pray in the synagogues, and on the street corners, in order to be seen by men. Truly they have their reward in full. But when you pray, go into your inner room, shut your door and pray to your Father who is in heaven . . . and do not use meaningless repetitions as the Gentiles do, for they suppose that they will be heard for their many words. Therefore do not be like them; for your Father knows what you need before you ask Him. (Matthew 6:5–8)

Jesus Teaches His Followers How to Pray the Lord's Prayer

Our Father who art in heaven, hallowed be Thy Name.
Thy kingdom come,

Thy will be done,

On earth as it is in heaven.

Give us today our daily bread

And forgive us our debts as we also have forgiven our
debtors.

And do not lead us into temptation, but deliver us from
evil. For Thine is the kingdom, and the power, and the
glory, forever. Amen.

For if you forgive men for their transgressions; your
heavenly Father will also forgive you. But if you do not
forgive men, then your Father will not forgive your
transgressions. (Matthew 6:9–14)

A notable thing about what Jesus teaches is that of a person's relationship
with God. Jesus teaches His followers to address God as "our Father."
What a privilege it is to come before the Creator of the universe as a son
or daughter loved by the Father unconditionally! We can come before
Him in the security of a close relationship. We can ask for all our needs
and even our wants, knowing that our Father hears us.

Teaching on Fasting

And whenever you fast, do not put on a gloomy face as
the hypocrites do, for they neglect their appearance in

order to be seen fasting by men. Truly I say to you, they have their reward in full. But you, when you fast, anoint your head and wash your face so that you may not be seen fasting by men, but by your Father who sees in secret. (Matthew 6:16–18)

Teaching on Money

Do not lay up for yourselves treasures upon earth, where moth and rust destroy . . . but lay up for yourselves treasures in heaven . . . for where your treasure is, there will your heart be also . . . No one can serve two masters; for either he will hate the one and love the other, or he will hold to one and despise the other. You cannot serve God and money. (Matthew 6:19–24)

Teaching on Anxiety

Do not be anxious for your life, as to what you shall eat, or what you shall drink, nor for your body, what you shall put on. Is not life more than food and the body more than clothing? Look at the birds of the air, they do not sow nor reap yet your heavenly Father feeds them. Are you not worth much more than they? Do not be anxious then, saying, "What shall we eat or what shall we drink," for your heavenly Father knows that you need all these things. But seek first His kingdom and His righteousness and all these things shall be added to you. Therefore do not be anxious for tomorrow; for tomorrow will care for itself. Each day has enough trouble of its own. (Matthew 6:25–34)

Teaching on Judging Others

Do not judge lest you be judged. For the way you judge, you will be judged; and by your standard of measure, it will be measured to you . . . How can you say to your brother, "Let me take the speck out of your eye, (correct your fault) and behold the log (bigger fault) is in your own eye?" You hypocrite, first take the log out of your own eye, and then you will see clearly to take the speck out of your brother's eye. (Matthew 7:1–5)

Praying to Your Heavenly Father

Ask and it shall be given you; seek and you shall find; knock and it shall be opened to you. For everyone who asks receives; and he who seeks finds, and to him who knocks it shall be opened. Or what man is there among you, when his son shall ask him for a loaf, will give him a stone? Or if he shall ask him for a fish, he will not give him a snake, will he? If you then, being evil, know how to give good gifts to your children, how much more shall your Father who is in heaven give what is good to those who ask Him! (Matthew 7:7–11)

Teaching on Treating Others

However you want people to treat you, so treat them, for this is the Law and the Prophets. (Matthew 7:12)

Teaching on the Kingdom of Heaven

Enter by the narrow gate; for the gate is wide, and the way is broad that leads to destruction, and many are those who enter by it. For the gate is small and the way is narrow that leads to life, and few are those who find it. Beware of the false prophets who come to you in sheep's clothing but inwardly are ravening wolves. You will know them by their fruits. Grapes are not gathered from thorn-bushes, nor figs from thistles. Even so, every good tree bears good fruit; but the bad tree bears bad fruit. A good tree cannot produce bad fruit, nor can a bad tree produce good fruit. Every tree that does not bear good fruit is cut down and thrown into the fire. So then you will know them by their fruits. Not everyone who says to Me, "Lord, Lord," will enter the kingdom of heaven; but he who does the will of my Father who is in heaven. Many will say to Me on that day, "Lord, Lord, did we not prophesy in Your name, and in Your name cast out demons and perform miracles?" And then I will declare to them, "I never knew you; depart from Me, you who practice lawlessness." Therefore everyone who hears these words of Mine and acts upon them may be compared to a wise man who built his house upon the rock. And the rain descended and the floods came and burst against this house; yet it did not fall, for it had been founded upon the rock.

And everyone who hears these words of Mine and does not act upon them will be like a foolish man, who built his house upon the sand. And the rain descended and the floods came, and the winds blew; and burst against that house; and it fell, and great was its fall. (Matthew 7:13–27)

Response to Jesus' Sermon

The multitudes were amazed at His teaching; for He was teaching them as one having authority, and not as the scribes.[36] (Matthew 7:28)

[36.] The scribes were teachers of the law who had to rely on the authority of tradition. Jesus Christ's authority was his own. It disturbed the Pharisees that he had no credentials as an official teacher in their system. His authority was his own!

Chapter Five

Muhammad and Jesus Meet a Blind Man

At the very beginning of his ministry, the Prophet of Islam was sitting with some of the important chiefs of the Quraysh in Mecca, trying to persuade them to join him in his new religion, Islam. He knew they were opposed to him and to his religion, but they were high-ranking people, and he wanted to gain their allegiance and lead them to Islam. He figured if he could attract leaders with status, he could gain many more followers. In the midst of his struggle to convince them, a blind man showed up, calling out loud to get the attention of the Prophet. Muhammad ignored him and was annoyed by the repeated interruptions.

Allah Reprimands Muhammad

Qur'an 80 Abasa ("He Frowned")[37]

Sura 80:1–10 records the story of Muhammad and the blind man.

1. He frowned and turned away.
2. Because the blind man came to him.

[37.] Every sura in the Qur'an is given a named title.

3. And what could make thee know that he might purify himself (i.e., become Muslim).
4. Or be mindful, so the reminder profit him?
5. As for him who considers himself free from need (the rich who did not care).
6. To him thou dost attend.
7. And no blame is on thee, if he purify himself not. (Muhammad, you will not be blamed for the one who refuses Islam.)
8. And as to him who comes to thee striving hard (the blind man).
9. And he fears.
10. To him thou payest no regard.

It is said that the blind man kept calling and repeating his plea, not knowing that the Prophet was busy facing someone else until the hatred appeared on the face of the messenger for being interrupted. The Prophet said to himself that these great people will say that his followers are but the blind and the slaves, so he turned away from him and faced the people he was talking to. Then the verses of sura 80 were revealed.

Sayyid Abul A'la Maududi explains and excuses Muhammad for his action. He says,

> The reason why the holy prophet had shown disregard for him (the blind man) is indicated by the word a'ma (blind) which Allah himself has used as the cause of the holy prophet's attention. That is, the Holy Prophet, thought that even if a single man from among the people whom he was trying to bring to the right path, listened to him and was rightly guided, he could become a powerful means of strengthening Islam. On the contrary, Ibn Um Maktum, was a blind man [who because of his disability could not prove to be as useful for Islam as one of the Quraysh elders]. This is the real point which the Holy Prophet had overlooked in preaching Islam on that occasion. [To instruct

Muhammad], Allah first reproved him on his behavior and told him what really deserved to occupy his attention as preacher of the Truth and what did not. There is a man whose apparent state clearly shows that he is a seeker after truth . . . therefore he comes all the way in search for knowledge of the true faith. There is another man whose attitude clearly reflects that he has no desire for the truth; rather on the contrary, he regards himself as self-sufficient, having no desire to be guided on the right way. Between these two kinds of men one should not see whose becoming a Muslim would be of greater use for Islam and whose becoming a believer could not be of any use in propagation . . . The first kind of man, whether he is blind, lame, crippled, or an indigent mendicant, who might apparently seem incapable of rendering any useful service in the propagation of Islam, is in any case a valuable man for the preacher of the Truth. To him therefore he should attend, for the real object of his invitation is to reform the people, and the apparent state of the person shows that if he was instructed he would accept guidance . . . This you should never do . . . The teaching of Islam is not such that it should be presented solicitously before him who spurns it, nor should a man like you try to invite these arrogant people to Islam in a way as may cause them the misunderstanding that you have a selfish motive connected with them, and that your mission would succeed only if they believed, otherwise not; whereas the fact is that the Truth is as self-sufficient of them as they are of the Truth.[38]

[38.] Sayyid Abul A'la Maududi in *The Meaning of the Qur'an*. Maududi was born in 1903 in India. He founded Jamaat-e-Islami. He and his party were pioneers in politicizing Islam and generating support for an Islamic state.

We actually do not know if Muhammad learned his lesson. Throughout his life, he catered to the rich and famous. It is interesting to know that many of the important chiefs Muhammad favored over the poor blind man remained his worst enemies till the end of their lives.

Jesus and the Blind Man

Some six hundred years before the time of Muhammad, another blind man needed help. We read his story in the gospel of Mark:

> And they came to Jericho. And as He (Jesus) was going out from Jericho with His disciples, and a great multitude, a blind beggar named Bartimaeus, the son of Timaeus, was sitting by the road. And when he heard that it was Jesus the Nazarene, he began to cry out and say, "Jesus, Son of David, have mercy on me."

> And many were sternly telling him to be quiet, but he kept crying out loud all the more, "Son of David, have mercy on me." And Jesus stopped and said, "Call him here." And they called the blind man, saying to him, "Take courage; arise! He is calling for you."

> And casting aside his cloak, he jumped up, and came to Jesus. And answering him, Jesus said, "What do you want Me to do for you?" And the blind man said to Him, "Rabboni (my Lord), I want to regain my sight!" And Jesus said to him, "Go your way; your faith has made you well." And immediately, he regained his sight and began following Him on the road. (Mark 10:46–52)

Two Blind Men and Two Great Leaders

The story of Muhammad and the blind man did not have a happy ending. Ibn Um Maktoum had not gone to the Prophet seeking healing of his sight, for he knew Muhammad could not perform a miracle. He went for spiritual questions but received no answers. The blind man remained blind, those to whom he tried to preach Islam remained resistant to his message, and Allah found it necessary to reprimand Muhammad, his prophet.

Like Muhammad, Jesus also had been busy, trying to teach his disciples everything he could before he would be taken away from them. These were the people he had chosen to carry on his message, just as Muhammad had hoped to spread his message through the Quraysh nobles.

Bartimaeus had gone to Jesus seeking healing of his sight, and he received more than that. His physical eyes were opened, and so was his spiritual vision. He repeated his cry even when he was told to be quiet. But he kept calling louder and louder. This blind man did receive a response. The people who were with Jesus had to wait because Jesus stopped and said, "Call the man."

We are told the beggar threw his cloak by the roadside and ran to Jesus. Meeting Jesus was worth more to him than all that he possessed.

When Bartimaeus came to Jesus, Jesus asked him a very important question: "What do you want Me to do for you?" Bartimaeus' response demonstrated great faith! He believed that Jesus could heal him. Bartimaeus was healed physically and spiritually. His eyes now open, Jesus told the blind man to go his way. But Bartimaeus wanted to stay near the One who had healed him and saved him.

Chapter Six

Purity of Heart

Muhammad's Heart Cleansed

When Muhammad was a small child playing with his nurse-mother's siblings, a very strange thing happened to him. It was narrated in a Hadith that Jibreel (the angel Gabriel) came to the messenger of Allah when he was playing with the other boys. Jibreel took hold of him and threw him to the ground; then he opened his chest and took out his heart, from which he took a clot of blood, and said, "This was the Shaytan's (Satan's) share of you." Then he washed it in a vessel of gold that was filled with *zamzam* (holy water), and he put his heart back together and returned it to its place. The boys went running to his mother (meaning the woman who nursed him) and said, "Muhammad has been killed!" They went to him, and his color had changed. Anas, the original narrator of this story, said, "I used to see the mark of that stitching on his chest."[39]

The Qur'an refers to this story: "(O Prophet), Did We not lay open your breast? And We removed from you your burden" (94:1–2).

---

[39]. Narrated by Sahih Muslim (162)

Did Muhammad experience a change of heart? Among the nobles of Quraysh that Muhammad was sitting with when the blind man approached him was Abu Jahl.

What Happened to Abu Jahl?

Abu Jahl was one of the chief nobles from Quraysh. He never agreed with Muhammad and remained one of his worst enemies. He was later murdered because of his animosity and leadership against Muhammad, as seen in the following story. Abu Jahl means the "Father of Ignorance." He was given that name by Muhammad as a twisting of his previous title, which was Abu Hakam, or "Father of Wisdom."

Two Young Boys Avenge Muhammad

The following is narrated by Abdul Rahman ibn Auf: "I was aligned in the ranks on the day of Badr, when I looked towards my right and left, I saw two young boys of the Ansar (the Helpers), and I thought I was stronger than them. One of them surprised me saying, 'O Uncle! Do you know Abu Jahl?' I said, 'Yes, what do you want from him, my nephew?' He said, 'I have been told that he insults the Messenger of God, by He in whose Hands my life is, (by Allah) if I should see him, I will not leave his body until one of us meets his fate.' I was astounded at his speech, then the other boy surprised me by saying the same as the other had said. After some time I saw Abu Jahl walking among the people. I said to the boys, 'Look! There is the man you enquired about.' So both of them set upon him with their swords and struck him until he died. (One of the boy's hands was slain. The hand was dangling, so he used his feet to step on the dangling hand, and he forcefully removed the hand so that it wouldn't cause him a problem in killing Abu Jahl). So both of them set upon him with swords and struck him until he died and then returned to the Prophet (PBUH)[40] to tell him about it. The Prophet said, 'Which one of you killed him?' They both said 'I killed him.' The Prophet (PBUH) said, 'Have you cleansed your swords?' They said, 'NO.' He looked at their swords and said, 'Indeed you have both killed him and the spoils of the deceased will be given to Mu'adh ibn Afra and Muadh ibn Jamuh.' The two boys were Mu'adh ibn Afra and Mu'adh ibn Amr ibn Jamuh" (Sahih Muslim, Hadith 1142 [passage edited to modernize punctuation]). Does this reflect a cleansed heart?

Jesus Publicly Approved by the Father

To fulfill the righteous requirement of the Jewish law and be the sacrificial substitute for sin, Jesus had to be perfect. Only then could He qualify to take the wrath of God on Himself in our place. Repeatedly, the New Testament says that Jesus was without sin. The apostle Paul writes, "For He made Him who knew no sin *to be* sin for us, that we might become the righteousness of God in Him" (2 Corinthians 5:21, NKJV). Jesus said, "Which one of you convicts me of sin?" (John 8:46a, NKJV). In other Scriptures, Jesus is called the spotless Lamb of God. Furthermore, God showed His approval of Jesus by speaking audibly on the following three occasions:

The first time was when Jesus was baptized by John the Baptist. The Bible tells us, "After being baptized, Jesus went up immediately from the water, and behold, the heavens were opened, and he saw the Spirit of God descending as a dove, and coming upon Him (Jesus), and behold, a voice out of heaven, saying, 'This is My beloved Son, in whom I am well pleased'" (Matthew 3:16–17).

Now people were coming to John to be baptized—praising God, condemning themselves, and willingly being baptized in the Jordan for forgiveness of their sins. Both the people and John were surprised to see

---

[40.] PBUH means "Peace be upon him."

Jesus coming to John to be baptized. What association did Jesus have with repentance, forgiveness, and sins? His baptism showed his identification with mankind—a visual of his coming death, burial, and resurrection. While Jesus had not given in to temptation and had no relation to sin, He wanted to display the strongest bond with sinners. He was willing to go down in the waters of the Jordan, as He would later be willing to die on the cross.

The second time we read of God audibly voicing His pleasure with Jesus is when Jesus took with Him His three closest friends—Peter, James, and John—"up into a high mountain by themselves. And He was transfigured before them; and His face shone like the sun, and His garments became as white as light. And behold, Moses and Elijah appeared to them talking to Him. And Peter answered and said to Jesus, 'Lord, it is good for us to be here. If You wish, I will make three tabernacles here, one for You, and one for Moses and one for Elijah.' While He was still speaking, behold a bright cloud overshadowed them, and behold, a voice out of the cloud, saying, 'This is My beloved Son in whom I am well pleased; listen to Him.' And when the disciples heard this, they fell on their faces and were much afraid. And Jesus came to them and touched them and said, 'Arise and do not be afraid'" (Matthew 17:1–7).

The third time was when Jesus was nearing the time of his death on the cross. He said, "Father glorify Thy name." There came therefore a voice out of heaven: "I have both glorified it and will glorify it again." Jesus answered and said, "This voice has not come for My sake, but for your sakes" (John 12:28–30).

The heart of Jesus did not need to be cleansed. He was approved by the Father.

Chapter Seven

Muhammad and the Sword

Muhammad said, "My daily sustenance comes from the shadow of my sword" (جعل رزقي تحت ظل رمحي).[41]

The sword accomplished several things for Muhammad:

1. Because of his sword, Muhammad became feared among his enemies.
2. Because of his sword, people converted to Islam to stay alive.
3. Because of his sword, Muhammad amassed a lot of wealth from the booty.
4. Because of his sword, Muhammad enjoyed many women as wives or sex slaves.
5. Because of his sword, Muhammad's followers today do not dare to leave Islam

Offensive or Defensive Battles?

This topic is controversial. Muslims believe that the prophet Muhammad engaged in wars only to defend himself for having been forced to flee

---

[41.] Sahih Bukhari, Al Jihad wa al Seyar, Section of Weapons, p. 116.

for his life, while others point out that the battles were primarily offensive in nature because it was Muhammad who started them.

Muhammad tried to introduce his Islam to the Quraysh of Mecca. At that time, Mecca was the center of worship, and still is, for the entire region. Before Muhammad, Mecca catered to worshippers of a variety of gods, including Allah. Muhammad insisted that only Allah should be worshipped and that he was the final prophet of Allah. But they did not want to accept his new religion. And as he insisted that he was Allah's only messenger, they mocked him, rejected him, and even attempted to kill him. He fled Mecca with a very few followers but *never forgot nor forgave the offenses.* From the day he left Mecca, he planned revenge against these people and held an unrelenting desire to return to Mecca *victorious.* So his many attacks on caravans and then battles against Mecca could be considered either defensive or offensive according to one's viewpoint. Muhammad's battles were offensive in nature, but in his mind, he considered his whole effort as defensive since he was forced to escape from Mecca.

What Happened after Muhammad's Success at the Battle of Badr?

In chapter 3, we read how Muhammad's conquest at the Battle of Badr made him famous among the Arabs and recognized as a successful general. But what were the consequences of this victory?

Meccans Retaliate in the Battle of Uhud

The Battle of Uhud was started by the Meccans in retaliation for their losses at the Battle of Badr. Badr forced the Meccans to realize that Muhammad, as a successful general, was a serious threat.[42]

[42.] Mubarakpuri, The Sealed Nectar, p. 181 (online at http://www.Webcitation.org)

The Meccans raised an army of three thousand and camped north of the city, hoping for the Muslims to come out to meet them.

A scout alerted Muhammad of the Meccan army's presence. The next morning, a Muslim conference of war was convened, and Muhammad and his senior leaders suggested that it would be safer to make the Meccans come to them and fight them in Medina. Then they could take advantage of Medina's heavily fortified strongholds. Younger Muslims disagreed, saying that huddling in the strongholds of Medina would destroy Muslim prestige. Muhammad agreed and got the Muslims ready for battle.

Muhammad ordered the Muslim archers to never, under any circumstances, leave their position on the hill of Uhud unless ordered to do so by him alone. He made this order very clear by saying, "If you see us prevail and start to take spoils, do not come to assist us. And if you see us get vanquished and birds eat from our heads, do not come to assist us."[43]

Some of Muhammad's Men Defect

A group of approximately one thousand Muslim men set out from Medina and took a position on the lower slopes of the hill of Uhud. One of Muhammad's leaders, Abd-Allah ibn Ubayy (chief of Khazraj), and all his followers withdrew their support from Muhammad, left the battlefield, and went back to Medina.

Allah was not happy with them, and later, Muhammad recited the following Qur'an verses: "What you suffered on the day the two armies met, (at Uhud) was with the leave of Allah, in order that he might test the believers and the Hypocrites also. They were told: Come fight in the way of Allah, or at least drive the foe from your city. They said: Had

---

[43.] The lesson of Uhud (defeat)

we known how to fight, we should certainly have followed you. They were nearer to unbelief than to faith saying with their lips what was not in their hearts, but Allah has knowledge of all they conceal. They are the ones that say (of their slain brethren) while they themselves sit (at ease): If only they had listened to us they would not have been slain. Say: Avert death from your own selves, if ye speak the truth" (Qur'an 3:166–168).

They basically did not want to fight knowing that they were outnumbered and simply defected.

The Meccan cavalry led by Khalid ibn al-Walid attacked the remaining minority of Muslim archers who were faithful to Muhammad's orders and were still positioned on the hill. Many Muslims were killed. (Later, Khalid ibn al-Walid eventually became Muslim and joined Muhammad. He was a very good fighter, and Muhammad nicknamed him سيف الله المسلول, or the Sharp Sword of Allah.)

While the Meccans were winning, rumors circulated that Muhammad too had perished; in fact, he had only been wounded by missiles of stone, which resulted in a gash on his forehead and lip. It is reported that Muhammad's son-in-law Ali ibn Abi Talib alone remained by his side, fending off the assaults of Khalid's cavalrymen. According to Ibn Atheer, the Prophet became the object of the attack of various units of the Quraysh army from all sides. Ali fiercely defended Muhammad from every attack made upon him.[44]

Some women had accompanied the Meccan fighters for support. One of them, Hind, and her companions are said to have mutilated the Muslim corpses, cutting off their ears and noses and making the relics

---

[44.] Reasons for the battle of Uhud (http/www.ezsflech.com/islamic'ohod.asp): Ali was Muhammad's cousin and son-in-law. He eventually became the fourth khalifa (successor) after Muhammad's death. Ali's followers are known as Shia Muslims today.

into anklets. Hind is reported to have cut open the corpse of Hamza, the paternal uncle of Muhammad, taking out his liver, which she attempted to eat.[45]

The Muslims incurred many casualties, but according to Qur'an 3:121–180, the misfortunes of Uhud were largely the result of the rear guard abandoning their position in order to seek booty and also were partly a punishment and partly a test for steadfastness.[46] Firestone observes that such verses provided inspiration and hope to the Muslims, sacralizing future battles that they would experience; and rather than demoralizing the Muslims, the battle seemed to reinforce the solidarity between them.[47]

The Three Major Jewish Tribes in Medina
Tribe of Banu Qaynuqa (بنو قيفاع)

The Banu Qaynuqa was one of the three major Jewish tribes and whose ancestors dated back to the tribe of Manasseh, the son of Joseph. They had been living in Medina for generations, and when Muhammad fled Mecca, they welcomed him in Medina. They were goldsmiths and armorers and had their own little compound and a small marketplace where they traded their goods. They had strong alliances with Arab tribes and expected to be helped by them. But by the time of Muhammad's victory in the Battle of Badr, most Arab clans had converted to Islam and were no longer loyal to the Jewish tribes. Abd-Allah ibn (son of) Ubbay, chief of Khazraj, had also converted to Islam but remained friends with the Qaynuqa tribe because they had previously helped him against his Arab enemies. Abd-Allah ranked high within the Muslims and was second in power only to Muhammad himself. He was eventually able to save the Qaynuqa tribe from death.

[45.] Ibn Ishaq (1955), 380–388, cited in Peters (1994), p. 218.
[46.] Watt (1974), p. 144.
[47.] Firestone (1999), p. 132.

The Jewish tribes were not showing allegiance to Muhammad and were not converting to Islam. They had violated a treaty with him that stated they would support him in his wars. (Initially, when Muhammad came, they signed a treaty of mutual aid in war. The Jews did not want to go to war to help Muhammad promote his religion. Muhammad regarded that as not keeping their end of the bargain.) He feared that as a group with substantial independent power, they could cause him danger. There had also been little incidents of fights between Jews and Muslims in the marketplace. Now strengthened by his victory at Badr, he decided to move against them.

The prophet Muhammad had reportedly said that he feared the Banu Qaynuqa, so Allah revealed these verses to him:

> And if thou fear treachery on the part of a people, throw back to them their treaty on terms of equality. Surely Allah loves not the treacherous. (Qur'an 8:58)

Ibn Kathir says that after Muhammad gained victory in the Battle of Badr and went back to Medina, he gathered the Jews in the marketplace of Banu Qaynuqa, and the following verse was revealed:[48]

> Say to those who reject faith: Soon will ye be vanquished and gathered together to Hell—an evil bed indeed (to lie on). (Qur'an 3:12)

By now, it was obvious to Muhammad that the Jews were not going to be his allies and supporters, and he was deciding to get rid of them. Then he marched against them and besieged them for fifteen days.

The Banu Qaynuqa submitted to the orders of the apostle of Allah, Muhammad, that their property would be for the Prophet while they

---

[48.] Ibn Kathir, Muhammad Saed Abdul-Rahman (2009), Tafsir Ibn Kathir Juz', part 3.

would take their women and children with them. Then under his orders, their hands were tied behind their backs.[49]

At that time, Abd-Allah ibn Ubbay (who was second only to Muhammad himself) rose up and said the following, which was reported by the Hadith of Al-Tabari:

> "Muhammad, treat my mawali (friends who are with me) well." The prophet delayed his answer, so Abd Allah repeated, "Muhammad, treat my mawali well." The prophet turned away from him so he put his hand into the messenger's collar. The messenger of Allah said, "Let me go!"—he was so angry that they could see shadows in his face (that is his face became red), then he said, "Damn you, let me go!" He replied, "No by God, I will not let you go until you treat my mawali well! Four hundred men without armor and three hundred with coats of mail, who defended me from the Arab and non-Arab alike, and you would mow them in a single morning? By God, I do not feel safe and am afraid of what the future may have in store." So the messenger of God said, "They are yours."[50]

The tribe of the Banu Qaynuqa marched out of Medina, first to the Jewish colonies in the Wadi Al-Qura, north of Medina, and later from there to Daraa in Syria.[51] (Wadi Al-Qura was later also attacked.)

Muhammad divided the property of the Banu Qaynuqa, including their arms and tools, among his followers, taking for himself the fifth. Some members of the Jewish tribes chose to stay and convert to Islam.

[49.] Ibn Sa'd in his book *Kitab al-Tabaqat al-Kabir*

[50] , Tabari, vol. 7, *The Foundation of the Community*, p. 86.

[51.] Wensinck, A. J., "Kaynuka, Banu" in the Encyclopedia of Islam.

Banu Nadir (بنو النضير)

The Other "Lucky" Jewish Tribe of Medina

When Muhammad expelled the Jewish tribe of Banu Qaynuqa, the Banu Nadir did not get involved, viewing the conflict as another example of tribal struggle.[52]

After the Battle of Badr, one of the chiefs of the Jewish Banu Nadir, Ka'b ibn al-Ashraf, went to Quraysh (Muhammad's tribe in Mecca) to lament about Mecca's loss at Badr. Ka'b was a gifted poet, and he wrote a poetic eulogy commemorating the slain of the Quraysh notables. This poetry influenced so many that it was considered an act of treachery by Muhammad.[53] Muhammad said, "Ka'b has openly assumed enmity to us and speaks evil of us and he has gone over to the polytheists (who were at war with Muslims) and has made them gather against us for fighting."[54]

Assassination of Ka'b ibn al-Ashraf

Muhammad called upon his followers to kill Ka'b. Muhammad ibn Maslama, who was called "Knight of the Prophet," volunteered for the job. He and four others pretended to have turned against Muhammad and enticed Ka'b out of his fortress on a moonlit night and killed him in spite of his vigorous resistance.[55] The Jews were terrified at his assassination, and as the historian Ibn Ishaq put it, "there was not a Jew who did not fear for his life."

52. Stillman, Norman, 1979, The Jews of Arab Lands.
53. William Montgomery Watt. Ka'ab ibn al-Ashraf. In P. J. Bearman's Encyclopedia of Islam online.
54. Al Zurqaani, Sharh al-Muwaahib, vol. 2, pp. 10–12.
55. Ibn Hisham 919550 Al-Sira al—Nabawiyya, vol. 2, Cairo, pp. 51–57. English translation from Stillman (1979), pp. 125–126.

After the defeat of Muslims at the Battle of Uhud, the Banu Nadir challenged Muhammad as the leader of Medina. During a skirmish in which the Muslims were involved, two men were killed. Muhammad went to the Nadir and asked them to pay blood money. To this day, compensation for a murdered kin by paying money is practiced in some Muslim countries. The Nadir postponed the contribution until later that day.[56] Muhammad left immediately, accusing the Banu Nadir of plotting to assassinate him. According to his biographer, he learned this either through revelation or from Muhammad ibn Maslama, who was a companion of the Prophet and was called "Knight of the Prophet." [57]

According to other sources, the Banu Nadir invited Muhammad to their habitations for a religious debate, on the condition that he bring no more than three men with him. Muhammad accepted. On his way there, he was notified by a Banu Nadir convert to Islam of a planned assassination attempt on his life at the debate.

Conquest of Banu Nadir

Muhammad besieged the Banu Nadir. He ordered them to surrender their property and leave Medina within ten days. The tribe at first decided to comply, but certain people of Medina who were not believers of Muhammad sent a message to the Banu Nadir, saying, "Hold out and defend yourselves; we shall not surrender you to Muhammad. If you are attacked, we shall fight with you and if you are sent away we shall go with you."[58] The Nadir were forced to surrender after a fourteen-day siege when the promised help did not come, and Muhammad ordered the burning and felling of their palm trees. Under the conditions of surrender, the Banu Nadir could only take with them what they

---

[56.] Watt (1956), pp. 211–212.

[57.] Al Halabi, Nur al-Din Sirat-i-Hallabiya, vol. 2, part 10, translated by Muhammad Aslam Qasmi.

[58.] The earliest biography of Muhammad by Ibn Ishaq

could carry on camels, with the exception of their weapons, which were not allowed.[59]

The Banu Nadir left on six hundred camels, parading through Medina to the music of pipes and tambourines. Al-Waqidi describes their impressive farewell: "Their women were decked out in litters wearing silk, brocade, velvet, and fine red and green silk. People lined up to gape at them."[60]

Most of Banu Nadir found refuge among the Jews of Khaybar, while others immigrated to Syria.

Muhammad divided their land between his companions who had emigrated with him from Mecca. Until then, the emigrants had to rely upon caravan plunders and the sympathizers of Medina for assistance. Muhammad reserved a share of the sizable land for himself, which also made him financially independent.[61]

After the Banu Nadir were banished from Medina, Muhammad recited a new Qur'an sura about the incident. It is Qur'an 59 and is called "The Banishment."

This Qur'an chapter deals explicitly with the expulsion of the Banu Nadir from their homeland in Medina. According to the Qur'an, Allah divided this chapter into three sections.

1. The exiled Jews (59:1–10)

> He it is who caused those who disbelieved (the people of the book, the Jews) to go forth from their homes at

---

[59.] Vacca V. Nadir, Banu "I," Encyclopedia of Islam Online.
[60.] Al-Waqidi (1966), Marsden Jones, ed. Kitab al—Maghaghazi, London, pp. 363–375. English translation from Stillman (1979), p. 136.
[61.] Stillman (1979), p. 14.

the first banishment. You deemed not that they would go forth while they thought that their fortresses would defend them against Allah. But Allah came to them from a place they expected not and cast terror into their hearts—they demolished their own homes with their own hands and the hands of the believers . . . and had it not been that Allah had decreed for them the exile, He would certainly have chastised them in this world; and for them in the Hereafter is the chastisement of fire. That is because they were opposed to Allah and his messenger . . . whatever palm tree you cut or leave standing it is by Allah's permission, that he may abase the transgressors . . . whatever Allah restored to his messenger from the people it is for Allah and his messenger and whatever the messenger gives you accept it, and whatever he forbids you abstain from . . . and Allah is severe in punishment. (Qur'an 59:2–4)

2. The hypocrites (59:11–17)

They say to their brethren who disbelieve from among the people of the book (Jews): If you are expelled we will go with you and if you are fought against we will certainly help you . . . and Allah bears witness that they are liars . . . if they are expelled they will not go with them . . . and if they are fought against they will not help them . . . so the end of both of them is that they are both in the Fire to abide therein and that is the end of the wrong-doer. (59:11–17)

3. An exhortation (59:18–24)

And be not like those who forget Allah, so he makes them forget their own souls. These are the transgressors. (59:19)

Submission of the Banu Nadir to the Muslim Troops—14th century painting.

Massacre of Banu Qurayza[62]

When the Prophet returned from the Battle of Al Khandaq, or the Battle of the Trench, and laid down his arms and took a bath, Gabriel came and said to him, "You have laid down your arms? By Allah, we angels have not laid them down yet. So set out for them." The Prophet said, "Where to go?" Gabriel said, "Toward this side," pointing toward Banu Qurayza. So the Prophet went out toward them.

The Banu Qurayza retreated into their stronghold and endured for twenty-five days. Then they surrendered to Muhammad's judgment. The Aws, the Arab tribe who had been their allies, asked Muhammad to treat them with leniency as he had treated the Qaynuqa for the sake of Abd-Allah ibn Ubbay. Muhammad then suggested to bring an arbitrator chosen from the Aws, to which they all agreed. Muhammad appointed Sa'ad ibn Muath to decide the fate of the Jewish tribe. Sa'ad had been one of the emissaries to the Qurayza but now was dying from a wound he had received from the Battle of the Trench, which he was fighting for Muhammad. When Sa'ad arrived, his tribe, the Aws, pleaded for leniency toward the Qurayza and, on his request, decided that they would abide by his decision.

Sa'ad dismissed the pleas for leniency because being close to death and concerned with his afterlife, he put what he considered his duty to Allah

---

62. Sahih Bukhari, vol. 5, book 59, number 443, narrated Aisha (Muhammad's favorite wife).

64

and the Muslim community ahead of the consideration for leniency. He pronounced that the men should be killed, the property divided, and the women and children taken captives. Muhammad approved of the ruling, calling it "similar to God's judgment." Other sources said that Muhammad did not want to show leniency as it would show weakness on his part, while others thought Muhammad had already made his decision to get rid of the tribe of Banu Qurayza.

Ibn Ishaq describes the killing as follows:

> The Apostle confined them in Medina . . . and went out to the market of Medina and dug trenches in it. Then he sent for them and struck off their heads in those trenches as they were being brought out to him in batches. Among them were the enemies of Allah, Huyyay ibn Akhtab and Ka'ab ibn Asad, their chiefs. There were 600–700 in all, though some put the figure as high as 800–900.

> Huyayy was brought out wearing a flowered robe in which he had made holes the size of finger-tips in every part so that it would not be taken away from him as spoil. With his hands bound to his neck with a rope, when he saw the apostle he said: "By God, I do not blame myself for opposing you, but he who forsakes God will be forsaken." Then he went to the men and said: "A book and a decree and massacre have been written against the sons of Israel." Then he sat down and his head was struck off.[63]

What did Muhammad do with the women, the boys, and the booty?

[63.] The text of Sirat Ibn Ishaq. p. 464. Ibn Ishaq was an Arab Muslim historian. He collected oral traditions that formed the basis of an important biography of the prophet Muhammad.

A Jewish boy by the name of Atiyah al-Qurayzah narrated the story of how he was spared: "I was among the captives of Banu Qurayza. They examined us and those who had begun to grow hair (pubes) were killed, and those who had not were not killed. I was among those who had not grown hair" (book 38, number 4390). The younger boys were sold as slaves.

The apostle had chosen one of their women for himself, Rayhana Bint Amr, and she remained with him till she died. The apostle had proposed to marry her, but she said, "Nay, leave me in your power, for that will be easier for me and for you." So he left her. She had shown repugnance toward Islam when she was captured and clung to Judaism.[64] In his book *Me, Muhammad, and Jesus* (direct translation from the Arabic), Mohammad Ghazoli reports, "Muhammad said to Rayhana when he captured her, 'Instead of you becoming my slave, I will release you and marry you.' She refused and said to him, 'It is more honorable for me to be one of your slaves, rather than to be a wife of a murderer like you.' Then she spat on him, because she was hoping he would order her to be executed. But Muhammad does not execute beautiful women, so he kept her as a slave. He exercised sex with her while her hands and legs were bound."[65]

Aisha, Muhammad's favorite young wife, narrated the following concerning killing captured women. She says, "No woman of Banu Qurayza was killed except one. She was with me talking and laughing extremely while the apostle of Allah, (peace be upon him) was killing her people with the swords. Suddenly a man called her name: 'Where is so and so?' I [Aisha] asked: 'What is the matter with you? She said: 'I did a new act.' The man took her and beheaded her. I will never forget

---

64. Ibn Ishaq, p. 466.
65. Ghazoli references *The Life of Muhammad* by Muhammad Hassanein Haykal, pp. 347–351.

that she was laughing extremely although she knew that she would be killed."[66]

The spoils were divided: "Then the apostle divided the property, wives, and children among the Muslims, and he made known on that day the shares of horse and men, and took out the fifth. A horseman got three shares; two for the horse and one for the rider. A man without a horse got one share. Then the apostle sent some of the captive women to Najd to be sold for horses and weapons."[67]

There are different variations on the account of why and how the tribe of Banu Qurayza was massacred; but the following Qur'an verses, which were revealed to Muhammad, help in explaining. Qur'an 33:26–27 says the following:

> And he drove down those of the people of the Book (Jews) who backed them from their fortresses (did not go to war with Muhammad) and he cast awe in their hearts; some you killed and you took captive some. And He made you heirs to their dwellings and their property, and to a land which you have not yet trodden. And Allah is ever possessor of power over all things.

> And kill them wherever you find them . . . and fight them until there is no more sedition and religion is only for Allah. (Qur'an 2:191–193)

> Fight those who believe not in Allah, nor in the last day, nor forbid that which Allah *and his messenger* have

---

[66.] Sunan Abu Dawud, book 14, number 2665, narrated by Aisha Ummul-Mu'minin (the mother of the believers). Rahman al-Mubarakpuri, Saifur (2005), The Sealed Nectar, Darussalam Publications, pp. 201–201 reports the woman was laughing because she had killed a Muslim warrior by flinging a grinding stone upon him.
[67.] Ibn Ishaq, p. 466

forbidden, nor follow the religion of truth (Islam) out
of those who have been given the Book, until they pay
the tax in acknowledgement of superiority (of Islam)
and they are in a state of subjection. (Qur'an 9:29)

Qur'an 9:29 refers to Christians who later on chose to fight Islam in order to remain Christians. They ultimately lost and became subjected to Muslims. They had three choices: (1) adopt Islam and be part of the ummah (worldwide nation of Islam), (2) pay the jizyah (a yearly tax levied on non-Muslims), or (3) be martyred. Many were killed, many converted to Islam, and many paid the jizyah.

The jizyah was discontinued in the nineteenth century by the Ottoman government. ISIS is now reinstating it wherever they have power.

Muslims, Jews, and Christians all revere and honor Abraham. Abraham was a man of peace. How did he handle conflict? We read in the Bible in the book of Genesis, chapter 13, that Abraham and Lot, his nephew, went toward the Negev and settled there. They both had a lot of flocks and herds, and the land could not sustain them both. And there was strife between the herdsmen of Abraham's flock and the herdsmen of Lot's flock. Then Abraham said to Lot, "Please let there be no strife between you and me; neither between your herdsmen and my herdsmen for we are brothers . . . please separate from me: if to the left, then I will go to the right; or if to the right, then I will go to the left."

Abraham avoided conflict and chose peace and came out a winner.

But neither Muhammad nor Jesus could walk away from conflict, for they each had a mission to accomplish.

To accomplish his mission, Muhammad used his sword.

To accomplish his mission, Jesus used his Word.

Chapter Eight

Jesus and His Word

Jesus left His home in heaven and came to the world in order to point people to God and give them eternal life. Muhammad also wanted to lead people to Allah, but to do so, he had to often coerce people by the use of his sword.

Jesus called people to follow God by using His spoken word. He demonstrated His power and care for people through the many miracles he performed. He spoke life and healing to the needy, condemnation to those who abused their power, and eternal life for those who trust in Him. He came to point us to God the Father, reveal His word, and do His will (Matthew 11:27, John 17:8). "For I have come down from heaven not to do my will, but the will of Him who sent me" (John 6:38).

Jesus Announces the Purpose of His Ministry

And Jesus returned to Galilee in the power of the Spirit; and news about him spread through all the surrounding districts . . . and He came to Nazareth where He had been brought up; and as was His custom, He entered the synagogue on the Sabbath, and stood up to read. He opened the scroll and found the place where it was written.

The Spirit of the Lord is upon Me, because He anointed Me to preach the gospel to the poor. He has sent Me to proclaim release to the captives, and recovery of sight to the blind, to set free those who are downtrodden, to proclaim the Favorable Year of the Lord . . . (Luke 4:14–21, quoting Isaiah 61:1–2)

After he had read, Jesus sat down, and everyone's eyes were fixed upon Him. And he began to say to them, "Today, this Scripture has been fulfilled in your hearing."

Jesus explains that the Holy Spirit anointed him for ministry. In the Old Testament, people were appointed to become kings, prophets, or priests by an authorized person pouring oil on their head. Jesus is the anointed Prophet, King, and Priest! In the verses that Jesus read in the synagogue, Isaiah goes beyond the normal boundaries of a prophet's ministry. The One capable of fulfilling these objects could be none other than the Messiah Himself. The Messiah's ministry is described through a series of objectives:

1. *To preach good tidings*, to announce or bring glad news. God's Son has come to the earth!
2. The Messiah *will bind up the brokenhearted*.
3. He will *proclaim liberty*. The Jews understood that Jesus was talking about the year of Jubilee, when land that had been mortgaged returned to the owner, debts were forgiven, and Israelite slaves released. This happened every fiftieth year (Leviticus 25:9–10).
4. *The opening of the prison* (captives released).
5. The Messiah *will proclaim the acceptable year of the Lord*. "The acceptable year of the Lord" was a reference to the year of Jubilee.

Jack Wellman, pastor of the Mulvane Brethren Church, writes,

The Jubilee year, contains many of the pictures of our salvation. Just as the land, the people and all the property was released, so we too have been released from a debt that we could not pay (our sins). We were once slaves to sin but now we've been released, once held captive but now set free. Christ's blood has atoned for our sins and satisfied the wrath of God that was due us. And as the land was given rest, we too have entered into His rest from all of our works for we could never save ourselves by our own works because salvation is fully the work of God.[68]

The synagogue incident was toward the beginning of Jesus' public life, and people were amazed at the gracious words that He was saying. Yet many were wondering, "Is this not the son of Joseph?" (Luke 4:22).

Miraculous Power of Jesus

Jesus had power to command healing from disease; He had authority over demons. He controlled nature and had authority even over death. In all His healings, Jesus never accepted payment or favors for the miraculous acts he performed and taught His disciples, saying: "Heal the sick, raise the dead, cleanse the lepers, cast out demons; Freely you have received, freely give" (Matthew 10:8).

Power over Disease

Jesus Heals a Paralytic by His Word

Jesus was speaking, and many people were gathered together. So there was no longer room, even near the door, and they came bringing to Him

---

[68] http://www.patheos.com/blogs/christiancrier/2014/06/01/what-is-the-meaning -of-jubilee-in-the-bible/

a paralytic carried by four men. Being unable to get to Him because of the crowd, they removed the roof above Him; and when they had dug an opening, they let down the pallet on which the paralytic was lying. And seeing their faith, Jesus said to the paralytic, "My son, your sins are forgiven."

The Scribes[69] React toward Jesus Forgiving Sins

But there were some of the scribes sitting there and reasoning in their heart, "Why does this man speak that way? He is blaspheming; who can forgive sins but God alone?" And immediately, Jesus, aware in his spirit that they were reasoning that way within themselves, said to them, "Why are you reasoning about these things in your hearts? Which is easier to say to the paralytic: 'Your sins are forgiven'; or to say, 'Arise and take up your pallet and walk?'"

(Was it so easy for Jesus to say, "Your sins are forgiven"? By no means! Jesus knew that He Himself would have to die in order for sins to be forgiven.) Which is easier to say "Your sins are forgiven," or "Get up and carry your bed and go"? But in order that they may know that the Son of Man has authority on earth to forgive sins, He said to the paralytic, "*I say to you*, rise, take up your pallet, and go home." And he rose and immediately took up the pallet and went out in the sight of all, so they were all amazed and glorified God, saying, "We have never seen anything like this" (Mark 2:1–12).

Jesus Heals a Man Born Blind

In a previous chapter, we talked about a blind man who was healed by Jesus. Jesus healed several blind men, but this story is different because the man was born blind.

---

[69]. The scribes were a group of individuals who enjoyed the authority of leadership in Israel.

Jesus and His disciples passed by a man who had been blind from birth. His disciples asked Jesus, "Who sinned, this man or his parents that he was born blind?" Jesus said, "It is neither him nor his parents, but it was in order that the works of God may be displayed in him. I must do the work of God who sent Me. As long as I am in the world, I am the light of the world." Jesus said that He was the light of the world, and now He demonstrated that before their own eyes. Jesus took some dirt from the ground and spat on it and made a little mud, which He put on the man's eyes, and told him to go wash in the pool of Siloam. The man went, washed, and came back seeing! Now the neighbors and everyone who knew him kept asking, "Is this not the blind man who sat here and begged?" Some said, "Yes, it is he, while others in disbelief said that it was probably someone who looked like him." When he was asked how he could now see, he told them that a man called Jesus made clay and anointed his eyes and told him to go wash in the pool of Siloam and that he did and immediately could see. Now this happened on the Sabbath, when the Jews were not supposed to work according to the law of Moses. The people then asked him where the one who opened his eyes was, and he said that he did not know. The people then took him to the Pharisees,[70] who asked him the same question, and the man gave the same answer. Some of the Pharisees said, "This man is not of God because he does not keep the Sabbath." Others said, "How could a man who is a sinner do such miracles?" And there was a division among them. Now they asked the man who had been blind, "What do you have to say about the man who opened your eyes?" He answered, "I say He is a prophet." The Jews still did not want to believe that he had been blind from birth, and they called his parents and asked them, "Is this your son who you say was born blind and now can see?" The parents said, "We know that this is our son and that he was born blind but by what means he can now see, we do not know. He is of age, why don't you ask him, he can speak for himself." The parents said this because

---

[70.] Religious leaders of the Jews who often insisted on following the letter of the law, but not the spirit of it

they were afraid of the religious leaders who had already agreed that if anyone confessed that Jesus was indeed the Christ, he should be put out of the synagogue.

Physical and Spiritual Sight

Now the Pharisees called the man who had been blind again and said to him, "Give God the praise. We know that this man is a sinner." He answered and said to them, "Whether he is a sinner or not, I do not know. One thing I know, that whereas I was blind, now I see." The blind man's spirit as well as his eyes were opening to see Jesus for who He really was. The story could have ended here, but they persistently asked him again, "What did he do to you?" Again, he answered, "I told you already, but you did not want to hear. Why are you asking again? Do you perhaps also want to be his disciples?" Then they reviled him and said, "You are his disciple, but we are the disciples of Moses. We know that God spoke to Moses. As for this fellow, we do not know where he is from." The man answered them, saying, "This is very interesting. You do not know where he came from, yet we know that he has opened my eyes. We know that God does not hear sinners, but if any man be a worshiper of God and does His will, He hears him. Since the world began, it has not been heard that any man opened the eyes of one who was born blind. If he were not of God, he could do nothing." They answered, "You were altogether born in sin, and do you now teach us?" They cast him out!

The Healed Man Worships Jesus

Jesus heard that they had cast him out, and when He found him, He said to him, "Do you believe in the Son of God?" The man answered and said, "Who is He, Lord, that I might believe in Him?" And Jesus said to him, "You have both seen Him, and it is He that talks with you." The man said, "Lord, I believe." And he worshipped Him (John 9:1–41)!

Power over Natural Elements

Jesus Calms the Storm

When evening had come, Jesus said to His disciples, "Let us go over to the other side." The disciples left the multitude and took Jesus along with them in the boat, and other boats went with them as well. Being exhausted, Jesus went down to the stern and fell asleep on the cushion. And there arose a fierce gale of wind, and the waves were breaking over the boat so much that the boat was already filling with water. They went down and woke Jesus up, saying, "Teacher, do you not care that we are perishing?" And being aroused, He rebuked the wind and said, "Hush, be still." And the wind died down, and it became perfectly calm. And He said to them, "Why are you so afraid? How is it that you have no faith?"

Who Is This?

The disciples became very much afraid and said to one another, "Who then is He that even the wind and the sea obey Him?" (Mark 4:35–41).

Jesus Walking on Water

Jesus had performed the miracle of feeding five thousand people[71] miraculously with five loaves and two fish. After Jesus had fed the multitude, He withdrew up the mountain to pray since He had heard of the death of John the Baptist.[72] The disciples of Jesus got into a

---

[71.] Matthew 14:15–21

[72.] John the Baptist was a prophet who came to announce the coming of Jesus. Herod (appointed king of Galilee by the Romans) ordered John's head cut off. John had reproved Herod for marrying his brother's wife, Herodia, so she became his enemy. When her daughter danced and pleased Herod during a party, he promised her a favor; after consulting her mother, she asked him to give her John's head on a platter (Mark 6:14–29).

boat to cross to the other side without Jesus. During the journey on the sea, the disciples were distressed by the wind and waves, but Jesus came to them walking on the sea. When the disciples saw him walking on the sea, they were frightened, saying, "It is a ghost," and they cried out for fear. But immediately, Jesus spoke to them, saying, "Take courage. It is I. Do not be afraid." Peter said to Him, "Lord, if it is You, command me to come to you on the water." Jesus said, "Come!" And Peter got out of the boat and walked on the water toward Jesus. But seeing the wind, he became afraid; and beginning to sink, he cried out, saying, "Lord, save me!" And immediately, Jesus stretched out His hand and took hold of him and said to him, "O you of little faith, why did you doubt?" And when they got into the boat, the wind stopped. Those who were in the boat worshipped Him, saying, "You are certainly the Son of God" (Matthew 14:22–33).

Christ walks on water (by Ivan Aivazovsky, 1888)

Power over Demons

Jesus Shows Compassion to a Desperate Father

A desperate father came to Jesus, saying, "Teacher, I brought You my son, possessed with a spirit which makes him mute; and whenever it seizes him, it dashes him to the ground and he foams at the mouth, and grinds his teeth and stiffens up . . ." And they brought the boy to Jesus. And when he saw Him, the spirit immediately threw him into a convulsion; and falling to the ground, he began rolling about and foaming at the mouth. Jesus asked the father how long this had been happening to him. The father said that it was since childhood. And it has often thrown him both into the fire and into the water to destroy him. "But, if You can do anything, take pity on us and help us!" Jesus said, "If You can! All things are possible to him who believes." The boy's father cried out, saying, "I do believe; help my unbelief." Jesus rebuked the unclean spirit, saying to it, "You deaf and dumb spirit, I command you, come out of him and do not enter him again." The evil spirit threw the boy into terrible convulsions and came out, and the boy became so much like a corpse that people thought that he was dead. But Jesus took him by the hand and raised him (Mark 9:17–27).

Jesus Orders the Evil Spirit to Be Quiet

And there was a man in the synagogue possessed by the spirit of an unclean demon, and he cried out with a loud voice, "Ha! What do we have to do with You, Jesus of Nazareth? Have you come to destroy us? I know who You are—the Holy One of God." And Jesus rebuked him, saying, "Be quiet and come out of him." And when the demon had thrown him down in their midst, he came out of him without doing him any harm. Amazement came upon them all, and they began discussing with one another, saying, "What is this message? For with authority and power He commands the unclean spirits and they come out." And the report about Him was getting out into every locality in the surrounding district (Luke 4:33–37).

The Gospels record many other miracles performed by Jesus. We will briefly mention some:

Jesus healed many lepers who had been living a lonely life away from family because of their contagious disease. He did not limit His healing power to his clan, the Jews, but whoever came to Him was not turned away. A Roman centurion (military officer who commanded one hundred men) told Jesus that his servant was ill. When Jesus offered to go heal him, the centurion said, "Lord, I am not worthy that you come to my house. Just say the word, and he will be healed." We also read of a timid woman who was suffering from hemorrhage for twelve years and said to herself, "If I only touch His garments I will be healed." Then she touched His cloak. Jesus knew a power had gone out of Him, and when He asked, "Who touched Me?" the trembling woman fell down before Him, confessing. And Jesus said, "Your faith has made you well."

Jesus was on His way to the house of a synagogue official named Jairus because his daughter was deathly ill, but the crowds were pressing on Him, and He stopped to address the woman with the hemorrhage. While He was still speaking, they came from the official's house, telling him not to trouble the teacher anymore because his daughter had already died.

Power of Jesus over Death

Hearing what was said to the official, Jesus said to him, "Do not be afraid any longer. Only believe." He allowed only Peter, James, and John to follow Him and went to the official's house. When they got there, they beheld a commotion, and people were loudly weeping and wailing. Entering in, He said to them, "Why make a commotion and weep? The child has not died but is asleep." And they began laughing at Him, but putting them all out, He took the child's father and mother along with His companions and entered the room where the child was. And taking the child by the hand, He said to her, "Talitha, Kum! (Little girl, I say to you, arise!)" And immediately, the girl got up and began to walk, and Jesus instructed them to give her something to eat (Mark 5:22–43).

Compassion of Jesus

Jesus and His disciples were going to a city called Nain. As He approached the gate of the city, a dead man was being carried out. He was the only son of his mother, and she was a widow. A sizeable crowd from the city was with her. When Jesus saw the mother, He felt compassion for her and said to her, "Do not weep." And He came up and touched the coffin, and the bearers came to a halt. And Jesus said, "Young man, I say to you, arise!"

The dead man sat up and began to speak, and Jesus gave him back to his mother. And fear gripped the people, and they glorified God, saying, "God has arisen among His people!" (Luke 7:11–17).

By His word, Jesus healed the sick, freed those possessed by demons, controlled the seas, and raised the dead.

Chapter Nine

Muhammad, the Qur'an, and Jesus

In the last chapter, we talked about some of the miracles that Jesus performed. What did Muhammad have to say about Jesus?

Who Wrote the Qur'an?

Once while talking to a bunch of college students in the Middle East, a young man asked me, "Who wrote the Bible?" Before I could answer, a very sharp and quick student answered him, saying it was written by Isa (Jesus). Looking at me, she realized I did not agree. They were all very surprised to know that Jesus did not write any part of the Bible, Old or New Testament, but that it was written by some forty men, inspired by the Holy Spirit. Then we talked about the prophet Muhammad who did not write but delivered the whole Qur'an in oral recitation.

The word "Qur'an" in Arabic (قرآن) means "recitation." Muhammad recited all the Qur'an verses, and many of his followers wrote them down; but by the time Uthman, the third khalifa (successor) of Muhammad, was in power, variances in the manuscripts were spreading among the peoples. Uthman sent for the manuscripts stored by Hifsa, Muhammad's wife. He copied and standardized them to the language of Quraysh and distributed them. He then ordered that any other fragments or copies be burned.[73]

What Did Muhammad Say about Jesus (Isa)?

Jesus is spoken of with the highest honor and dignity in the Qur'an. Muhammad recited many chapters about Jesus and about His mother, Mariam. Women alluded to in the Qur'an are all nameless, except for Mary, who was privileged to have sura 19 titled after her name, as well as other references. The whole of the Qur'an has 114 chapters (suras) in which Muhammad recited many nice things about Jesus and His mother.

Speaking about Mariam, the mother of Jesus, Muhammad says the following:

1. "And Mary the daughter of Imran, who guarded (protected) her private part, and we breathed into it from our spirit and she believed her Lord's words and His books and was of the obedient ones" (Qur'an 66:12).

وَمَرْيَمَ ٱبْنَتَ عِمْرَٰنَ ٱلَّتِىٓ أَحْصَنَتْ فَرْجَهَا فَنَفَخْنَا فِيهِ مِن رُّوحِنَا وَصَدَّقَتْ بِكَلِمَٰتِ رَبِّهَا وَكُتُبِهِۦ وَكَانَتْ مِنَ ٱلْقَٰنِتِينَ ﴿١٢﴾

Muhammad used very explicit words to describe *the virgin birth* in the above verses. Also, in Qur'an 19 (sura "Mariam"), he says that when Mariam's people confronted her for being pregnant out of wedlock, Mariam pointed to Jesus and said, "Ask Him." And when they said,

[73] Bukhari, vol. 6, Hadith 510, pp. 478–479, book 61. Narrated by Anas bin Malik.

"How can we speak to one in the cradle?" Jesus reportedly answered, "I am indeed a servant of Allah. He has given me the Book and made me a prophet" (19:29–30).

2. Mariam said, "How shall I have a son, since no mortal has touched me, neither have I been unchaste?" He said, "Even so thy Lord has said, 'It is easy to Me, and that we may appoint him *a sign unto men and a mercy from Us*. It is a thing determined'" (Qur'an 19:20–21, "Mariam").

3. The Qur'an calls Jesus *"Word of Allah and a Spirit from Him"* (كلمة الله وروح منه). The Word of God is only used in the Qur'an in reference to Jesus. And the word "Spirit from Him" was translated by Muslims saying,[74] "He is the Spirit of God because He is the giver of life in their religions, and because he used to raise the dead"[75] (Qur'an 4:171).

4. The Qur'an calls Jesus *"Worthy"* (وجيه). Qur'an 3:45 says, "Oh Mary, Allah gives Thee good news with a Word of Him whose Name is the Messiah, Jesus, son of Mary, worthy in this world and in the hereafter . . ." Muslim expositors agree that Jesus is "Worthy because of His prophecy in the world and His intercession in the after-life."[76] This is while the Qur'an attributes intercession to Allah alone. All expositors of Islam agree that the reason why Jesus was called worthy is that He is worthy in this world (during his life) because of His prophecy, and in the afterlife, it is His intercession. "Allah's is the intercession altogether . . ." (Qur'an 39:44).

5. The Qur'an calls Jesus *"sinless."* The angel told Mary, "I am the bearer of a message from my Lord: that I will give thee a Pure Boy"

[74.] Imam Al-Razi and Imam al-Baidawi

[75.] Ibid.

[76.] Al- Baidawi, p. 99

(Qur'an 19:19). Muslim expositors[77] agree that the word "pure" refers to Jesus being a sinless prophet. All prophets had sinned, and their sins were mentioned in the Qur'an, but Isa was the only sinless one. There is no Qur'an verse that tells of Jesus ever asking for forgiveness, whereas in Qur'an 47:19, Allah tells Muhammad to ask for forgiveness for himself and for the other believers.

6. The Qur'an attributes the *ability of creation* to Jesus, where He made a bird from mud and breathed life into it.[78] The same verse says that Jesus has the *ability to reveal the unknown*, for He knows what people eat and what they store in their homes.[79] To have revelation of the unknown is a power the Qur'an attributes to God alone.

7. The same verse attributes to Jesus' *miracles*, such as healing the blind and the leprous and raising the dead.

8. The Qur'an quotes Jesus as saying about the people, "I said to them: *'I said not to them except what You commanded me*—to worship Allah, my Lord and your Lord.' And I was a witness over them as long as I was among them; but when You took Me up, You were the Observer over them, and You are, over all things Witness."[80] This verse indicates that *there was an exchange of responsibility between Jesus and God.* While Jesus was on earth, He was a witness; and when He was called up to heaven, God became the witness over the people.

9. The following Qur'an verses are the source of many different interpretations by Islamic scholars and contain major differences between Muslim beliefs versus Christian beliefs:

---

[77] 71. Al Tabari, Al Razi, and Al Zamkhashari
[78] This story is not in the Bible.
[79] Qur'an 3:49 (family of Amran)
[80] Qur'an 5:117, Al-Ma-ida (the table)

And for their saying (referring to Christians), "We killed Christ Jesus the son of Mary, the Messenger of Allah, but they killed Him not, nor crucified him, but He was made to appear to them as such. And certainly those who differ therein are in doubt about it. They have no knowledge about it but only follow the doubt; and they killed Him not for certain. But Allah raised him up unto Himself and Allah is ever Mighty, Wise."[81]

The crucifixion of Jesus is denied by all Muslim sects. The majority claim that the likeness of Jesus was placed on another human being (whose looks were changed to look like Jesus and who then was crucified instead of Jesus). Some specify it was Judas who was crucified. Others claim that Jesus asked for someone to volunteer to be crucified instead of Him.

Al-Baidawi writes that Jesus told His disciples in advance that whoever volunteered would go to heaven. Ibn Kathir, whose Hadith is rated as authentic (Sahih), related that before Allah raised Him up to heaven, Jesus went to His disciples and asked for a volunteer . . . When the Jews came looking for Jesus, they found that young man and crucified him . . . Yet others disagree, saying that Allah does not use deceit.

The question then arises as to what Muslims believe really happened to Jesus. Did He die a natural death, or was He lifted up to heaven, bypassing death?

In Qur'an 19:33, Muhammad quotes Jesus as saying, "And peace on Me the day I was born, and the day I die, and the day I am raised to life."

Again, most scholars believe that Jesus did not die but ascended to heaven in His bodily form and that He will eventually come back to

---

[81] Qur'an 4:157–158. al-Nissa'a (the women)

the world at the end-times to judge the living and the dead. It is narrated that the messenger of Allah, Muhammad, said, "By the One in whose hand is my soul, soon the Son of Mariam will descend among you as a judge. He will break the cross and kill the pigs (Jews) and abolish the Jizyah (taxes levied on non-Muslims to be able to live without accepting Islam) and wealth will be abundant . . ."[82] And Abu Hurayra[83] said recite if you wish:

> And there is no one of the Jews or the Christians but must believe in Jesus son of Mary, only as a messenger of Allah and a human being . . . and Isa (Jesus) himself will be a witness against them.[84]

This means that Christians would be forced to acknowledge that Jesus is merely a human prophet, and even Jesus Himself would be against the ones who say He is God. This is the second main difference between Islam and Christianity. *Muslims do not accept that Jesus is God, and they do not believe He died on the cross.*

Many Muslims, like many Christians, do not necessarily know or understand much of their sacred books; but they do know the main differences between Islam and Christianity. In summary, Muslims believe the following:

1. Jesus was a good prophet sent by Allah.
2. Jesus was born without an earthly father of a morally chaste virgin in whom Allah breathed His Spirit. Some Muslim women in Egypt go to shrines of the virgin Mary to petition for miraculous favors.
3. Jesus came as a sign from Allah and mercy to the world.

[82.] Al Bukhari, 3129; Muslim, 220.
[83.] One of the companions of Muhammad and the most frequent narrator of Hadith per *Wikipedia*.
[84.] Qur'an 4:159

4. Jesus was not deity, but fully human since He ate, slept, and relieved Himself.
5. Jesus was not crucified.
6. Jesus will come back at the end-times to judge the living and the dead.

In Egypt, I personally heard some pious Muslims swear "by the living Messiah."

In spite of the many good verses Muhammad recited about Jesus, the Qur'an refers to Christians as the descendants of the monkeys and the pigs. Then they say, "Should I inform you [people of the Book] of those, who will have even worse recompense from Allah than the transgressors? They are those whom Allah has cursed; who have been under His wrath; some of whom were turned into apes and swine; who worshipped taghut [the devil or idols]; those are the people who are in a far worse plight and who have turned farthest away from the Right Way" (Maududi's translation, Qur'an 5:60).

Jesus lived about six hundred years before Muhammad and did not say anything about him, but according to Islamic teaching, the Bible does speak about Muhammad. This will be discussed in chapter 24, titled "Jesus in the Marketplace."

What Did Muhammad Say about Himself?

In Qur'an 33:21, Muhammad tells the people, "Certainly you have on the Messenger of Allah an excellent exemplar for him who hopes in Allah and the Latter day, and he remembers Allah much."

> Surely Allah and His angels bless the Prophet. O you who believe, call for blessings on him sand salute him with a becoming salutation. (Qur'an 33:56)

Whoever obeys the Messenger, he indeed obeys Allah. And whoever turns away, We have not sent thee as a keeper over them. (Qur'an 4:80)

Allah has sent me as an apostle so that I may demonstrate perfection of character, refinement of manners and loftiness of deportment. (Malik, Mawatta; Ahmed, Musnad; Mishket)[85]

I am a Prophet of Allah but I do not know what will be my end. (Sahih Bukhari, chapter "Al-Janaiz")

O people of Quraysh be prepared for the hereafter, I cannot save you from the punishment of Allah; O Bani Abd Manaf, I cannot save you from Allah; O Abbas, son of Abdul Mutalib, I cannot protect you either; O Fatima, daughter of Muhammad, even you I cannot save. (Sahih Bukhari and Sahih Muslim)

He used to pray, "O Allah! I am but a man. If I hurt anyone in any manner, then forgive me and do not punish me." (Musnad Ahmad ibn Hanbal, vol. 6, p. 103)

[85.] http://www.islamweb.net/en/article/136184/prophet-muhammads-manners-and-disposition

Chapter Ten

Jesus in the Bible

What Did Jesus Say about Himself?

I remember Ali (not his real name), a young college student in a Middle Eastern country. Ali loved Islam and the Prophet of Islam, but he also had read some of the Bible and had many unanswered questions regarding what the Bible said about Jesus. Ali came with a long list of questions and challenges. First, he wanted to know why if Jesus was really the Son of God, He did not say, "People, listen to Me. I am God," like the prophet Muhammad said, "I am Allah's prophet from Allah." I asked him if he had ever heard of a king who went around saying, "Look at me. I am a king!" Maybe Jesus wanted people to find out for themselves that He was who He claimed to be, both king and God through His actions and His words. However, Jesus said and did enough to demonstrate that His actions and identity were indeed supernatural.

Jesus heard what people were saying about Him, but He wanted to know what his disciples thought, so he said to them, "And who do *you* say that I am?" Simon Peter answered, "You are the Christ, the Son of the living God." And Jesus answered, "You are blessed, Simon son of Jonah, because flesh and blood did not reveal this to you, but my Father in heaven" (Matthew 16:15–17).

What Jesus Said about Himself

1. "I am the way, and the truth and the life; no one comes to the Father, but through Me" (John 14:6).
2. "I am the light of the world; whoever follows Me will not walk in darkness, but shall have the light of life" (John 8:12).
3. "I am the good Shepherd and I know My sheep and My own know Me. Even as the Father knows Me and I know the Father; and I lay down My life for the sheep" (John 10:14).
4. "I am the door of the sheep. All who came before Me are thieves and robbers, but the sheep did not hear them. I am the door, if anyone enters through Me he shall be saved and shall go in and out and have pasture. The thief comes only to steal, and kill and destroy; I came that they might have life and have it more abundantly" (John 10:7–10).
5. "I am the bread of life; he who believes in Me shall never hunger, and he who believes in Me shall never thirst" (John 6:35).
6. "I am the resurrection and the life. He who believes in me shall live even if he dies; and everyone who lives and believes in Me shall never die. Do you believe this?" (John 11:25–26).
7. "I am the First and the Last, and the living One and I was dead, and behold I am alive for evermore . . ." (Revelation 1:17–18).

Jesus also called Himself the Son of Man because He had a human body. He was a real human person. He got hungry and tired, felt a need to pray, and experienced grief and pain. But Jesus was also divine because He did not have a human father, but unlike all humans, His physical body was begotten by the Spirit of God. As God, He accepted worship and answered prayer. He could heal, walk on water, raise the dead, and forgive sins.

What the Prophets Predicted about Jesus

Many Old Testament prophets wrote specific details regarding the coming Messiah. At the end of this book is an appendix with a chart of forty-four such prophecies,[86] showing how Jesus fulfilled them all.

What Jesus Said He Came to the World to Do

1. "For the Son of Man came to seek and to save what was lost" (Luke 19:10).
2. "I came into the world to bear witness to the truth. Everyone who is of the truth hears My voice" (John 18:37b).
3. "My food is to do the will of Him who sent Me, and to accomplish His work" (John 4:34).
4. "This is the work of God; that you believe in Him whom He has sent" (John 6:29).
5. "The Son of Man did not come to be served, but to serve and to give His life a ransom for many" (Matthew 20:28).
6. "I did not come to call the righteous, but sinners" (Mark 2:17b). (No human is altogether righteous, but the one who confesses finds salvation.)
7. "Let not your heart be troubled; believe in God, believe also in Me. In My Father's house are many dwelling places . . . I go to prepare a place for you" (John 14:1–2).
8. "All that the Father gives Me shall come to Me, and the one who comes to Me I will certainly not cast out. For I have come down from heaven, not to do My own will, but the will of Him who sent Me. And this is the will of Him who sent Me, that of all that He has given Me I lose nothing, but raise it up on the last day. For this is the will of My Father that everyone who beholds the Son and

---

[86.] See "Prophecies of Jesus Fulfilled" by H. L. Willmington in the appendix for additional material.

believes in Him, may have eternal life; and I Myself will raise him up on the last day" (John 6:37–40).

9. "For just as the Father raises the dead and gives them life, even so the Son also gives life to whom He wishes. For not even the Father judges anyone, but He has given all judgment to the Son, in order that all may honor the Son, even as they honor the Father. He who does not honor the Son does not honor the Father who sent Him. Truly, truly, I say to you, he who hears My word and believes Him who sent Me, has eternal life And does not come into judgment, but has passed out of death into life. Truly, truly I say to you, an hour is coming and it is now when the dead shall hear the voice of the Son of God; and those who hear shall live. For just as the Father has life in Himself, even so He gave to the Son also to have life in Himself; and He gave Him authority to execute judgment, because He is the Son of Man" (John 5:21–27).

10. "Come unto Me, all who are weary and heavy-laden, and I will give you rest. Take My yoke upon you, and learn from Me, for I am gentle and humble in heart; and you shall find rest for your souls" (Matthew 11:28–29).

11. "Truly, truly I say to you, unless one is born again, he cannot see the kingdom of God . . . unless one is born of water and the Spirit; he cannot enter into the kingdom of God. That which is born of the flesh is flesh and that which is born of the Spirit is spirit. Do not marvel that I said to you, 'You must be born again'" (John 3:3–7).

Did Jesus Himself Say He Was God?

When Jesus told the Jews, "I and the Father are One," the Jews tried to stone Him. And when Jesus asked them, "I showed you many good works, for which of them are you stoning Me?" The Jews answered Him, "For a good work we do not stone You, but for blasphemy; and because, You being a man, make Yourself out to be God" (John 10:30–33).

Philip, one of the disciples, said to Jesus, "Lord, show us the Father and it is enough for us." Jesus said to him, "He who has seen Me has seen the Father . . . and whatever you ask in My Name, I will do it" (John 14:8–14).

Jesus said to the Jews, "Your father Abraham rejoiced to see My day; and he saw it and was glad." The Jews said to Him, "You are not yet fifty years old, and have You seen Abraham?" Jesus said to them, "Truly, truly I say to you before Abraham was born, I am" (John 8:56–58). One of the most important names of God in the Old Testament was I AM, given to Moses at the burning bush (Exodus 3:14). Jesus applied this name of God, I AM, to Himself.

After Jesus rose from the dead, the disciples of Jesus were gathered together, and the door was shut because they were afraid of the Jews. Thomas was not with them at the time, and Jesus walked in through the closed doors and greeted them, saying, "Peace be with you." When the disciples told Thomas that the Lord had been there, Thomas refused to believe and said, "Unless I shall see in His hands the imprint of the nails and put my finger into the place of the nails, and put my hand into His side, I will not believe." (He was later called doubting Thomas.) Eight days later, the disciples were again gathered; and this time, Thomas was with them. Jesus came in with the doors shut, stood in their midst, and said, "Peace be with you." Then He said to Thomas, "Reach here your fingers, and see My hands, and reach here your hand and put it into My side; and be not unbelieving, but believing." Thomas answered, "My Lord and My God" (John 20:21–28).

Jesus was asked by the high priest, "Are You the Christ, the Son of the Blessed One?" And Jesus said, "I Am; and you shall see the Son of Man sitting at the right hand of power, and coming with the clouds of heaven" (Mark 14:61–62).

Jesus Commissions His Disciples

The Great Commission

Jesus had asked His disciples to go to Galilee to the mountain that He had designated, and Jesus came up and spoke to them, saying, "All authority has been given to Me in heaven and on earth. Go therefore and make disciples of all nations, baptizing them in the name of the Father and the Son, and the Holy Spirit, teaching them to observe all that I commanded you; and lo, I am with you always, even to the end of the age" (Matthew 28:18–20).

Chapter Eleven

Women in the Life of Muhammad

In chapter 1, we talked about Muhammad's first wife, Khadija, and the influence she had on his life. Fifteen years his senior, she offered him her love, her wealth, and the tenderness of the mother he had missed in his childhood. While married to her, he did not marry any other woman; and to her memory, he remained forever faithful.

After twenty happy years of marriage, Muhammad watched Khadija die, leaving him alone to raise their four daughters. That same year, Muhammad's uncle also died; and the prophet of Islam faced the saddest year of his adult life, which has been remembered as the year of sadness.

Sawda and Aisha

Whether you know little or much about the life of Muhammad, the prophet of Islam, you probably know that he was a great warrior and a successful general. But what do you know about his personal and family life? In this chapter, we will learn the story of Muhammad as the husband and lover of three of the first women he married after Khadija's death. At one time, he was married to eleven wives and had an estimated total of fifteen in his lifetime.[87] Later on, there will be references to some of his other wives. Sawda and Aisha were the next two wives who lived under his roof, and they were subsequently joined by more wives and concubines/sex slaves. Each of these women had a different story and a unique place in Muhammad's life; however, Sawda and Aisha had a special relationship with each other, unlike the other wives.

Muhammad Marries Sawda

After Khadija's death, Muhammad's followers desired to see him married; but due to his obvious grief, they did not dare approach him with the subject except for Khawla bint Hakim. She came to Muhammad one evening, suggesting that perhaps he should marry Sawda while he waited to consummate his marriage to Aisha, the daughter of his best friend, until she was old enough. Aisha was six years old at the time.

Sawda was twenty-seven years old (thirty-seven according to some accounts) when she married Muhammad, who was by then fifty, in the year AD 620. There was great surprise in Mecca that Muhammad would choose to marry a widow who was neither young nor beautiful, but Sawda was delighted to be his wife after Khadija's death. She knew that it would not be easy to follow in the footsteps of Khadija, the prominent lady of Quraysh. She also knew that soon she would have Muhammad's young wife, Aisha, join her as her rival. But she took pleasure in keeping house for him and caring for his four children, restoring to him the family life he was missing. By and by, however, Sawda had to share her husband with other younger wives; and she

---

[87.] According to Anas ibn Malik, the prophet Muhammad used to visit all eleven of his wives in one night, but he could manage this as he had the sexual prowess of thirty men. The historian Al-Tabari calculated that Muhammad married a total of fifteen women, though only ever eleven at one time, and two of these marriages were never consummated. This tally of fifteen does not includeat least four concubines (https://wikiislam.net/wiki/List_of_Muhammads_Wives_and_Concubines).

knew that they, not her, were favored by him and enjoyed more of his love, emotion, and attention. She knew he barely tolerated her as a wife, yet she loved him and would do anything to keep him as her husband. Muhammad was good and kind toward Sawda but had no romantic love to share with her. Knowing that she felt unloved as a wife, he pitied her and wanted to spare her the feeling of rejection and tried to be loving toward her, but his human heart was unable to deliver emotions he did not have for her. So the best he could do for his wife Sawda was to give her equal material provisions. He finally decided that perhaps he should divorce her and spare her heart from pain even though she had never complained. So Muhammad waited till it was her designated night[88] and kindly told her of his intent to divorce her. Sawda was struck by grief and begged the apostle of Allah to keep her in his household, promising that she would forfeit her lawful designated night to his favorite young wife, Aisha.

Muhammad accepted her plea and kept her in his household. Then Allah gave him the following verse:

> And if a woman fears ill-usage from her husband or desertion, no blame is on them if they effect a reconciliation between them. And reconciliation is better. And avarice is met with in (men's) minds. And if you do good (to others) and keep your duty, surely Allah is ever Aware of what you do. (Qur'an 4:128)[89]

Although there really was no spousal reconciliation, Sawda continued to live in Muhammad's house because she expressed her desire to be known as the Prophet's wife on the Day of Resurrection. She survived Muhammad by many years and died in Medina in the year 674. (Muhammad died in 632.)

[88.] Men with more than one wife designate a night for each of the wives, treating them equally.

[89.] Translation by Maulana Muhammad Ali

There was a special bond of appreciation between Sawda, Muhammad's oldest wife (after Khadija), and Aisha, his youngest and favorite wife. Aisha loved Sawda and always remembered how she had given her the extra night with Muhammad.[90] Unlike Muhammad's other wives, there was never rivalry between these two!

Muhammad's Marriage to Aisha

Aisha was the daughter of Abu-Bakr, Muhammad's closest friend and the first to embrace Islam outside his own family. Abu-Bakr eventually became the first khalifa (successor) after Muhammad's death.

Aisha was engaged to Muhammad when she was six years old, but they did not have sex until she was nine. Muhammad was then fifty. Aisha describes her marriage to Muhammad in the following way:[91] "The prophet of Allah came to our house with the Helpers[92] and some women. My mother came to get me while I was outside swinging on a swing. She got me down and fixed my hair and wiped my face with some water. Then she led me until I was by the door and waited until I could take a breath. Then she took me to the prophet of Allah, Peace Be upon Him, who was sitting on a bed in our house and she sat me in his lap saying to me: 'These are your relatives and may Allah bless you in them and bless them in you.' And the men and women quickly left and the prophet of Allah had me (consummated the marriage) in my house." Muhammad then took his bride to his house, where she always had a special place in the life of Muhammad and in Islam.

Aisha grew up in his house, and her personality developed under his care. He raised her from childhood to maturity. He used to bring her

---

[90.] Sahih Muslim, book 17h, 1463, and its translations by Ibn Sa'ad.

[91.] *The Wives of the Prophet*, Dr. Aisha Abdul-Rahman, professor of Higher Education, College of Al-Shariah, University of Al-Karaweyeen: Morocco, 8th edition (written in Arabic).

[92.] Those who joined Muhammad in Medina

friends to play with her. He would carry her on his shoulders to watch some Ethiopians playing with their weapons.[93] Later on, he also took her to watch his battles.

Muhammad loved Aisha and favored her over his other wives. She was intelligent, witty, and very jealous of his other women, especially the beautiful ones. Muhammad was amused by it and excused her by saying, "If she could help it, she wouldn't be jealous." However, when it came to his deceased wife, Khadija, Muhammad did not allow any criticism and sternly reprimanded Aisha when she spoke negatively about Khadija, referring to her as the "old lady." Aisha quickly apologized and learned that she should never dishonor Khadija's memory.

Muhammad's Marriage to Hifsa

Hifsa was the daughter of Umar ibn Al-Khattab, a close companion of Muhammad, who later became the second khalifa (successor) after Muhammad's death. She was eighteen years old when her husband died in the Battle of Uhud. Muhammad chose to marry the young woman, and she became the third wife in the Prophet's house.

Aisha Meets Her New Rival, Hifsa

Sawda welcomed Hifsa; however, Aisha was upset and jealous that her husband brought a rival, which he never did during his marriage to Khadija. She had been upset about Sawda sharing her husband, but soon, Sawda gave up her right to Muhammad. But now, she had to share her husband with another beautiful young woman. Soon, however, she had to deal with even more rivals as Muhammad brought new wives into the marital house. Aisha then chose to befriend Hifsa and team with her against the other wives. Hifsa was also sharp-tongued and

---

[93.] Sahih Bukhari 3/182, Alsharqiah, and Musnad Ahmad.

often made Muhammad angry. One day, as he was sitting with friends who had made a pact with him under the tree, he said to them, "None of those who made the pact with me under the tree will go to hell." Hifsa, contradicting her husband, recited a verse Muhammad had previously delivered that said:

و ان منكم الا واردها كان علي ربك حتما مقضيا (مريم 17)

> And there is none of you but shall come to it (hell). This
> is an unavoidable decree of thy Lord. (Qur'an 19:71)

Muhammad in Trouble with His Wives

Qur'an 66, "The Prohibition"

Later on, with a household of eleven wives and one husband, there arose much conflict and bickering. Sometimes a few of them would gang against him and cause him trouble. But another big trouble was caused by Hifsa and Aisha, which spread among all the wives. One day, while Hifsa had gone to visit her mother, she came back to find Maria,[94] the Coptic slave girl, with Muhammad in her own bedroom. When she became very upset, the prophet of Allah promised Hifsa that he would never again have relations with Maria on condition that she kept this incident to herself. But Hifsa told Aisha, and soon, everybody knew about the incident.[95]

[94.] Maria later gave Muhammad a son, Ibrahim, whom he loved immensely; but Ibrahim died before age two.

[95.] Al-Tabakat Al Kobra, 8/186–187 related by A'isha Abdul-Rahman in her book *The Wives of the Prophet*, p. 139.

Muhammad Abandons His Wives

Muhammad decided to abandon all his wives for a month. News spread about it, and people thought he had divorced them all. Then Allah revealed chapter 66 of the Qur'an, "The Prohibition."

> And [remember] when the Prophet confided to one of his wives a statement; and when she informed [another] of it and Allah showed it to him, he made known part of it and ignored a part. And when he informed her about it, she said, "Who told you this?" He said, "I was informed by the Knowing, the Acquainted." (Qur'an 66:3, Sahih International at Quran.com)

Allah apparently informed Muhammad that his secret was out, and he was very upset and confronted his wife. When the wife asked him who told him so, he replied it was Allah.

> If you two [wives] repent to Allah, [it is best], for your hearts have deviated. But if you cooperate against him—then indeed Allah is his protector, and Gabriel and the righteous of the believers and the angels, moreover, are [his] assistants. (Qur'an 66:4)

The two guilty wives were told in this verse that they should repent because Allah, Gabriel, the angels, etc., were Muhammad's assistants.

And when Muhammad had abandoned all his wives, Allah spoke to them through Muhammad, reciting the following:

> Perhaps his Lord, if he divorced you [all], would substitute for him wives better than you—submitting [to Allah], believing, devoutly obedient, repentant, worshipping, and traveling—[ones] previously married and virgins. (Qur'an 66:5)

The wives repented, and after a short separation, Muhammad got his wives back.

When Aisha and Hifsa caused Muhammad trouble, demanding more of the world's comforts and leading the other wives to follow suit, Allah gave the following verse:

> O prophet say to thy wives, "If you desire this world's life and its adornment, come, I will give you a provision and allow you to depart a goodly departing (divorce)." (Qur'an 33: 28)

Muhammad's household returned to normal, but the jealousy and bickering continued, and Aisha remained the favored wife.

Aisha and the Distress of the *Ifk*[96] (Slander)

Privileged to be Muhammad's favorite wife, Aisha still lived her life competing with other women for Muhammad's heart. But this was not now her biggest problem. Aisha was confronted with the accusation of committing adultery. In Arabia and all over the Middle East, this is a very serious charge for which a woman should be stoned to death. In the West, a husband or wife could secure a divorce and go on with life—not so in Arabia and especially during that period. Adultery touches a man's honor, and he is expected to deal with it not only for himself, but for the whole community. But Muhammad was no ordinary man, and this only added to his already-big problem! Aisha, the favorite jealous wife (and who in her shoes wouldn't be jealous) was accused of committing adultery! Whether a true or false accusation, it was a trying time for her as well as her husband, the Prophet of Islam.

[96.] The story of *ifk* was described by Sahih Bukhari 5:59, 42, and Sahih Muslim 37:6673 in their most reliable Hadith.

In her book *Women of the Prophet*, Aisha Abdul-Rahman tells the grievous story of Aisha and Muhammad and the reactions of Muslims in Medina at that time:

> The prophet was going on one of his battles, the invasion of Bani Mustaliq, and as usual he cast lots to determine which of his wives would accompany him. The lot fell on Aisha who happily accompanied him, and as his lucky charm, she witnessed his victory. Upon their victorious invasion, Muhammad and his soldiers headed back to Medina. Aisha was supposed to be transported on top of a camel's back in her Hawdaj.[97] When they reached Medina, they gently lowered Aisha's camel in front of her house and waited for her to come out of her Hawdaj, but found out that she was not in it. Muhammad and his friends waited anxiously while others went looking for her until she appeared riding a camel led by Safwan Bin Al-Muattal Al Selmy. Muhammad was happy to see her safe and listened to her as she explained why she was late. She said: "I went out for my 'business'[98] before they started on the trip back. When I was finished, my necklace fell off my neck and I went to look for it till I found it. But by the time I came back the people had led away my camel not knowing I was not in it, because I was thin and light weight. So when I found no one, I huddled in my clothes and stayed in my place knowing that sooner or later they would come after me. Then came by me Safwan bin Al Muattal, one of the fighters. He had been delayed from coming back with the other soldiers and did not spend the night with them. When he saw me he knew me because he had

---

[97.] Covered bed or litter on top of the camel, which was prepared to transport women when they accompanied their husbands in battle

[98.] Go to the bathroom

seen me before the Hijab[99] was imposed on us. So he brought his camel and asked me to ride and drove me back on his camel."

Aisha slept safely in her bed that night, but not the people of Medina who began the slander led by Abd Allah bin Abi Saloul. The conversation around the Ifk (slander) spread from house to house, but no one dared to tell Aisha because since her return she had been feeling very sick. But what was mostly troubling her, was Muhammad's uncharacteristic silent treatment toward her which was something she had never before experienced. He would go in to her while her mother was caring for her and coldly ask how they were doing and quickly leave. When she could take it no more, Aisha asked her husband permission to go to her mother's house. After twenty some days there she got better and went out for her "business" with a friend who then told her that she had been the subject of gossip all over town. Aisha was devastated and spent many sleepless, tearful nights, but she was not the only one. Muhammad was also miserable between listening to his heart that told him his wife was innocent, and his ears listening to the many accusations against her.

Muhammad gathered the people and stood on the platform addressing them saying, "Listen, O ye people. Why are there some men slandering me in my family?" As he went on speaking, the people were feeling his pain and their voices mingled, some shouting for revenge and retribution (which could mean stoning), while others

---

[99.] Veil covering the head and chest, worn in the presence of nonfamily men

demanded the death of those who spread the slanderous news.

Muhammad then went to his home taking with him two men to consult them in the matter. Oussama gave Muhammad a favorable report on Aisha, but Ali said, Prophet of Allah, there are many women.[100] A few days later, Muhammad, unable to come to a decision in spite of his love for Aisha, went to see her at her father's house, his best friend Abu Bakr. He found her crying and for the first time after the slander he talked to her directly asking her if what she was accused of was true; for if she were innocent Allah would free her, and if she were guilty, she'd better confess her guilt and Allah is ever forgiving. At that Aisha stopped crying and asked her parents to answer him in her defense, but they both said that they did not know how to answer Muhammad. Aisha said that she would never confess to what the people are accusing her of because she was not guilty, "but if I deny what they say, you will not believe me." She then turned around and lay on her bed.

The prophet of Allah did not move from his place and the symptoms of revelation came upon him. Whenever Muhammad had revelations from Allah, he would have cold sweats, shake and foam.

When Muhammad regained his composure he sat up wiping the sweat on his forehead and addressed Aisha saying, "Be of good cheer, Aisha, for Allah has declared your innocence."

[100.] Muhammad's son-in-law, who later became a successor of Muhammad and was killed in the Battle of Jamal. Aisha never liked him, and after Muhammad's death, she led a battle against him.

Her mother then asked her to go to her husband, but Aisha said: "By Allah, I will not go to him, for I am grateful only to Allah who declared my innocence."

Then the *ifk* verses were revealed. You can read them in Qur'an 24:11–20.

The verses basically say the following:

1. The people who did this thing will have terrible punishment in hell.
2. Why did they not bring out four witnesses?[101]
3. Allah's message is clear to you.

Then Muhammad had another verse revealed: "And those who accuse free women and bring not four witnesses, flog them with eighty stripes and never accept their evidence, and these are the transgressors" (Qur'an 24:4).

والذين يرمون المحصنات ثم لم يأتوا بأربعة شهداء فاجلدوهم ثمانين جلدة و لا تقبلوا لهم شهادة ابدا
4 النور سورة) الفاسقون هم ولئك (وا

And by Muhammad's order, the slanderers received eighty stripes.

Aisha returned to her home, proudly declaring to her rivals, "Which woman is favored by her husband like me?"

---

101. Four eyewitnesses are required before the judgment of stoning.

Chapter Twelve

Women in the Life of Jesus

While Muhammad had a big household with many women, Jesus did not have a home to call His own. When a certain scribe said to Him, "Teacher, I will follow You wherever You go," Jesus said to him, "Foxes have holes, and the birds of the air have nests; but the Son of Man[102] has nowhere to lay His head" (Matthew 8:20).

While Jesus had no wives or women living with Him, He had many dealings with women. He loved them and respected them and dealt kindly with them. The Bible tells us that when Jesus went out with His disciples proclaiming the good news, some women accompanied Him. "And also some women who had been healed of evil spirits and sicknesses; Mary who was called Magdalene, from whom seven demons had gone out, and Joanna the wife of Chuza, Herod's steward, and Suzanna, and many others who were contributing to His support out of their own private means" (Luke 8:2–3). He never used them to enhance His power but demonstrated to them the unconditional love

---

[102.] Son of Man is the name that links Jesus to the earth and to His mission. It was His favorite designation of Himself, used over eighty times, and was based on the prophet Ezekiel's title and also Daniel 7:13–14. It emphasizes His lowliness and humanity, His suffering and death (Luke 19:10), and His future reign as king (Matthew 24:27).

of God toward all humans, male and female. At the cross, there were women weeping for Him.

Stagg writes that of all founders of religions and religious sects, Jesus stands alone as the One who did not discriminate in some way against women. By word or deed, He never encouraged the disparagement of a woman.[103]

In a previous chapter, we read about the woman who was hemorrhaging for twelve years. She came up in the crowd to Jesus, thinking to herself if she could only touch the hem of His cloak, she would be healed. At that time, the Jews considered a woman with blood to be defiling, and she was not supposed to touch a man. When she did, Jesus—instead of being upset with her—gently addressed her, saying, "Daughter, your faith made you well; go in peace" (Mark 5:25–34, Matthew 9:20–22, Luke 8:43–48). She must have felt secure to hear the Master call her "Daughter"!

But other than the many women who followed Him, Jesus had friends whom He often visited in their homes.

Mary and Martha

This story is found in Luke 10:38–42. Mary and Martha were two sisters who lived with their brother Lazarus in Bethany, a town about two miles away from Jerusalem. Jesus probably visited them many times, but the Bible gives us three specific encounters. Because they were His friends and lived in a convenient location, Jesus often stopped at their house to rest and perhaps have a meal. One day, as Jesus was travelling with His friends, He entered Bethany and went to the house of Lazarus, Mary, and Martha. Mary and Martha loved Jesus and

---

[103.] Stagg, Evelyn, and Frank. *Women in the World of Jesus.* Westminster: John Knox Press, 1978. ISBN 978-0-664-24195-7.

rushed to prepare a meal for Him and His friends. But while they were busy in the kitchen, Mary heard Jesus teaching and rushed to take her place at His feet. Mary loved Jesus so much that she wanted to hear everything He said and learn all that she could from Him. For Mary to sit at the feet of Jesus meant that Mary occupied the place of a student, which was unusual for a woman in first-century Judaism. But Jesus allowed her this privilege and even commended her for it. Thus, He elevated the place of women, allowing them equal opportunities to aim and achieve a place that had been previously granted only to men. Martha also loved Jesus very much, yet she had chosen to express her love by serving Him. But she was so burdened with the preparation of food that she came out in frustration, saying to Jesus, "Lord, don't you care that my sister has left me to do the work by myself?" Jesus answered Martha, saying, "Martha, Martha, you are worried and upset about many things, but only one thing is needed. Mary has chosen what is better, and it will not be taken away from her." By saying this, Jesus affirmed Mary's position as a disciple, sitting at His feet to hear and learn everything He taught.

The second encounter of Jesus with Mary and Martha is recorded in John 11:1–44.

Lazarus, the brother of Mary and Martha, was sick; and the two sisters sent word to Jesus, telling Him that their brother, whom He loved, was sick. But Jesus delayed going there, and Lazarus died. Jesus said to His disciples, "Our friend Lazarus is asleep." They answered and told Him if he were asleep, he would wake up. But Jesus said, "Lazarus is dead, and I am glad for your sakes that I was not there that you may believe." Jesus wanted to show His disciples that even though Lazarus was dead, He had the power to raise Him from death so their faith in Him would increase.

Mary and Martha were at home mourning for their brother, and many of the Jews were there with them to console them. Martha heard that Jesus was coming, and she quickly went out to meet Him. Jesus meant so much to Martha, so who but He could better comfort them at this time of grief? Wishing He had been present with them at the time of their brother's death, she said to Him, "Lord, if You had been here my brother would not have died. Even now I know that whatever You ask of God, God will give You." Jesus said to her, "Your brother shall rise again." But as if it were too much to believe, Martha told Him that she knew her brother would be raised in the Day of Resurrection. Jesus said to Martha, "I am the resurrection and the life; he who believes in Me shall live even if he dies, and everyone who lives and believes in Me shall never die. Do you believe this?" To this, Martha confirmed her faith, saying, "Yes, Lord; I have believed that You are the Christ, the Son of God, even He who comes into the world." What a great and reliable promise of eternal life Jesus gives all who believe in Him!

Martha went back to the house and told her sister that Jesus was in town. Mary quickly rose and went to meet Him, followed by those who were comforting her. Mary fell at the feet of Jesus, weeping and telling Him the same as Martha had said—that had He been there, their brother would be still living. Jesus loved these two women so much and, feeling their grief, asked, "Where have you laid Him?" Jesus wept. He then told Mary and Martha, "Did I not say to you, if you believe you shall see the glory of God?" Again being deeply moved within, Jesus came to the tomb. It was a cave, and a stone was lying against it. Jesus said, "Remove the stone." Martha said, "Lord, by this time there will be a stench, for he has been dead four days." When they removed the stone, Jesus raised His eyes and in a loud voice said, "Father, I thank You that You have heard Me. And I knew that You always hear Me; but because of the people standing around I said it, that they may believe that You did send Me." And Jesus cried out with a loud voice and said, "Lazarus come forth." He who had died came forth, bound hand and foot with wrappings, and His face was wrapped around with cloth. Jesus said, "Unbind him and let him go."

Many who witnessed what Jesus had done believed in Him, but some of the Jews went to the religious leaders and told them the things that

Jesus had done. Therefore, the leaders convened a council and were saying, "If we let Him go on like this, all men will believe in Him, and the Romans will come and take away both our place and our nation" (John 11:48).

Another encounter by Jesus with Mary and Martha took place about a week before His crucifixion. Again, the supper was prepared, Martha was serving, and Lazarus was one of the people reclining at the table with Him. This suggests that there were many other people eating there. This family appears to be well-off, and their home was open to many. Again, Mary was not serving but chose to express her love toward Jesus by pouring out perfumed ointment over His feet and wiping them with her hair. Some of the people present were angry. Judas (the disciple who later betrayed Him) was offended the most and said that this expensive perfume worth eleven months' wages should have been sold and the money given to the poor (not that he loved the poor, but because he held the money box and used to pilfer from it). Jesus, therefore, said, "Let her alone; why do you bother her? She has done a good deed for me. For the poor you always have with you, and whenever you wish, you can do them good; but you do not always have Me. She has done what she could; she has anointed My body beforehand for the burial. And truly I say to you, wherever the gospel is preached in the whole world, that also which this woman has done shall be spoken of in memory of her" (John 12:1–8). Jesus affirms women by encouraging their good judgment.

Jesus Heals the Daughter of a Syrophoenician Woman

A woman whose little daughter had an unclean spirit came and fell at the feet of Jesus and kept asking Him to cast the demon out of her daughter. And Jesus was saying to her, "Let the children be satisfied first, for it is not good to take the children's bread and throw it to the dogs.[104]

[104.] Jews of that day referred to Gentiles (non-Jews) as dogs.

(Knowing she was not a Jewish woman, Jesus wanted to test her faith.) But she answered and said to Him, "Yes, Lord, but even the dogs under the table feed on the children's crumbs." Jesus said to her, "O woman, great is your faith. Because of your answer go your way; the demon has gone out of your daughter." Going back to her home, the woman found the child lying on the bed, the demon having departed (Matthew 15:21–28, Mark 7:25–30).

Jesus and the Woman at the Well

In the gospel of John, chapter 4, we read the story of Jesus speaking to a Samaritan woman. Jesus left Judea and was going back to Galilee. He had to pass by Samaria and came to a city called Sychar, near the parcel of ground that Jacob gave to his son Joseph. Jacob's well was there, and being tired from His journey, Jesus sat by the well. It was about noontime. His disciples had gone away into the city to buy food. While He sat, a woman of Samaria came to draw water, and Jesus said to her, "Give me a drink." The Samaritan woman then said to Him, "How is it that you, being a Jew, ask me for a drink, since I am a Samaritan woman?" Jesus answered and said to her, "If you knew the gift of God and who it is who says to you give Me a drink, you would have asked Him, and He would have given you living water." She said to Him, "Sir, You have nothing to draw with and the well is deep; where then do you get that living water? You are not greater than our father Jacob, who gave us the well and drank of it himself and his sons and his cattle, are You?" Jesus answered and said to her, "Everyone who drinks of this water shall thirst again; but whoever drinks of the water that I shall give him shall never thirst; but the water that I shall give him shall become in him a well of water springing up to eternal life." The woman said to Him, "Sir, give me this water, so I will not be thirsty, nor come all the way here to draw." Jesus said to her, "Go, call your husband, and come here." The woman answered and said, "I have no husband." Jesus said to her, "You have well said, 'I have no husband'; for you have had five husbands, and the one whom you now have, is not your husband; this you have said well." The woman said to Him, "Sir, I perceive that You are a prophet. Our fathers worshipped in this mountain, and you people say that in Jerusalem is the place where men ought to worship." Jesus said to her, "Woman, believe Me, an hour is coming when neither in this mountain, nor in Jerusalem, shall you worship the Father. You worship that which you do not know; we worship that which we know, for salvation is from the Jews. But an hour is coming and it is now, when the true worshippers shall worship the Father in spirit and truth . . . God is spirit and those who worship Him must worship in spirit and truth." The woman said to Him, "I know that Messiah is coming (He who is called Christ); when that One comes, He will declare all things to us." Jesus said to her, "I who speak to you am He." And at this point, his disciples came, and they marveled that He had been speaking with a woman; yet no one asked him why He was speaking to her and what He was seeking.

Living in our world, Jesus had to understand and feel loneliness. He was a sinless Person living among sinful people in a sinful world. "He was despised and rejected by men; a man of sorrow and acquainted with grief" (Isaiah 53:3). No one on earth could identify with Him, but He could identify with the nameless lonely woman who came to the well to fetch water. She came alone because she had a bad reputation and maybe had no friends to come with. She came in the heat of the day rather than in the cool time when others came to fetch water to avoid the looks and whispers of women who might have judged her as a sinner living with a man. But Jesus knew her inside and out and yet wanted to talk to her. He was thirsty and asked her for a drink of water. Surprised, she asked Him why He, being a Jewish man, would want to talk to her, a Samaritan woman.[105] There was animosity between the

---

[105.] The Samaritans were descendants of colonists whom the Assyrian kings planted in Palestine after the fall of the Northern Kingdom in 721 BC. They were despised by the Jews because of their mixed Gentile blood and their different location of worship, which centered at Mount Gerizim (NASB study Bible note on Luke 10:33).

Jews and the Samaritans because the Samaritans were former Jews who had intermarried with invading foreigners and adopted their pagan gods. The Jews hated the pagan gods and the Samaritans, who were considered half-breeds. Besides being a Jew, Jesus was a man, and men were not supposed to speak to women without the presence of their husbands. But wanting to steer her mind away from the conflicts and into the right spiritual direction, Jesus told her that if she only knew who He was, she would be the one asking Him for water—not the water she was drawing from the well, but spiritual water that would satisfy her thirsty, lonely heart. Yet the woman did not get it. She confronted Jesus with His physical limitations; He had nothing with which He could draw water, and His simple humanity did not compare with that of Jacob, who provided the well. Jesus again steered her away from the physical to the spiritual. Again, He told her of the spiritual water that He alone could give—water that would not only satisfy her thirst, but also become in her a well of water springing up to eternal life. Now Jesus had her attention, for she begged Him for this water that would quench her thirst to a point she would not have to come to the well anymore.

Jesus did the right thing and asked her to go get her husband. The woman told the truth about having no husband. Jesus acknowledged her honesty and revealed His knowledge of her life; she had had five husbands, and now she was living with a man who was not her husband. The woman sensed no judgment in the words of Jesus. She inferred he must be a prophet to know everything about her. Yet she still went back to the differences people imposed on one another. "We worship in this mountain and you Jews worship in Jerusalem." At this point, Jesus revealed to her that salvation came from the Jews, and those worshipping God would worship Him in spirit and in truth. At this point, the Samaritan woman still had unanswered questions and said to Jesus that when the Messiah came, He would give us all the answers we needed. Jesus answered her longing heart by saying to her, *"I am He. I am the Messiah for which people have been waiting!"* At this, the woman left her past and her search for water and ran back to the village, inviting her people to come and see the

Savior Messiah for themselves. "Come see a Man who told me all the things that I have done, this is not the Christ, is it?"

The men of the city came out to see Jesus. They asked Him to stay with them, and He stayed there two days. And from that city, many of the Samaritans believed in Him, and they were saying, "It is no longer because of the word of the woman who testified that we believe, but because of what He said that we believe, for we have heard for ourselves and know that this One is indeed the Savior of the world."

Meanwhile, the disciples came back with food, saying, "Rabbi, eat." But he said to them, "I have food to eat that you do not know about." The disciples, therefore, were saying to one another, "No one brought Him anything to eat, did he?" Jesus said to them, "My food is to do the will of Him who sent Me, and to accomplish His work."

The unnamed Samaritan woman was the first evangelist in John's gospel. Jesus liberated this woman and gave her a new life, which she not only received herself, but also shared with others. "From that city many of the Samaritans believed in Him because of the word of the woman who testified, 'He told me all the things that I have done.'"

Two people met. This woman's sins caused the village women to avoid her. Jesus purposely connected with her. (Not only did he break custom to speak with a woman alone, but He also went directly through Samaria, when Jews took a longer route around the area to avoid contact.)

She was tired, and Jesus was tired and sat down.

She was thirsty and came for water, and He was thirsty and asked for water.

She was searching for pleasure that did not satisfy.

He poured out His life to troubled souls and satisfied His Father's will to be the Savior of mankind.

She was unfulfilled in her sinful life, and Jesus was committed to give meaning to her life.

Jesus said, "Behold, I stand at the door and knock; if anyone hears My voice and opens the door, I will come in to him, and will dine with him, and he with Me" (Revelation 3:20).

Chapter Thirteen

What Muhammad taught about Marriage, Divorce, and Remarriage

Marriage in Islam

The prophet Muhammad was a big advocate of marriage. He said, "Marry, because marriage is the tradition of the prophet." He also said, "Whoever likes to follow my tradition, then, he should know that marriage is from my tradition."[106] Muhammad also said, "When a man marries he has fulfilled half of the 'deen' (religion); so let him fear Allah regarding the remaining half."[107]

In several Qur'an verses, Muhammad advocates marriage. He says, "And marry those among you who are single and those who are fit among your male slaves and your female slaves; if they are needy, Allah will make them free from want out of His grace; and Allah is ample-giving, knowing" (Qur'an 24:32). The Islamic term for "marriage" literally means "sexual intercourse."[108]

[106.] Wasa 'il ul-Shia Hadith, vol. 14, pp. 3–4, 6.

[107.] At-Tirmidhi Hadith 3096 narrated by Anas ibn Malik.

[108.] *Marriage and Morals in Islam*, Sayyid, Muhammad Rizvi (in Arabic).

Qur'an 2:221–223 says, "And do not marry polytheistic (non-Muslim) women until they believe. And a believing slave woman is better than a polytheist, even though she might please you. And do not marry polytheistic men [to your women] until they believe. And a believing slave is better than a polytheist, even though he might please you. Those invite [you] to the Fire, but Allah invites to Paradise and to forgiveness, by His permission. And He makes clear His verses to the people that perhaps they may remember. And they ask thee about menstruation. Say: 'It is harmful.' Some keep aloof from women during menstrual discharge and do not go near them until they are clean. But when they have cleansed themselves, go in to them as Allah has commanded you. Surely Allah loves those who turn much (to Him) and He loves those who purify themselves. Your wives are a place of sowing of seed for you, so come to your place of cultivation however you wish and put forth [righteousness] for yourselves. And fear Allah and know that you will meet Him. And give good tidings to the believers."

A man is allowed to have up to four wives at a time. If he divorces one, he can replenish the number up to four if he chooses to. Of course, not all Muslims do that, but it is permissible and lawful. For Muhammad, however, the limit was much higher, maybe because he wanted to build special relationships with which he would promote Islam. Qur'an 4:3–5 says, "And if you fear that you will not deal justly with the orphan girls, then marry those that please you of [other] women, two or three or four. But if you fear that you will not be just, then [marry only] one or those your right hand possesses. That is more suitable that you may not incline [to injustice]. And give the women [upon marriage] their [bridal] gifts graciously. But if they give up willingly to you anything of it, then take it in satisfaction and ease. And do not give the weak-minded your property, which Allah has made a means of sustenance for you, but provide for them with it and clothe them and speak to them words of appropriate kindness" (Sahih International). Sahih Bukhari 62:2 provides the context for verse 4:3 of the Qur'an. "Dealing justly" is defined within a financial context. It refers to providing a fair dowry to secure marriage—not to the equal or fair treatment of wives (which is impossible according to Qur'an 4:129).[109]

Mahr (Bridal Money) Condition for Marriage

The Qur'an says that you should give *mahr*, or "bridal money," to the woman you will marry. Mahr is a mandatory payment in the form of money or possessions (paid or promised to be paid) by the groom to the bride at the time of marriage and becomes her legal property. Qur'an 4:24 says, "Also forbidden are women already married, except those whom your right hand possesses (captives and slaves). Thus Allah ordained for you. All others are lawful, provided you seek them (in marriage) with Mahr from your property, desiring chastity, not committing illegal sexual intercourse, so with those of whom you have enjoyed sexual relations, give them their Mahr as prescribed; but after a Mahr is prescribed you agree mutually (to give more) there is not sin on you. Surely Allah is ever All Knowing, All Wise."

Part of the mahr can be deferred to a later date after the marriage but has to be paid in full in case of divorce. However, many abusive husbands force the wife to surrender part or all of it during the marriage. Many Muslim women in Egypt tried to save some secret money behind their husband's back to help them in case of a divorce. Another fear they had was that a husband might have enough money to pay mahr, allowing him to take a second wife. They had a saying among themselves, "Clip his wings so he will not fly" (meaning don't let him accumulate money).

Mahr is a religious requirement according to Sharia (Islamic law). Some educated modern women do not like the idea of mahr because it implies that they are being bought by the husband but still have to comply with it because it is Sharia. Recently, I was told that the mahr of a certain educated affluent bride was set at a token one dollar.

[109.] https://www.thereligionofpeace.com/pages/quran/polygamy.aspx

The Muslim woman does not take her husband's last name but remains forever the daughter of so-and-so. When she has children, she is referred to as the mother of her oldest son's name. A few Muslim women in the West, however, are opting to take their husband's name.

The marriage ceremony is executed by a cleric in the presence of two witnesses. The prophet Muhammad said, "There is no marriage except with a guardian (wali) and two just witnesses."[110] *Wali* means "protector" or "custodian." The groom does not have to have a wali at the time of the marriage contract but enters into the marriage contract by himself. It is the woman who needs to have a wali because the Prophet said, "Any woman who gets married without a Wali, her marriage is invalid, invalid, invalid."[111]

Under Islamic law, there is no concept of joint marital property. A Muslim man and woman do not merge their legal identity upon marriage. The assets of the man before the marriage and earned during the marriage remain his in case of a divorce because the husband had to pay mahr to the bride before marriage, as ordered by the prophet Muhammad. In American courts, this has been contested by Muslim women who have been living in the United States for a long time and believe they should enjoy the American way, where assets are divided equitably between husband and wife in case of divorce.

One such case was that of a Muslim couple who married in Pakistan and moved to New Jersey. After divorce, the court concluded that the wife was not entitled to any of her physician husband's marital assets because she had already signed a contract in Pakistan specifying her entitlements in marriage. They found no public policy reason that would justify refusing to enforce the mahr agreement, which they viewed as a prenuptial contract, in accordance with Sharia. As a result,

---

[110] Ibn Hibban

[111] Hadith by Aisha, narrated by al-Tirmidhi, 1102 classed as unproven by Abu Dawood, 2083; ibn Naajah, 1879.

the wife was left with the $1,500 specified in the mahr agreement. She parted with no maintenance, equitable distribution of assets, or alimony.[112]

Urfi Marriage

Besides regular marriage, a second type of marriage in Islam is called *urfi*. This marriage bypasses the law of mahr, divorce laws, and any financial obligation on the part of the man. The only condition to this marriage being halal[113] is that the girl's father or guardian knows about it and that it is not made in secret. The *urfi* marriage is not registered in or recognized by most Arab states, so they do not grant legal divorces from it. *Urfi* marriage is not defined by Sharia but has existed by custom. "In the past, it was common among the widows of soldiers who had huge pensions and did not want to lose it by officially remarrying."[114] Currently, it is becoming popular in Egypt among young people who cannot afford the mahr of a regular marriage.

Mut'a Marriage

The word *mut'a* means "enjoyment." A marriage of *mut'a* is a marriage that the contract stipulates will last for a fixed period of time—a day to perhaps even a year or more. Muhammad started this when his men were on the battlefield away from their wives, and it continues to the present time among the Shia Muslims. Although it is part of the Qur'an, Sunni Muslims do not practice it anymore and argue it should not be legal because it is a form of prostitution. Shia Muslims still practice *mut'a*, saying it is legal and remains part of the Qur'an that Muhammad recited; therefore, it is valid. The verse in question is Qur'an 4:24. "So for whatever you enjoy [of marriage] from them, give them their due

---

[112.] Chaudry v. Chaudry, 388 A.2d 1000 (NJ Superior Court Appeal, Div. 1978).

[113.] "Halal" means allowed and not sinful vs. "haram," which means sinful and not allowed.

[114.] https://en.wikipedia.org/wiki/Nikah_%27urfi

compensation as an obligation. And there is no blame upon you for what you mutually agree to beyond the obligation. Indeed, Allah is ever Knowing and Wise" (Qur'an 4:24, Sahih International).

Divorce in Islam

Muhammad did not like divorce, nor did he advocate it. He said, "The most hated of permissible things to Allah is divorce." A lot has been written about this Hadith.[115]

Muhammad also said, "Marry and do not divorce, for verily Allah does not love the male and female tasters (those who marry and divorce different people).[116] However, at one time, Muhammad was willing to divorce his wife Sawda because he was not sexually attracted to her. He also was willing to divorce all his wives when they ganged up against him.

In Qur'an 4:34–35, Muhammad gave instructions to be followed before divorce. "Men are in charge of women by [right of] what Allah has given

---

[115.] A Hadith (Arabic "report") is one of the sayings, actions, or habits of Muhammad, the prophet of Islam. Hadith are second only to the Qur'an in developing Islamic jurisprudence. The sayings of Muhammad are divided into four categories: Sahih (trustworthy), Hasan (good), Da'if (weak), or Maudu (fabricated). In order to be of the highest-ranking (Sahih), the material must have a continuous chain of transmission by people of good character and sound mind and must not conflict with any other reliable reports. Hasan also comes from an unbroken chain of transmission from people of sound character, but perhaps weak memory. Dai'f reports lack one of the elements—a broken chain of narration or a narrator of poor character or memory. Maudu are considered wrongly attributed to Muhammad (https://en.wikipedia.org/wiki/Hadith). This particular Hadith was recorded by Abu Dawood, Ibn Maajah, and Al Hakim from Ibm Umar. Al Albani graded it Da'if (weak) in Da'if ul-Jaami #44, Al Irwaa #2040, and Al-Mishkaat #3280 (https://en.wikipedia.org/wiki/Hadith_terminology; http://www.islamic-awareness.org/Hadith/Ulum/asb7.html).

[116.] Hadith recorded by Al-Tabaraani in Al-Kabeer and is said to be Hasan.

one over the other and what they spend [for maintenance] from their wealth. So righteous women are devoutly obedient, guarding in [the husband's] absence what Allah would have them guard. But those [wives] from whom you fear arrogance—[first] advise them; [then if they persist], forsake them in bed; and [finally], strike them. But if they obey you [once more], seek no means against them. Indeed, Allah is ever Exalted and Grand. And if you fear dissension between the two, send an arbitrator from his people and an arbitrator from her people. If they both desire reconciliation, Allah will cause it between them. Indeed, Allah is ever Knowing and Acquainted [with all things]" (Qur'an 4:34–35, Sahih International).

After unsuccessful attempts at reconciliation, the Qur'an allows divorce.

Rules for Divorce in Islamic Law (Sharia)

The husband has the power to divorce his wife whether she is present or absent. To do so, he has to pronounce the formula of divorce in Arabic: you are *talik* (divorced), or my wife so-and-so is *talik*. If the husband is enraged out of his senses, or the wife is menstruating, the divorce is not valid.[117]

Qur'an 2:229 says, "A divorce is only permissible twice: after that, the parties should either hold together on equitable terms, or separate with kindness. It is not lawful for you, (Men), to take back any of your gifts (from your wives), except when both parties fear that they would be unable to keep the limits ordained by Allah. If ye (judges) do indeed fear that they would be unable to keep the limits ordained by Allah, there is no blame on either of them if she give something for her freedom. These are the limits ordained by Allah; so do not transgress them if any do transgress the limits ordained by Allah, such persons wrong (themselves as well as others)" (Qur'an 2:229, Yusuf Ali

---

117. Al-Islam.org, Ahlul Bayt digital Islamic Library, "Divorce."

translation). This verse is speaking to the husbands, telling them to go through divorce peacefully and to let the wife keep her mahr.

The "limits of Allah" (2:229) are the two times Allah allows a couple to divorce because a third divorce from the same woman has more serious consequences, as in Qur'an 2:230, which will be discussed later. So if they do not think they can make it, then the husband should let the wife go and let her keep all or part of the mahr.

Woman-Instigated Divorce

Under Islamic law in Egypt, if a woman wants to separate from her husband, she has two options: seek a *tafriq* (separation) or seek *khull* (no-fault divorce).

Tafriq is allowable under certain conditions only and has to be approved in an Islamic court with the consent of a religious qadi (judge). In this case, the wife may be entitled to the mahr given her at the marriage. The second option is *khull*.[118] *Khull* is when the wife seeks divorce through a court order. *Khull* divorce is gaining popularity among educated Muslim women. It is still not easy to get. This is a divorce without cause, by mutual consent, and it must be supported by consideration that passes from the wife to the husband. This consideration almost always results in the wife forfeiting her mahr.[119] (She abandons the money since she chose the divorce.) The word *khull* is relatively new. However, there are stories of women telling Muhammad they wanted a divorce; and he said, "Okay, give back the mahr." Sahih Bukhari cites the story of the wife of Thabit, who didn't want to live with him any longer. So she went to the prophet of Allah. "[He] said to

---

[118.] In 2000, Egypt liberalized their laws granting women the right to a "no fault" divorce, or *khull*. It is still difficult to obtain and requires the woman to give up all her *mahr*.

[119.] Wael B. Hallaq, Sharia Theory, Practice, Transformations (2009), p. 271.

her, 'Will you give back the garden which your husband has given you (as Mahr)?' She said, 'Yes,' Then the Prophet said to Thabit, 'O Thabit! Accept your garden, and divorce her once.'"[120]

Islamic Divorce for Men

While a woman can only get a divorce through court action,[121] a man-initiated divorce is simple and easy. All the man has to do is say, "I divorce you," and the woman is divorced. The woman does not have to be present to be divorced. A Muslim man can say "I vow to divorce my wife so-and-so (giving her name)" in front of two witnesses, and the wife is considered divorced. The husband then goes home and tells his wife that he has just divorced her and asks her to cover up because she has now become estranged to him. However, if he changes his mind, he may marry her back.

A man is free to marry anytime after the divorce if he has less than four wives. A woman has to wait three months before she can remarry to make sure she is not pregnant by her husband. For wives under the age of nine or a woman in menopause, there is no time restriction. A woman who is pregnant can be divorced but cannot remarry until she has delivered.

Who Gets the Children

The mother has the right of custody of a male child until he is capable of taking care of himself. This has been judged to occur at seven years

120. Sahih al Bukhari 5273; vol. 7, book 63, Hadith 197.
121. Gabriel Sawma, attorney specializing in Muslim divorce law and professor at Farleigh Dickinson University in "'Let's talk about sex, divorce' in Egypt," CNN.com.

of age, and the fatwa (legal verdict) has been issued since at this age, most children are able to take care of themselves.[122]

In the case of a female, the mother has the right of custody until she reaches puberty. This has been declared to occur at age nine years of age.[123]

Conditions for the Mother's Right of Custody to Be Taken Away[124]

1. She leaves Islam.
2. She indulges in sin.
3. She often leaves the house.
4. She marries another man.
5. She demands custody payment if there is another woman to raise the child for free. Often, one of the husband's wives volunteers.

Divorce for the Third Time

A Muslim man cannot divorce his wife and remarry her as many times as he pleases. This can only work up to two times as mentioned in Qur'an 2:229. If he divorces her for the third time, he and his divorced wife have to face serious consequences should they decide to remarry. Regarding this, Allah gave his prophet more stringent rules:

> If he has divorced her [for the third time], then she is not lawful to him afterward until [after] she marries a husband other than him. And if the latter husband

---

[122.] Radd-al-Mutar 3/566.

[123.] Al-Mawsili, al-Ikhtiyar li Ta'lil al-Mukhtar, 3/237.

[124.] daruliftaa.com (Institute of Islamic Jurisprudence), "Child Custody after Divorce." Muhammad also said, "You are . . . entitled to him so long as you do not get married." Abu Dawwod in Sunan 2276.

divorces her [or dies], there is no blame upon the woman and her former husband returning to each other if they think that they can keep [within] the limits of Allah. These are the limits of Allah, which He makes clear to a people who know" (Qur'an 2:230)

The limits Allah gives is that a woman whose husband has divorced her three times and wishes to marry her back cannot do so at will. She has to marry another man, and the marriage has to be consummated and then divorced before her original husband can marry her again (for the fourth time).

The following story is narrated by Aisha, Muhammad's young wife, regarding this type of marriage:

> Rifa'a Al Qurazi divorced his wife irrevocably (the divorce was final because it was the third). Later on, Abdur-Rahman bin Az-Zubair married her after him. She came to the prophet and said, "O Allah's Apostle! I was Rifa'a's wife and he divorced me thrice, and then I was married to Abdur-Rahman bin Az-Zubair, who by Allah has nothing with him except something like this fringe,[125] O Allah's Apostle" showing a fringe she had taken from her covering sheet . . . Allah's apostle did nothing except smile and then said to the lady, "Perhaps you want to go back to Rifa'a (her first husband)?" No, it is not possible unless and until you enjoy the sexual relation with Abdur Rahman (the current temporary husband), and he enjoys the sexual relation with you.[126]

[125.] Referring to his private male organ
[126.] Translation of Sahih Bukhari, Good Manners and Form (Al-Adab), vol. 8, and book 73, number 107.

Another story specifically says that the woman accused her new temporary, interim husband of impotence so she could get the divorce without having the mandatory sexual relationship. The man denied the charge against him and came to the Prophet with his two sons from another wife. The Prophet then asked if these were his sons, to which he replied, "Yes." The Prophet then said to the woman, "You claim that he is impotent; but by Allah, these boys resemble him as a crow resembles a crow."

The solution to the marriage of a woman whose husband has divorced her three times is that if she and her husband wanted to get back together, the woman has to have sex with another husband. And if and when the new husband chooses to divorce her, then she can go back to her original husband who divorced her three times. This marriage is called *hulla*.

Hulla means to render halal (acceptable) by the temporary marriage and allow the wife to go back to her previous husband.

But Muslims do not like this arrangement one bit; neither did Muhammad, the prophet of Islam, in spite of Allah giving him the Qur'an verse.

The following conversation took place between the Prophet (PBUH) and the companions:

The Prophet said, "Shall I inform you about the makeshift male goat?"

The companions answered, "Yes."

The Prophet said, "He is the temporary husband. Allah curses the temporary husband and the husband for whom *hulla* is practiced."

Qur'an 2:230 allows a marriage that Muhammad claims is cursed by Allah! Muslims, in general, do not like or approve of this *hulla*, but it is still practiced in Islam to this day.

I watched an interview between a talk show host and one who performs *hulla* for a living. They call him *muhallal* (makes halal), rendering permissible what otherwise would not be. This guy performs the role of the *muhallal*, or interim husband. The *muhallal* marries the woman for a short period of time, performing sexual relations with her so she can return to her husband, but agrees beforehand to divorce her. The talk show host asked him how he liked his job. He said he enjoys a halal good time with a woman, especially since he gets paid for it too! Once in a while, he says the woman even wants him to have sex with her multiple times before he divorces her but asks him to keep it a secret from her husband. Asked what he does then, he said, "I gladly do it and keep it a tight secret from everyone, especially my wife." When asked what his wife thinks of his role of *muhallal*, he said that she did not like it at all, but the money was good.

Egypt is a country that produces the most Arabic movies and theatrical plays in the Middle East, which is why the Egyptian dialect is well understood in all Arabic-speaking countries. Adel Imam is a very famous Egyptian cinema and theater actor. He is primarily a comedian but does other serious roles as well. One of his most popular plays was about the subject discussed above. The play is called *El Wad Sayed El Shaghal* (Sayed the Servant). Adel Imam plays the role of a young man who leaves the village and goes to the capital to work as a servant in a very wealthy home, where the young husband and wife always argue. The wife's father reminds his daughter that she did not have the luxury of yet another divorce because she had already been divorced and remarried twice by her husband. A third divorce would require the intervention of a *muhallal* to make it possible for her to return to her husband. The spoiled rich daughter forgets and once again asks her husband for a divorce, to which he replies, "You are divorced." Now she is legally divorced! When her father hears of it, he is devastated and tries to keep it a family secret because of the scandal this divorce would bring to his political career. After a lot of thought, he calls Sayed, their servant, and offers him some money to become the *muhallal* (temporary husband of his daughter) and then divorce her so she can be free to remarry her husband. Sayed the servant (comedian-actor Adel Imam) drives a hard bargain, continuously raising the price of his services as temporary husband of his mistress. The father agrees to the high price, and the marriage ceremony quietly takes place. His mistress, the bride, however, refuses to sleep with her servant; and the comedy becomes hilarious! When the sheikh (religious man who performs weddings, divorces, etc.) is called to perform the divorce and asks the servant if he has had intercourse with his wife (his mistress), he says no. Upon which, the sheikh refuses to give divorce papers until the marriage has been consummated, saying, "It is Allah's law," and leaves. The servant now demands his new role as the husband and refuses to go ahead with the planned divorce. The comedy continues with the servant taking over and bossing everyone around. He then exercises his right as the husband to take his wife to Beit El Ta'ah (house of obedience), which gives him the right to demand that his wife live with him, in his own house, under his own rule.

We shall leave the rest to your imagination to see how funny the play continues, with the servant now the husband, who has the upper hand. The last scene of the play is with Adel Imam (the servant) at his very humble home sitting down while his wife (previous mistress) is sitting on the floor, rubbing his feet in a tub. Needless to say, it was on stage for many consecutive years!

Adel Imam is both very much loved by most Egyptians yet is hated by some for his many controversial roles about society, politics, and religion. He was sentenced to jail for three months while he was out of the country.

The BBC[127] reported the following: "On April 25, 2012, a court in Egypt upholds a three-month prison sentence handed to leading comic actor Adel Imam convicted of insulting Islam in his films and plays." Later that year, he won his appeal, and the sentence was lifted.

[127.] www.bbc.com/news/world-middle-east-17832703

Chapter Fourteen

What Jesus Taught about Marriage, Divorce, and Remarriage

What Did Jesus Teach?

When questioned about divorce and remarriage, Jesus directed their attention to what God had to say about the matter in the Jewish Scriptures. We read in the gospel of Matthew, chapter 19, "Some Pharisees came to Jesus, testing Him and asking, 'Is it lawful for a man to divorce his wife for any reason at all?' And He answered and said, 'Have you not read that He who created *them* from the beginning MADE THEM MALE AND FEMALE, and said, "FOR THIS REASON A MAN SHALL LEAVE HIS FATHER AND MOTHER AND BE JOINED TO HIS WIFE, AND THE TWO SHALL BECOME ONE FLESH"? So they are no longer two, but one flesh. What therefore God has joined together, let no man separate.' They said to Him, 'Why then did Moses command to GIVE HER A CERTIFICATE OF DIVORCE AND SEND her AWAY?' He said to them, 'Because of your hardness of heart Moses permitted you to divorce your wives; but from the beginning it has not been this way. And I say to you, whoever divorces his wife, except for immorality, and marries another woman commits adultery.'

"The disciples said to Him, 'If the relationship of the man with his wife is like this, it is better not to marry.' But He said to them, 'Not all men can accept this statement, but only those to whom it has been given'" (Matthew 19:3–11, NASB, referring to Genesis 1:27, Genesis 2:24, and Deuteronomy 24:1–4).

Thanks to John MacArthur's online sermons at Grace to You for many of these insights. The Pharisees (religious leaders) hated Jesus and attacked Him. They wanted to do everything they could to discredit Him, and they wanted Him dead! So they came to him with a carefully prepared question designed to do just that. They already knew that he advocated a strong message against divorce. Divorce was a common thing among the Jews and the Pharisees as well. They were divorcing their wives and teaching that you could divorce your wife for any reason.

There had been a rabbinical feud on the question of divorce. There was a rabbi by the name of Shammai, who said there was to be no divorce. But he did not find a large following because his view was not popular. But there was another rabbi by the name of Hillel, who had died twenty years before Jesus' ministry, and his view was that you could divorce your wife for any reason. For example, he said you could divorce your wife for taking her hair down, for speaking to men, or even for saying something unkind about her mother-in-law. You could divorce her for not giving you a son or if you found somebody prettier or younger than she was.[128]

Now the Pharisees knew that Jesus did not teach this because he had said it before. In Matthew, chapter 5, He had said to them, "You say you don't commit adultery. I say you are the worst kind of adulterers and you proliferate adultery all over the place, . . . because you get divorce without cause. And when you divorce without cause, you cause adultery everywhere, because the person divorced who remarries is an

---

[128.] https://www.gty.org/library/sermons-library/2336/jesus-teaching-on-divorce-part-1

adulterer and makes an adulterer of the one they marry. You are making adultery all over the place by your divorces without cause."[129] So they already knew where Jesus stood on the question of adultery. However, they were hoping that by his answer, he would come across as intolerant and lose popularity with the crowds or, even better, run afoul of Herod Antipas, whose territory Jesus had just crossed into. The Pharisees hoped he would say something entangling like John the Baptist did and similarly get himself killed.

John the Baptist had been thrown in prison by Herod Antipas, who ruled that area. Herod had seduced Herodias, the wife of his brother Philip, and was now married to her. But John the Baptist, following God's law, did not recognize the adulterous (and also, for Herod, incestuous) union and call it marriage. So when John said to him it is not lawful for you to have her, he was put in prison and ultimately had his head chopped off because he had confronted Herod's actions. Herodias ultimately was the one who wanted his head (Mark 6:14–29).

So in this setting, when the Pharisees asked Jesus, "Is it lawful for a man to divorce his wife for any cause at all?," He shrewdly did not answer their question from His own viewpoint. He went all the way back to the beginning, and He quoted God. "Have you not read[130] that He who made them from the beginning made them male and female and said for this reason a man shall leave his father and mother and shall cleave to his wife, and the two shall become one flesh? Consequently they are no longer two, but one flesh. What therefore God has joined together let no man separate." Then Jesus gave four reasons from the foundational text in Genesis why it is not lawful to divorce for any cause.

[129.] Ibid.

[130.] This was a special dig at the Pharisees because it was the line they used for their students.

1. The first reason is that God created one woman for one man. "Have you not read that He who made them at the beginning made them a male and a female?" (Genesis 1:27). Jesus asked them if they have read the Scriptures. God did not make plans for polygamy and did not make plans for divorce by making any extra people or uneven ratios. In Adam's case, polygamy or divorce was not an option, and that is God's intention for His creation.

2. The second reason why divorce is not permitted is the strong bond. God says, "For this reason a man shall leave his father and his mother and cleave to his wife" (Genesis 2:24). To "cleave" means to be stuck to something firmly to the point that it grows together. The man is to leave his family and cleave to his wife. Marriage, then, is a union between two people who are bonded and utterly devoted to each other. That's why 1 Corinthians 7:4 says your body does not belong to yourself, but to your spouse, and your spouse's body belongs to you.

3. The third reason why marriage does not allow itself to be broken is because the husband and wife become one flesh. "And the two shall become one flesh." They are not two anymore. You cannot separate them. That oneness ultimately is best seen in the child they produce, which is the emblem of their union. When you break up a marriage, you slice a person in half.

4. The fourth reason why a marriage should not be broken is that it is God's creation. "What therefore God has joined together let no man separate." Every time a couple comes together in the joy of their relationship, it is an act of God. Divorce kills a creation of God. When the Jewish leaders asked Jesus, "Is it lawful for a man to get a divorce for any reason?" He told them to listen to what God said: one man, one woman, strong bond, one flesh, and if you tear them up, you are tearing what God made; and you are in a very serious position.

So when the Pharisees asked why Moses allowed them to write a certificate of divorce, Jesus pointed them to their evil hearts. It is because of the hardness of their hearts that Moses permitted, not condoned, divorce. Deuteronomy 24 says that when the divorced wife goes and marries another and he divorces her or he dies, she cannot return to her first husband. So Deuteronomy 24 does not actually authorize divorce; it only stipulates no remarriage. The point in the Old Testament is that divorce, except for the cause of adultery, leads to adultery. The innocent spouse is allowed to remarry because the marriage has already been broken. Although painful, grace can be extended when the guilty spouse sincerely repents and seeks forgiveness and reconciliation.

What happens in the case of divorce and remarriage for reasons other than adultery? Does God forgive those who willfully break His command? Before we answer this, let us examine ourselves. Have we ever willfully broken any of God's commands? Has God refused to grant us forgiveness? Never! Forgiveness was granted in the atoning sacrificial death of Jesus Christ on our behalf. But we have to repent of our sin. So it is with divorce. We have to know that when we divorce and remarry for other than adultery, we sin against God and against our spouse. We have to repent from our hearts and ask for God's forgiveness as well as the spouse we sinned against.

While we do not always understand all the reasons for God's commands, it is certainly obvious that divorce causes heartache to everyone involved. Is there anyone who has not heard a friend, a child, or a parent describe the agony of divorce? Children are torn apart when they have to choose between living with either their father or their mother when they would rather enjoy the security and undivided love of both. When I was widowed at age fifty-two, I thought about my divorced friends and the pain they must have gone through, not only losing their spouse, but feeling rejected by them as well.

A dear friend of mine experienced the agony of divorce when her husband divorced her to marry her friend and neighbor and moved across the street to his new wife's house. The children were devastated and felt deeply hurt when they visited their father, whom they loved, in a strange house with a strange wife; and children who used to be their friends.

Polygamy also causes great grief to the family. The children hate to see their father share his love with a woman other than their mother and find themselves having to compete for their father's attention and love with other siblings who come into their family. But I cannot even begin to understand the pain of the wife who finds herself forced to share her husband's heart, resources, and their sacred marriage bed.

When I was teaching in a Middle Eastern country, I was invited to a party given by some of the college students I taught. They were all in their twenties except a mother who was probably in her forties. I sat beside her, and she opened her heart to me and poured out her grief with tears running down her cheeks as she told her story. In spite of the custom of arranged marriages, she and her husband had married for love. They had four lovely children, now in college, and a good marriage till one day she learned that her husband had married another younger wife. When the husband saw her crying incessantly, he gave her the choice to either stop crying or, if she could not control herself, he would divorce her. She chose to stay and shed her tears only when he was not around.

Is it any wonder that God's design for marriage is one man for one woman?

The followers of Jesus wrote about what the relationship between husband and wife should be. The apostle Paul wrote, "Husbands love your wives, just as Christ also loved the church (the believers) and gave Himself up for her . . . So husbands ought also to love their own wives as their own bodies. He who loves his own wife loves himself. For no one ever hated his own flesh, but nourishes and cherishes it, just as Christ also does the church; because we are members of His body. For this cause a man shall leave his father and mother and shall cleave to his wife; and the two shall become one flesh . . . let each individual among you also love his own wife even as himself; and let the wife see to it that she respect her husband" (Ephesians 5:25–33).

The apostle Paul gives further instructions on the principles of marriage in 1 Corinthians. "Nevertheless, because of sexual immorality, let each man have his own wife, and let each woman have her own husband. Let the husband render to his wife the affection due her, and likewise also the wife to her husband. The wife does not have authority over her own body, but the husband *does*. And likewise the husband does not have authority over his own body, but the wife *does*. Do not deprive one another except with consent for a time, that you may give yourselves to fasting and prayer; and come together again so that Satan does not tempt you because of your lack of self-control . . . Now to the married I command, *yet* not I but the Lord: A wife is not to depart from *her* husband. But even if she does depart, let her remain unmarried or be reconciled to *her* husband. And a husband is not to divorce *his* wife. But to the rest I, not the Lord, say: If any brother has a wife who does not believe, and she is willing to live with him, let him not divorce her. And a woman who has a husband who does not believe, if he is willing to live with her, let her not divorce him . . . But if the unbeliever departs, let him depart; a brother or a sister is not under bondage in such *cases*. But God has called us to peace" (1 Corinthians 7:2–5, 10–15, NKJV). "Do not be unequally yoked together with unbelievers" (2 Corinthians 6:14, NKJV).

The principles Paul gives are that the ideal Christian marriage is one man and one woman for life, only marry another believer, do not sexually deprive each other, and cherish and honor each other. If two unbelievers marry and one subsequently becomes a follower of Jesus, it is preferable to stay together as long the unbeliever is willing.

Chapter Fifteen

Muhammad and Adoption

Muhammad loved children. "Wealth and children are an adornment of the life of this world" (Qur'an 18:46). Qur'an 6:151 says, "I will recite what your Lord has forbidden to you: . . . do good to parents and slay not your children for (fear of) poverty—we provide for you and for them . . . and kill not the soul which Allah has made sacred except in the course of justice." Muhammad used to play with his grandchildren, Hassan and Hussein, kissing them and carrying them on his back. He even cut his prayers short because of crying children. He did not want to kill captured children. Instead, he just sold them.

Orphans constitute approximately 1.7 percent of the Egyptian population, according to figures released in 2009 by UNICEF. Save Our Souls (SOS), an NGO working on this issue, says these numbers are on the rise. However, the media representative of Al-Orman orphanage, Mohamed Farid, believes this is a conservative estimate. "The number of orphans in Egypt is much higher; I would actually suggest it is between three and five million" (3.5 to 6 percent).

Orphans in Egypt are often referred to as *laqeet* (foundling), a term which in the past was written on their birth certificates. Sometimes they were even known by the negative label *awlad haram* (children of sin).

Egyptian law, in adherence with the Qur'an and Islam as well as the tradition of the prophet Muhammad, forbids adoption but follows the practice of *kafala*.[131]

Fostering (*kafala*) means "to assume partial or complete responsibility for a child who has been temporarily or permanently deprived of parental care," explains Imam Faizul Khan. He clarifies that adoptions where the child assumes the family name of the foster family or inherits from them are forbidden in Islam, whereas fostering (*kafala*) is highly recommended.

Due to Islamic restrictions on gender mixing, *kafala* has its problems too, for when a male child is placed in a Muslim home, the mother is not free to appear in her home without the hijab (covering) in front of the child as soon as he reaches puberty at age twelve or so.

Islamic *kafala* is a grueling process overseen by the Ministry of Social Affairs.

Why then, one might ask, does Islam not allow adoption? It all started with the founder of Islam, the prophet Muhammad. In order to make it clear, we must begin with the original story so the reader can understand how this custom got started and how it eventually resulted in the forbidding of adoption.

The Story in a Nutshell

Muhammad adopted a slave boy and gave him his name. Once the boy grew up, Muhammad, like any Arab father, wanted to secure a good wife for his son. Muhammad chose his own cousin to be the wife of his son, but the girl refused to marry one who was beneath her in status.

[131.] *Kafala* is taking financial responsibility or fostering the orphan but not adopting the orphan or giving him the name of the one fostering him.

Allah gave Muhammad a Qur'an verse, and the girl then married Muhammad's son in obedience to Allah. Later on, Muhammad was attracted to his daughter-in-law, and his son offered to divorce her so his father could marry her. Muhammad did not want people to gossip, so he told his son to keep his wife. But once again, Allah intervened with more Qur'an verses that said that he should marry her and gave additional verses that forbid adoption altogether.

The Story of Muhammad and Adoption

Muhammad had four daughters and two sons by his first wife, Khadija. The girls survived, but the sons died in their first two years. Later on, he had a son by the Egyptian Coptic slave who was gifted to him, and Muhammad called him Ibrahim. But that son also died at age two. So Muhammad never enjoyed any grown biological sons in his lifetime, but he did adopt one during his marriage to his first wife, Khadija.

Zaid, the Freed Slave

Muhammad's first wife, Khadija, went to visit her nephew, who had come back from a business trip where he had purchased slave boys, among whom was eight-year-old Zaid. Khadija's nephew offered to give her a slave boy of her choice as a gift. Khadija selected Zaid. When Muhammad, her husband, saw the boy, he liked him and asked Khadija to give him the boy, which she did. At that time, Zaid's biological father heard that his son was sold as a slave and that he had ended up with Muhammad. So he went to Muhammad, trying to redeem the boy. Muhammad did not object to returning the boy to his father if the boy chose to return. Zaid, however, preferred to stay with his master, Muhammad. This made Muhammad very happy. The Prophet's eyes were full of thankful and compassionate tears. He held Zaid's hand and walked to the Kaaba,[132] where the Quraysh were holding a meeting, and cried out, "I bear witness that Zaid is my son, and in case I die first, he will inherit from me, and in case he dies first, I will inherit from him."[133] This happened before the migration of Muhammad to Medina.

So Zaid was known to all as the son of Muhammad, and he was one of the first to embrace Islam, the religion of his adoptive father. When Zaid grew up, Muhammad chose for him his beautiful cousin Zainab Bint Jahsh as wife. But both Zainab and her brother refused to allow the marriage of the honorable lady Zainab to Zaid based on his previous status as a slave. Then Allah revealed the following verse to Muhammad:

> It is not for a believing man or a believing woman, when Allah and His Messenger have decided a matter, that they should [thereafter] have any choice about their affair. And whoever disobeys Allah and His Messenger has certainly strayed into clear error. (Qur'an 33:36)

وَمَا كَانَ لِمُؤْمِنٍ وَلَا مُؤْمِنَةٍ إِذَا قَضَى اللَّهُ وَرَسُولُهُ أَمْرًا أَن يَكُونَ لَهُمُ الْخِيَرَةُ مِنْ أَمْرِهِمْ وَمَن يَعْصِ اللَّهَ وَرَسُولَهُ فَقَدْ ضَلَّ ضَلَالًا مُّبِينًا ﴿٣٦﴾

So upon the revelation of this verse, Zainab married Zaid in obedience to the decree of Allah and his apostle. However, Zaid and Zainab did not live together happily ever after.

Zaid Divorces Zainab So Muhammad Can Marry Her

There have been many controversial stories regarding Muhammad's marriage to Zainab. In spite of some different interpretations, all

---

[132.] Shrine of multiple gods in Mecca where all the townspeople met
[133.] Al-sira1/264 and history of Al Tabari 2/215; also Qur'an.com/Zaid Ibn-Harithah.

Muslim accounts agree that it was Allah who orchestrated the divorce of Zaid and Zainab, and it was Allah who instigated Zainab's marriage to Muhammad, her former father-in-law. They all agree that Allah made Zaid divorce Zainab and Zainab marry the Prophet to remove the barrier set up by ties of adoption and render invalid adoption altogether! Apparently, Allah wanted to change the custom of adoption exercised by the Arabs in Muhammad's time. So he ordered Zainab to marry Zaid, then ordered Zaid to divorce her and allowed Muhammad to marry his daughter-in-law in order to abolish adoption altogether.

According to the Muslim historians Ibn Sa'd and at-Tabri,[134] this is how the divorce between Zaid and his wife, Zainab, happened. On one occasion, Muhammad sought Zaid at his house (went to visit him) but did not find him there. He happened to come upon Zainab when she was not fully clothed and surprised her, so he left. When she found out it was Muhammad, Zainab went after him and asked him to come in, but he did not. Instead, he left, uttering, "Hallelujah, glory of the Great Bank of hearts . . . Praise be to Allah who disposes the hearts." (Allah is the one who instigated in Muhammad's heart the desire to have Zainab.) When Zaid came home, his wife told him that Allah's prophet had come to the house to see him. Zaid then asked her if she had invited him in, to which she answered that she did, but he refused to come in. She also told him that Muhammad had said, "Praise be to Allah who disposes the hearts." Zaid then went to his father and said, "Prophet of Allah, I heard that you went to my house." And he then asked him, "Shall I divorce her?" Muhammad said, "Keep your wife to yourself and fear Allah."

But Allah had another plan for Muhammad and Zainab; so when Zaid had divorced his wife, Zainab, Muhammad was commanded by Allah to marry her. The Qur'an refers to this marriage in sura 33:37:

[134.] Tabakat Ibn Sa'd 8/101 and the history of Tabari, year 6 3/42 Ta. (Tabari is a Muslim historian and religious scholar whose annals are the most important source for the early history of Islam.)

And (remember) when you (Muhammad) said to him (Zaid), "Keep your wife to yourself, and fear Allah." But you did hide in yourself what Allah has already made known to you that He will give her to you in marriage. That which Allah will make manifest, you did fear the people who say Muhammad married the divorced wife of his son, whereas Allah had a better right that you should fear Him. So when Zaid had accomplished his desire from her (i.e., divorced her), We gave her to you in marriage, so that (in the future) there may be no difficulty to the believers in respect of the marriage of the wives of their adopted sons when the latter have no desire to keep them (they have divorced them). And Allah's Command must be fulfilled.

وَإِذْ تَقُولُ لِلَّذِى أَنْعَمَ اللَّهُ عَلَيْهِ وَأَنْعَمْتَ عَلَيْهِ أَمْسِكْ عَلَيْكَ زَوْجَكَ وَاتَّقِ اللَّهَ وَتُخْفِى فِى نَفْسِكَ مَا اللَّهُ مُبْدِيهِ وَتَخْشَى النَّاسَ وَاللَّهُ أَحَقُّ أَنْ تَخْشَىٰهُ فَلَمَّا قَضَىٰ زَيْدٌ مِنْهَا وَطَرًا زَوَّجْنَكَهَا لِكَىْ لَا يَكُونَ عَلَى الْمُؤْمِنِينَ حَرَجٌ فِى أَزْوَجِ أَدْعِيَائِهِمْ إِذَا قَضَوْا مِنْهُنَّ وَطَرًا وَكَانَ أَمْرُ اللَّهِ مَفْعُولًا ٣٧

This verse allows fathers-in-law to marry their daughters-in-law.

Although this marriage brought some disgrace to Muhammad, it brought pride to Zainab. Later on, she would brag, saying to her rivals, "All of you were given to marriage by your fathers, as for me I was given to Muhammad by Allah in the seventh heavens."[135]

And the jealous young wife of Muhammad, who was his favorite, would tell him, "I feel that our Lord hastens in fulfilling your wishes."[136]

---

[135] Tabakat ibn-Sa'd.8: 73; a-l Muhbber 86 al-isti'ab al-Isaba Oyoun al-Athar
[136] Sahih Bukhari book 60, Hadith 311

Muslims have felt the need to justify Muhammad's marriage to his daughter-in-law, and so many explanations have been offered. One is from the book *Ash-Shifa* of Qadi, who quotes the story related by Ali Ibn Husayn:

> Allah knew better than his prophet that Zainab would be one of his wives. When Zaid complained about her to the Prophet, and he told him, "Keep your wife and fear Allah," Muhammad had hid in himself what Allah had intimated to him about his marriage to her; but Allah brought it into the open by bringing her marriage to an end by Zaid's divorcing her.[137]

So apparently, Muhammad knew that Allah wanted him to marry his daughter-in-law, Zainab; but he was concealing it in his heart. Some suggest that he was embarrassed and afraid that people would criticize him for marrying his former daughter-in-law.

So Allah, wanting to abolish adoption and remove the old customs, gave Muhammad the following verse:

> Muhammad is not the father of any of your men, but he is the Messenger of Allah and the seal of the prophets (the last prophet). And Allah is ever knower of all things. (Qur'an 33:40)

مَّا كَانَ مُحَمَّدٌ أَبَا أَحَدٍ مِّن رِّجَالِكُمْ وَلَٰكِن رَّسُولَ اللَّهِ وَخَاتَمَ النَّبِيِّينَ وَكَانَ اللَّهُ بِكُلِّ شَيْءٍ عَلِيمٌ

Allah says, "Neither has he made your adopted sons your real sons. These are the words of your mouths . . . call them by the names of their fathers, but if you know not their fathers, then they are your brethren in faith and your friends. And there is no blame on you in that you

---

[137.] Iyad (Muhammad, Messenger of Allah), Medinah Press, Grenada (1991), pp. 352–354. The work was translated by Aisha Bewley.

made a mistake . . . and Allah is ever forgiving, merciful" (Qur'an 33:4–5).

Those verses say that adopting Zaid was a mistake that Allah wanted to straighten out by saying that Muhammad was not the father of anyone. Then regarding those who had been formerly adopted (by mistake), their names should be changed back to that of their biological father, if known. If not, they will be called friends and brothers in the faith.

So Zaid was no longer called Muhammad's son, but his name was changed to Zaid bin Harithah, which was his biological father's name. Abdullah bin Umar said, "Zaid, bin (son of) Muhammad may Allah be pleased with him, the freed servant of the Messenger of Allah, was always called Zaid bin Muhammad, until the words of the Qur'an were revealed."

So with the referenced Qur'an verses recited by Muhammad, Zaid lost his wife, Zainab; his adoptive father, Muhammad; as well as his inheritance because Allah wanted to change the old custom of adoption.

It seems that Allah caused Muhammad to have desires for his adopted son's wife and caused his son to divorce his wife so that Muhammad could marry her and show others that it was permissible for them to marry their adopted sons' former wives. Why was this involved set of circumstances necessary to remove adoption before Allah would abolish adoption altogether according to Qur'an 33:4–5?

What Were People to Do with Their Adopted Sons?

The plan worked well for Muhammad. However, at the same time, it also created unexpected problems for many others. For example, Abu Huthayfa and his wife, Sahla, had an adopted son called Salim. Salim used to work and live freely in the house. As Salim was like a son to her,

Sahla used to rely on him to help in the housework. She could stay with him in the same room without having to cover herself with the veil (hijab) to remove herself from his gaze. However, when Muhammad made the practice of adoption illegal in Islam, Salim suddenly became a stranger in his own house. He could no longer be alone with Sahla, his adoptive mother. Sahla complained to Muhammad about this unexpected dilemma caused by the new Islamic ruling.

Women Breastfeeding Adult Men

Muhammad immediately provided her with a solution. He asked her to breastfeed Salim, after which she would be allowed to keep him as her son in the house. She replied, "But Salim is a man and has a beard!" Muhammad smiled to her and said, "I know that."

The following Hadith carefully details how adult breastfeeding came to be sanctioned in Islam:

Imam Malik's Muwatta, book 30, number 30.2.12:

> Yahya related to me from Malik from Ibn Shihab that he was asked about the suckling of an older person. He said, "Urwa ibn az-Zubayr informed me that Abu Hudhayfa ibn Utba ibn Rabia, one of the companions of the Messenger of Allah, may Allah bless him and grant him peace, who was present at Badr, adopted Salim (who is called Salim, the mawla of Abu Hudhayfa) as the Messenger of Allah, may Allah bless him and grant him peace, adopted Zayd ibn Haritha. He thought of him as his son, and Abu Hudhayfa married him to his brother's sister, Fatima bint al-Walid ibn Utba ibn Rabia, who was at that time among the first emigrants. She was one of the best unmarried women of the Quraysh. When Allah the Exalted sent down in His

Book what He sent down about Zayd ibn Haritha, "Call them after their true fathers. That is more equitable in the sight of Allah. If you do not know who their fathers were then they are your brothers in the deen and your mawali" (sura 33 ayat/verse 5). People in this position were traced back to their fathers. When the father was not known, they were traced to their mawla (owner).

So if a woman breastfeeds a grown man, he becomes her son, and she does not have to cover up in his presence.

> Aisha took that as a precedent for whatever men she wanted to be able to come to see her. She ordered daughters of her sisters and brothers to give milk to whichever men she wanted to be able to come in to see her. [She had a sister also married to Muhammad.] The rest of the wives of the Prophet, may Allah bless him and grant him peace, refused to let anyone come in to them by such nursing. They said, "No! By Allah! We think that what the Messenger of Allah . . . ordered Sahia bint Suhayl to do was only an indulgence concerning the nursing of Salim alone. No! By Allah! No one will come in upon us by such nursing!" This Hadith is Sahih (authentic).[138]

In May 2007, Dr. Izzat Atiya, head of Egypt's Al Azhar University's Department of Hadith, issued a fatwa (Islamic legal decree), saying that female workers should "breastfeed" their male coworkers in order to work in each other's company. According to the BBC, he said that if a woman fed a male colleague "directly from her breast" at least five times, they would establish a family bond and thus be allowed to be alone together at work. "Breast feeding an adult puts an end to the problem of the private meeting, and does not ban marriage," he ruled. "A woman

---

138. Musnad Ahmad bin Hanbal, p. 192, Hadith number 26208.

at work can take off the veil or reveal her hair in front of someone whom she breastfed."[139]

Atiya based his fatwa on a Hadith, a documented saying or action of Muhammad. Many Egyptians naturally protested this decree—Hadith or no Hadith—though no one could really demonstrate how it was un-Islamic, for the fatwa conformed to Islamic jurisprudence. Still, due to the protests (not many Egyptian women were eager to "breastfeed" their male coworkers), the fatwa receded; and that was that. However, because it was never truly repudiated, it kept making a comeback. Though the fatwa of breastfeeding adult males did not gain popularity, the reason that had triggered it in the first place continues to the present day. Not allowing adoption changed the status of Zainab from daughter-in-law to non-daughter-in-law, therefore allowing Muhammad to marry her. As a consequence, there is no adoption in Islam.

[139.] http://news.bbc.co.uk/2/hi/6681511.stm

Chapter Sixteen

Jesus and Adoption

What Jesus Said about Children

We read the following in the gospel of Mark, "And they were bringing children to Him (Jesus) so that He might touch them; and the disciples rebuked them. But when Jesus saw this, He was indignant and said to them, 'Permit the children to come to Me; do not hinder them; for the kingdom of God belongs to such as these. Truly I say to you, whoever does not receive the kingdom of God like a child, will not enter it at all.' He took them up in His arms, put His hands upon them and blessed them" (Mark 10:13–16).

> See that you do not despise one of these little ones, for I say to you that in heaven their angels continually behold the face of My Father who is in heaven. (Matthew 18:10)

> So it is not the will of your Father who is in heaven that one of these little ones perish. (Matthew 18:14)

> Whoever shall offend one of these little ones that believe in Me, it were better for him that a millstone were hanged around his neck, and that he were drowned in the depth of the sea. (Matthew 18:6)

Taking a child, Jesus set him before them; and taking him in His arms, He said to them, "Whoever receives one child like this in My name receives Me, and whoever receives Me, does not receive Me, but Him who sent Me (God the Father)" (Mark 9:36–37).

What Jesus had to say about children laid the foundation for Christian adoptions. From statistics, we see that countries with a Christian heritage have a larger share of adoptions.[140]

Following the call of Jesus to care for children, a brave young American girl went to Egypt to raise orphaned children. While she could not place them for adoption because of Islamic law, Lillian Trasher took in the children and raised them up in the faith to be adopted into God's family.

Lillian Trasher's Orphanage in Asyut, Egypt

On February 10, 2011, Egypt celebrated the one hundredth anniversary of Lillian Trasher Orphanage in Asyut, Egypt. The orphanage, one of the largest in the world, continues to accomplish to this day a great service to orphans and abandoned children.

The Story of Lillian Trasher

When Lillian sought the Lord's guidance for where she should go to serve Him, the Lord gave her Acts 7:34: "I have certainly seen the oppression of My people in Egypt, and have heard their groans, and I have come down to deliver them; come now, and I will send you to Egypt."

[140.] https://en.wikipedia.org/wiki/Adoption#cite_note-52

Orphanage Celebrates 100 Years Ago TODAY

Lillian Trasher with orphans

A great compassion ministry started on February 10, 1911, 100 years ago today.

On that day, Lillian Trasher, a 23-year-old single American missionary in Egypt, went to visit a dying woman. She saw the woman's baby daughter and was touched by her pitiful cry. When the woman died, Trasher took the tiny orphan to raise. To provide space for her new "family," she rented a small house in Assiout. That day—February 10, 1911, was the beginning of the Lillian Trasher Orphanage.

Over the next 51 years, about 10,000 children were raised in her home; and since her death in 1961, many more thousands of children have called Lillian Trasher Orphanage their home.

THE BEGINNING

Lillian Trasher was born September 27, 1887, and grew up in Brunswick, Georgia. One day, as a young girl, she knelt by a log in the woods and prayed, "Lord, if ever I can do anything for you, just let me know and I'll do it."

In her younger years she worked for Miss Perry in an orphanage and, later, at a training institute where she also worked with children, learning to trust God for the needs of everyday life.

Lillian later attended God's Bible School in Cincinnati, Ohio, pastored a church in Georgia and did evangelistic work in Kentucky. In 1909 she returned to Miss Perry's orphanage in Marion, North Carolina.

She had been praying about a call to missions, and during that time became engaged to be married. Ten days before her wedding day, in June of 1910, she accompanied Miss Perry to hear a missionary from India. At that service she sensed God telling her now was the time to get involved in missions.

Since her fiancé didn't feel the call as she did, she made the painful decision of breaking off her engagement to "the most wonderful young man in the world."

Knowing little about where she was to go, she gathered her few possessions and a few dollars and went to a missionary convention in Pittsburgh, Pennsylvania. She was sure God would provide as He had always done before.

He did. In a short time she arrived in Brooklyn, New York, on her way to Egypt. In the fall of 1910 she sailed for the land of her calling.

After starting the orphanage, since Lillian had no means of support, she begged. Her first donation was thirty-five cents. It was enough for that day's food.

She traveled by donkey throughout the region pleading for money for the children. The government officials were amazed that no one did anything to alarm or hurt Lillian.

LILLIAN TRASHER JOINS THE NEW ASSEMBLIES OF GOD

In 1914 she became affiliated with the new movement, the Assemblies of God. They sent barrels of clothing and an occasional check, but Lillian still relied on the generosity of her Egyptian neighbors.

By 1915 she had 50 children in her orphanage. She had to build on, and the children helped with the construction, even making bricks.

By 1923 she housed 300 orphans and widows but had still not seen a great spiritual harvest. In 1927 it finally came, and she witnessed the revival she had long prayed for. In the meantime, she continued sewing, washing, feeding and building. She continuously relied on God for all things.

In January 1960 she began a new year, her 50th in Egypt. She remembered that as a young, happy girl in 1910, she dreamed of having 12 children of her own.

She did not realize what her life was going to be like when she ended her engagement. Even though she loved him, she said good-bye to Tom, the young preacher who was to be her husband. She wanted to put God first. Now, 50 years later, as a gray-headed woman, she looked out her window to her 1,200 children.

This loving missionary lady, known as "Mama Lillian," or "Mother of the Nile," went on to be with the Lord on December 17, 1961.

EARLY LETTER FROM LILLIAN TRASHER

A 1936 letter from Lillian Trasher gives us a glimpse of the way in which the Heavenly Father provided for the 700 children she had at that time in her orphanage. Here are some excerpts from her letter:

"We are still looking to the Lord for our hourly needs. He is a wonderful caretaker! About 2 weeks ago I was rushing out early for an appointment when one of our boys, who is in charge of the meals, stopped me, saying, 'Mama, what is the orphanage to have for dinner.' I said, 'Fize, I haven't one cent and I have to hurry out now.'

"Soon I was attracted by a man waving an umbrella; he came toward me, took out his wallet and handed me $50, saying that someone who did not wish to reveal his identity had sent it to me to buy food for the children. Fize was soon on his way to town for supplies.

"That day I was invited out for dinner where the subject of God's care for His children came up. Someone mentioned how the Lord had provided for the orphanage that day. A rich young man at that dinner heard the story and gave me $50.

"Yesterday we were without any money for bread and the mail brought us only $5. I was very busy taking care of a very ill baby, so I cried out, 'Oh, Lord, surely you would not have me leave this sick child to go out to try to find bread for the children. I'll take care of the baby, and you

please send in the food.' I called the post office to see if there might be something more and received word that they had a money order for me for $40. It had come from South Africa.

"Last Sunday we had no money for bread. I went to visit a lady who had been ill. She gave me $25 to buy beef for the children's dinner and $25 for anything else.

"The next day I was again without money. We were out of soap, sugar and flour. Our flour costs $560 a month. That day a stranger handed me $25 and a friend handed me $5, so I was able to get all I needed for that time.

"Twenty-five years ago this month I arrived in Egypt and He has never failed me all these years. We are being fed like the sparrows which have no barns nor storerooms."

A WARTIME MIRACLE

It was September 1941. World War II was raging. At that time "Mama Lillian," as she was now called, cared for 900 orphans, 80 widows, plus staff members and some refugees she had taken in.

They were not in danger of the fighting, but the war had cut off the mail which brought money from friends around the world to care for the orphans.

She had rationed food for days trying to make it last as long as possible. Not only were the children hungry, but their clothing was in tatters and their bath towels and bed sheets were worn full of holes.

In desperation Mama did what she had done in every crisis. She called a prayer meeting on a Monday. The note she passed around read: "The children can pray as long and as hard as the Lord puts it on them. We have nothing. The need is very great indeed, but our God is greater. 'Ask and it shall be given.' Lillian."

The next day the prayers continued. Wednesday morning, Mama Lillian received an urgent appeal to come to Cairo and meet with the American ambassador.

She arrived in Cairo on Thursday morning. The ambassador had startling news! A Red Cross ship, loaded with relief supplies for Greek refugees, had turned back and come into port at Alexandria, Egypt. Its cargo included thousands of dresses for women and girls, shirts and pants for men and boys, layettes for b abies, scarves, sweaters, towels, washcloths, bedding, hundreds of kegs of powdered milk, huge sack of rice, flour and beans."

"Could you use any of these things?" the ambassador asked Mama Lillian.

After lunch the ambassador took Mama Lillian to the docks. Crates and boxes were lined up on the sand as far as Mama could see. A convoy of trucks was loaded with food and other urgently needed supplies. More was being loaded on a train.

On Saturday when the supplies reached the orphanage every box and crate held answers to their prayers. That night, for the first time in days, the children could eat all they wanted. They slept on new bedding. On Sunday every child went to church wearing sparkling new clothes.

Mama Lillian helped save lives of orphans and gave them a good home until they grew up and were able to provide for themselves; and even then she was always there for them.

The Lillian Trasher Orphanage has provided a loving home, hope and Christian training to more than 25,000 children during these past 100 years. Today it is one of the largest and finest orphanages in the world.

Adoption in God's Family

The Biblical foundation for the act of adopting children is found in the New Testament of the Bible. Jesus did not specifically talk about adoption, but Jesus' followers developed the concept of adoption very early in their New Testament writings. "The deepest and strongest foundation of adoption is not in the act of humans adopting humans, but is in God adopting humans; *for adoption is at the very heart of the gospel of Jesus Christ.*"[141] We read in the Bible, "But when the fullness of time had come, God sent forth His Son, born of a woman (the virgin Mary) born under the law, to redeem those who were under the law, so that we might receive adoption as sons" (Galatians 4:4–5). This means that God appointed the time for Jesus to come into the world to redeem the human race, who was separated from God because of sin. Christ reconciled the human race with God the Father through His perfect life and death on the cross as payment to satisfy the Father for the sins of the world. Paying the death penalty for their sins, humans were liberated and became eligible to be adopted into the family of God.

The Bible tells us that as we place our trust in Jesus, we are spiritually removed from our natural family in Adam and adopted into the family of Jesus forevermore. "But to all who did receive Him (Jesus) who

---

[141.] http://www.desiringgod.org/messages/adoption-the-heart-of-the-gospel. (This quote and several of the titled sections in this adoption chapter come from John Piper's sermon.)

believed in His name, He gave the right to become children of God, who were born, not of blood, nor of the will of the flesh, nor of the will of man, but of God" (John 1:12–13).

This verse contrasts the natural birth that happens as a result of the union of a man and a woman with the spiritual birth that results as one puts his trust in Jesus Christ as the Savior-Redeemer. This is why Jesus said, "You must be born again" (John 3:3, 7). You must be born spiritually, just like you were born physically.

There are many similarities between what God did to adopt us in His family and what happens in the physical adoption of a child into a new family.

Adoption Was Costly to God

"God sent His Son to redeem those who were under the law." To "redeem" means to obtain or set free by paying a price. What price did God pay to liberate us and adopt us? It cost God the price of His Son's life. "Christ redeemed us from the curse of the law by becoming a curse for us—for it is written, 'Cursed is everyone who is hanged on a tree'" (Galatians 3:13). Jesus died on the cross a cursed death to purchase us from the curse of sin, and He adopted us into His redeemed family when He rose victorious from the dead.

Adoption Is Costly to Humans

There are huge costs in adopting children. Some are financial; some are emotional. There are costs in time and stress for the rest of the life of parents who adopt. They never stop being a parent till they die. The stresses of caring for adult children can even be greater than the stresses of caring for young children. God's cost to adopt us is far greater than any cost we will endure in adopting and raising children.

Adoption and the Legal Status of the Adopted

"God sent His Son . . . so that we might receive adoption as sons. And because you are sons, God has sent the Spirit of His Son into our hearts crying, 'Abba Father'" (Galatians 4:4–6). In order to adopt sinners into His family, God had to satisfy His justice and His law. He allowed the painful death of His Son on the cross as payment for sin so we can be adopted in the family of God.

So it is with our adopted children today. The legal process may seem long and hard before our adopted child may call us Father Daddy.

The Aramaic term for "father," "Abba" (which also happens to be the same in Arabic), is a very endearing term that God never takes away from His adoptive children. I think back on Zaid, the adopted son of the prophet Muhammad, and how hard it must have been for him to be stripped of the use of this very endearing term, "Abba."

Inheritance: A Benefit of God's Adoption

We read in the Bible, "The Spirit Himself bears witness with our spirit that we are children of God, and if children, then heirs—heirs of God and fellow heirs with Christ provided that we suffer with Him in order that we may also be glorified with Him" (Romans 8:16–17). Jesus provided spiritual adoption, giving His children His name and inheritance. Have you been adopted into God's family? Can you call Him Abba Daddy?

Chapter Seventeen

Muhammad and Deception

People from all nations and all religions sometimes lie or do not tell the whole truth, in some communities more than others. As humans, we understand this whether we like it or not. In addition, all major religions advocate being truthful, and Islam is no exception. But Muhammad allowed some exceptions to this rule, called taqiya, based on Allah's revelations. Taqiya allows, condones, and even encourages Muslims to lie when deemed necessary. Interestingly, the Qur'an says, "And they (the disbelievers) schemed, and Allah schemed (against them): and Allah is the best of schemers" (Qur'an 3:54). The Arabic word *makr* (deceit) translated "scheme" means "sly," "cunning," "wily," or "deceptive."[142]

Growing up in Egypt, a Muslim country, we were perhaps unaware of the principle of taqiya; however, the culture was influenced by it in many ways. People were following taqiya in their everyday living without knowing where it originated from. Of course, I had no idea either until I started studying Islam. Then I remembered the charge our sponsor had given us the first day we arrived in New York: "Never, never lie!"

[142.] https://wikiislam.net/wiki/Allah_the_Best_Deceiver

My husband and I landed in New York, awaiting our destiny to unfold in a new country we had only heard about and formed ideas about in our imagination. We had left Egypt, our country of birth, and gone to Beirut, Lebanon, to seek passage to the United States as political refugees.

After some months, we arrived in New York in December 1962, homeless and penniless.[143] We were met by our sponsors, who hosted a dinner reception for us. The speaker gave a welcome speech and told us about what we should and should not do in America. One of the important things he said, which I always remembered, was that in America we should always tell the truth. To drive the point home, he went as far as saying that in the States, lying is considered worse than killing! This sounded very extreme, and as a thirty-year-old, I could not understand his reasoning. Perhaps our speaker knew that coming from Middle Eastern countries, lying was not only tolerated, but also accepted and, in some cases, encouraged.

So what is taqiya exactly?

Taqiya was mostly sanctioned for protecting and expanding Islam.

From Islamic law, we read the summary: "One should compare the bad consequences entailed by lying to those entailed by telling the truth; and if the consequences of telling the truth are more damaging, one is entitled to lie."[144]

The word "taqiya" has several meanings:

1. Saying something that is not true
2. *Kitman,* or lying by omission or telling half the truth
3. *Tawria,* or intentionally creating a false impression

[143.] The Nasser regime allowed us to take only $150 per adult and $75 per child.

[144.] Ahmad Ibn Naquib al-Misri, Reliance of the Traveler (p. 746; 8.2). *Reliance of the Traveler* is a classical manual of the Shafi'i school of Islamic jurisprudence written in the fourteenth century.

Taqiya serves to mislead the enemy in times of war, to reconcile quarreling parties, or to placate one's wife. In these three circumstances, Muhammad states it is permissible to lie. The following is from Sahih Muslim 32:6303: "He did not hear that exemption was granted in anything what the people speak as lie but in three cases: in battle, for bringing reconciliation amongst persons and the narration of the words of the husband to his wife, and the narration of the words of a wife to her husband (in a twisted form in order to bring reconciliation between them)."[145]

The Qur'an contains two verses that are the foundation for the principle of taqiya. The first one is Qur'an 16:106: "Whoso disbelieves in God (Islam) after having believed, *unless it be one who is forced and whose heart is quiet in the faith*—but whoso expands his breast to misbelieve—on them is wrath from God and for them is mighty woe" (emphasis added).[146]

This verse permits the pious Muslim to conceal his Islamic faith from non-Muslims or even pretend to be an infidel in cases of coercion. According to the commentators, this verse was revealed concerning an incident about Ammar, an early follower of Muhammad. Ammar became a Muslim in the beginning of Muhammad's call but then denied his faith before the people of Quraysh to escape their persecution after they killed his father and his mother, as reported by al-Razi.[147] When a crying Ammar returned to Muhammad, Muhammad wiped his tears and said, "If they repeat it to you, repeat to them what[ever] you said before." In other words, Muhammad gave Ammar permission to lie to avoid persecution. This story is supported by most of the major Islamic scholars. Al-Tabari[148] concludes, "As for one who is forced to

145. https://www.thereligionofpeace.com/pages/quran/taqiyya.aspx
146. Taqiya: Deliberate Deception by Mohamed El-Tayeb, p. 10.
147. Al Razi 20:123
148. Al Tabari 14:376

pronounce by his tongue [blasphemy or infidelity] but has faith in his heart, so he can escape from his enemy, there is no guilt on him."

$$\text{لَا يَتَّخِذِ ٱلْمُؤْمِنُونَ ٱلْكَٰفِرِينَ أَوْلِيَآءَ مِن دُونِ ٱلْمُؤْمِنِينَ ۖ وَمَن يَفْعَلْ ذَٰلِكَ فَلَيْسَ مِنَ ٱللَّهِ فِى شَىْءٍ إِلَّآ أَن تَتَّقُوا۟ مِنْهُمْ تُقَىٰةً ۗ وَيُحَذِّرُكُمُ ٱللَّهُ نَفْسَهُۥ ۗ وَإِلَى ٱللَّهِ ٱلْمَصِيرُ ﴿٢٨﴾}$$

Yusuf Ali translates Qur'an 3:28 as follows: "Let not the believers Take for friends or helpers Unbelievers rather than believers: if any do that, in nothing will there be help from Allah: except by way of precaution, that ye may Guard yourselves from them. But Allah cautions you (to remember) Himself; for the final goal is to Allah."

Qur'an 3:28 tells Muslims not to take those outside the faith as friends unless it is to "guard themselves" against danger, meaning that there are times when a Muslim should appear friendly to non-Muslims even though they do not feel that way.

Regarding this verse, Ibn Kathir writes[149] (d. 1373) "Whoever at any time or place fears evil from non-Muslims may protect himself through outward show." As proof of this, he quotes Muhammad's close companion Abu Darda, who said, "Let us grin in the face of some people while our hearts curse them." Another companion said, "Doing taqiya is acceptable till the day of judgment."[150]

A more compelling expression of deceiving the infidels is the following: Ka'b ibn Ashraf (a poet), offended Muhammad, prompting him to exclaim, "Who will kill this man who has hurt Allah and his prophet?" A young Muslim volunteered on condition that in order to get close

---

[149.] Ibn Kathir is a highly regarded authority on the Qur'an.
[150.] 'Imad ad-Din Isma'il Ibn Kathir, Tafsir al-Qur'an al-Karim (Beirut: Dar al-Kutub al-'Ilmiya, 2001), vol. 1, p. 350 (noted in the online Middle East Quarterly, winter 2010, article by Raymond Ibrahim, pp. 3–13, to which I am indebted for much of this material).

enough to Ka'b to assassinate him, he be allowed to lie to the poet. Muhammad agreed, and the young man travelled to Ka'b and began to insult Islam and Muhammad. He carried on till he convinced Ka'b, the poet, of his hatred of Muhammad and gained his confidence. The boy then appeared with another Muslim and, while Ka'b's guard was down, killed him.[151]

Another example of lying is when Muhammad used deception to trick his personal enemies into letting down their guard and exposing themselves to slaughter by pretending to seek peace. This happened in the case of Ka'b bin al-Ashraf (as previously noted) and again later against Usayr ibn Zarim, a surviving leader of the Banu Nadir tribe, which had been evicted from their home in Medina by the Muslims.

> At the time, Usayr ibn Zarim was attempting to gather an armed force against the Muslims from among a tribe allied with the Quraysh (against which Muhammad had already declared war). Muhammad's "emissaries" went to ibn Zarim and persuaded him to leave his safe haven on the pretext of meeting with the prophet of Islam in Medina to discuss peace. Once vulnerable, the leader and his thirty companions were massacred by the Muslims with ease, probably because they were unarmed, having been given a guarantee of safe passage (Ibn Ishaq, 981).[152]

War Is Deceit

So when did this notion that war is deceit start? Deceit in warfare is nothing new; however, what is different is that according to Muhammad,

[151.] Ibn Ishaq, *The Life of Muhammad* (Karachi: Oxford University Press 1997), pp. 367–8.

[152.] https://www.thereligionofpeace.com/pages/quran/taqiyya.aspx

Islam regards itself in a state of perpetual warfare with infidels (non-Muslims). He said, "I have been commanded to fight against people till they testify that there is no god but Allah, that Muhammad is the messenger of Allah, and they establish prayer, and pay Zakat and if they do it, their blood and property are guaranteed protection on my behalf except when justified by law, and their affairs rest with Allah" (Sahih Muslim, book 1, number 33). So because of perpetual warfare, you can also expect perpetual deception.

> This Muslim notion that war is deceit goes back to the Battle of the Trench (627), which pitted Muhammad and his followers against several non-Muslim tribes known as Al-Ahzab. One of the Ahzab, Na'im ibn Mas'ud, went to the Muslim camp and converted to Islam. When Muhammad discovered that the Ahzab were unaware of their co-tribalist's conversion, he counseled Mas'ud to return and try to get the pagan forces to abandon the siege. It was then that Muhammad memorably declared, "For war is deceit." Mas'ud returned to the Ahzab without their knowing that he had switched sides and intentionally began to give his former kin and allies bad advice. He also went to great lengths to instigate quarrels between the various tribes until, thoroughly distrusting each other, they disbanded, lifted the siege from the Muslims, and saved Islam from destruction in an embryonic period. Most recently, 9/11 accomplices, such as Khalid Sheikh Muhammad, rationalized their conspiratorial role in their defendant response by evoking their prophet's assertion that "war is deceit."[153]

[153.] http://www.meforum.org/2538/taqiyya-islam-rules-of-war#_ftn15

Islam teaches that deceit is integral to jihad.[154] In the Hadith and actions of Muhammad, practicing deceit in war is well demonstrated. Indeed, its need is more stressed than the need for courage. Ibn Al-Munir writes, "War is deceit, i.e., the most complete and perfect war waged by a holy warrior (mujahid) is a war of deception, not confrontation, due to the latter's inherent danger, and the fact that one can attain victory without harm to oneself."[155]

Tawria (concealing): Lying does not have to be for wartime or among Allah's enemies only. It can be for any other reason.

The first chapter of the Qur'an, "Al-Fatihah" (The Opening), is recited by Muslims in each of their five daily required prayers. Qur'an 1:5–7 says, "Guide us on the right path; The path of those upon whom thou hast bestowed favor;_not those upon whom wrath is brought down, nor those who go astray." The Qur'an explains that "those" refers to the Jews and the Christians. But if you ask a Muslim why in their daily prayer they demean Christian and Jews, a Muslim will quickly practice *tawria* (hiding) under taqiya and tell you that the verse never mentions Jews or Christians even though he and everyone else know full well that this is the meaning given in the Qur'an.

Kitman (telling only part of truth) is if someone asks if you have seen so-and-so and you may answer no even if you have seen him, but in your mind, you mean that you have not seen him today!

Abrogation and Deception

What does the word "abrogation" mean? "Abrogation" means "to annul by official means (such as a law)," "to abolish," or "to repeal."

---

154. Fighting for the cause of Allah
155. Ibn Al-Munir (d. 1333)

When it comes to Islam, this is a word that has led to a lot of misunderstanding and confusion. Let me explain why and how. We have all heard a president and other people say, "Islam is a religion of peace." You may or may not agree with this statement. You may have also heard that Islam is not a religion of peace because of all the killings that occur in the name of Islam. So what does the Qur'an, the authority on Islam, have to say? We all know some very sincere, good Muslims who are really peaceful and live peacefully among us. On the other hand, we hear of terrible acts of violence committed in the name of Islam by religious Muslims who shout "Allahu Akbar" as they behead, kill, or stone their victims. So which is the true Islam? Peaceful Muslims may show you a verse in the Qur'an to prove to you that Islam is indeed a religion of peace. On the other hand, radical Muslims insist that *they* are the ones who follow the teachings of Muhammad, the prophet of Islam; and they back it up with Qur'an verses as well. Ironically, both are right, and the answer lies in the theory of abrogation.

A Saudi student at the university with whom I had become friends was trying to convince me that Islam was a religion of peace and that the Qur'an accepts Christians and Jews and speaks kindly about them. She quoted me a Christian-friendly verse from the Qur'an, which says, "Surely those who believe and those who are Jews and the Christians and the Sabeans, whoever believes in Allah and the Last Day and does good, they have their reward with their Lord, and there is no fear for them, nor shall they grieve" (Qur'an 2:62). According to this verse, Islam is peaceful, and Muslims accept Christians and do not seek to harm or kill them.

I told my friend that this verse sounded very good, but in spite of the fact that it is still in the Qur'an, it does not function as part of it anymore because it has been abrogated and replaced by another verse that says, "And whoever seeks a religion other than Islam, it shall not be accepted from him, and in the hereafter he shall be one of the losers" (Qur'an 3:85).

My friend turned pale and quickly changed the subject because she did not expect a Christian to know about abrogation. In fact, not too many Muslims know about it either.

There are over a hundred verses in the Qur'an that have been abrogated—repealed, annulled, and replaced—by other verses (rendered ineffective) even though they are physically not removed from the Qur'an. How did this happen? Well, Muhammad received a verse from Allah telling him that whenever the devil causes him (Muhammad) to forget a verse or if Allah wants to bring down a better verse, Allah will replace the earlier one with a new and better one.

Allah told Muhammad, "Whatever verse we abrogate or cause to be forgotten, we bring one better than it or one like it. Knowest thou not that Allah is possessor of power over all things?" (Qur'an 2:106).

So the above verse allowed Muhammad to change many verses he had recited earlier and replace them with new ones in the Qur'an. So which verses in the Qur'an are to be followed? Having encountered this problem, the commentators of Islam developed the doctrine of abrogation, which basically maintains that verses revealed later to Muhammad take precedence over earlier verses whenever there is a discrepancy. This is known in Arabic as *an-Nasikh wa'l Mansukh* (the abrogator and the abrogated). Unfortunately, both the old verse and the new remain in the Qur'an even though only the newer verses are legitimate. This creates confusion for the reader.

As a general rule, during his early mission, Muhammad was reciting conciliatory and peaceful verses in an attempt to win people to join him in his call to embrace his new religion, Islam. By and by, however, Muhammad gained some supporters and established the Islamic ummah (a nation under the banner of Islam regardless of geographic location). With the ummah, he gained power, fought his enemies, and won many battles against those who refused Islam; and he subdued them. So when Muhammad gained power, so did his Qur'anic verses.

They became powerful and aggressive, demanding destruction of those who are the enemies of Allah, his prophet Muhammad, and Islam. This is why the Qur'an has many contradictory verses. This is not only confusing to non-Muslims, but to most Muslims who have not studied Islam in depth. Peaceful people read the peaceful verses, believe them, and want to live by them. So when they hear of the atrocities committed by radical Muslims, they respond with, "This is not Islam! Islam is a religion of peace!" Radical Muslims argue that they indeed are the true followers of the instructions of their prophet Muhammad. They know too well that the earlier friendly verses have been replaced by the later jihad verses. By emphasizing abrogated verses, peaceful Muslims can present Islam as a religion of peace.

The Qur'an and Abrogation

The following are some examples where the old peaceful verses were abrogated and replaced with jihad verses:

Qur'an 2:256 states, "There is no compulsion in religion . . ." This verse was abrogated and replaced with: "So when the sacred months have passed, slay the idolaters wherever you find them, and take them captive and besiege them and lie in wait for them in every ambush . . ." (Qur'an 9:5).

Qur'an 5:99 states, "The duty of the messenger is only to deliver . . ." This verse was also abrogated and replaced with verse 9:5 above.

Qur'an 29:46 states, "And argue not with the people of the book (Christians and Jews) . . . But say: we believe in that which has been revealed to us and revealed to you; and our Allah and your Allah is one . . ." This verse was abrogated and replaced with: "Fight those who believe not in Allah, nor in the last day; nor forbid that which Allah and his messenger have forbidden nor follow the religion of truth (Islam), even if they are of the people of the book, until they pay the Jizya with willing submission, and feel themselves subdued" (Qur'an 9:29).

Qur'an 2:83 states, "And when we made a covenant with the children of Israel: 'You shall not serve any but Allah . . .'" This verse was abrogated and replaced with: "So, when the sacred months have passed, slay the idolaters . . ." (Qur'an 9:5).

The above verse is known as "Ayat as-Sayf" (the verse of the sword) and has abrogated about 113 verses, including every other verse in the Qur'an that commands or implies anything less than a total offensive against nonbelievers.[156]

So in order to document which verses abrogated which, a religious science devoted to the chronology of the verses of the Qur'an evolved as *an-Nasikh wa'l Mansukh* (the abrogater and the abrogated).[157]

Jihad

The word "jihad" is well-known in the West. What does it really mean? The following few words from Ibn Khaldun help explain jihad:

> In the Muslim community, Jihad is a religious duty because of the universalism of the Muslim mission and the obligation to convert everybody to Islam either by persuasion or by force. The other religious groups did not have a universal mission, and the jihad was not a religious

[156.] David Bukay, Peace or Jihad? Abrogation in Islam. *Middle East Quarterly*, Fall 2007, pp. 3–11, fn58; David S. Powers, "The Exegetical Genre nsikh al-Qur'an wa mansukhuhu, in Approaches to the History of the Interpretation of the Qur'an, Andrew Rippin, ed. (Oxford: Clarendon Press, 1988) pp. 130–131.

[157.] For a complete listing, see https://wikiislam.net/wiki/List_of_Abrogations_in_the_Qur%27an.

duty for them, save only for purpose of defense. But Islam
is under obligation to gain power over other nations.[158]

Many well-meaning Muslims argue that verses of the Qur'an that call
for fighting and jihad were given by Muhammad only in periods of war.
This may be true, except that Islam vows to be in perpetual war until
Islam prevails over all religions. "He it is who has sent his messenger
with the guidance and the religion of truth that He may make it prevail
over all religions. And Allah is enough for a witness" (Qur'an 48:28,
9:33, 61:9). Yes, this verse has been repeated three times, and radical
Muslims will continue to kill in hope of making Islam prevail over all
religions.

[158.] The Muqadimah, An Introduction to History, Frantz Rosenthal, trans., New
York: Pantheon, p. 473.

Chapter Eighteen

Jesus and Truth

The Bible, like the Qur'an, has many stories of lies and deceit by people for personal gain. However, there is a major difference between the lying and deception in the Qur'an and that of the Bible. What Muhammad sanctioned in the Qur'an Jesus unequivocally forbade in the New Testament of the Bible. Jesus never told a lie and did not condone lying for any reason—not to save one's life during wars or persecution nor to try to achieve peace between quarreling people nor to say something with your tongue when meaning something else in your heart.

Telling the Truth

Throughout the books of the Bible, God's word admonishes His people to tell the truth. We read the following in the Old Testament:

> Lying lips are an abomination to the Lord, but those who act faithfully are His delight. (Proverbs 12:22)

> Truthful lips endure forever, but a lying tongue is but for a moment. (Proverbs 12:19)

These are the things that you shall do: Speak the truth to one another. (Zechariah 8:16)

You destroy those who speak lies; the Lord abhors the bloodthirsty and deceitful man. (Psalm 5:6)

From Psalm 15, we find the characteristics of the one who will dwell with God. "He that walks uprightly, and works righteousness, and speaks the truth in his heart . . . He that swears to his own hurt, and changes not" (Psalm 15:2, 4).

God is not man, that he should lie, or a son of man, that he should change his mind. Has he said, and will he not do it? Or has he spoken, and will he not fulfill it? (Numbers 23:19, ESV)

And in the books of the New Testament, we read the following:

But speaking the truth in love, we are to grow up in all aspects into Him who is the Head, even Christ. (Ephesians 4:15)

Therefore, having put away falsehood let each one of you, speak the truth with his neighbor . . . (Ephesians 4:25)

Do not lie to one another since you laid aside the old self with its evil practices. (Colossians 3:9)

Speaking to the multitudes about making an oath Jesus said to them, "Make no oath at all but let your statements be, 'Yes, yes, and 'No, no' and anything beyond that is from the evil one" (Matthew 5:37).

Truth in communication is very important because it is the foundation for trust and connection. The God of the Bible is called Father. His desire is to have loving fellowship with His children.

Jesus Is the Truth

Jesus said, "I am the way, the truth and the life; no man comes to the Father except through Me" (John 14:6). This statement goes far beyond instructions to tell the truth. It is a claim of deity because the ultimate truth in the universe is God. The Bible says of Jesus, "In the beginning was the Word, and the Word was with God and *the Word was God*. He (Jesus) was in the beginning with God" (John 1:1–2). Perfection and total truthfulness are only found in the divine being of God. Truthfulness is fundamental to God's nature. This is why devout followers of Jesus place high value on being truthful.

Satan: The Father of Lies

Speaking to a group of Jewish leaders, Jesus told them, "You are of your father the devil, and you want to do the desires of your father. He was a murderer from the beginning, and does not stand in the truth, because there is no truth in him, whenever he speaks a lie he speaks from his own nature; for he is a liar and the father of lies" (John 8:44).

So when Jesus called Satan a liar and the father of lies, He said so because he knew Satan well. He knew that he was a fallen angel who had rebelled against God and became His enemy and the enemy of His creation. What about the Jews? Why did Jesus tell them, "You are of your father, the devil"? How had they become children of the devil? They were children of the devil because they were acting like him. To understand what Jesus was referring to, we need to go back to the original story in Genesis, chapter 3.

God created Adam and Eve and had fellowship with them in the Garden of Eden. Satan was jealous and set out to destroy this relationship between God and man, whom He loved. To separate God's creation from their Creator, Satan schemed and came out with his first lie to mankind. That is why Jesus called him the father of lies! Before his lie, he first went to Eve and planted doubt in her mind by asking her if God had really forbidden them from eating from the fruit of the trees in the garden. Eve replied that God had forbidden them to eat of one tree only because if they did, they would die. Then Satan quickly delivered to Eve the first lie. He contradicted God and said, "You surely shall not die, for God knows that the day you eat from it, your eyes will be opened, and you will be like God, knowing good and evil." With that lie, Satan led Eve to her spiritual death (separation from God) and ultimately to her physical death. Adam followed, and so have we all. Adam lost his spiritual life and could not pass on what he did not have.

But Jesus came to save humanity from their condition of spiritual death, which happened the day they believed Satan's lie and acted upon it by disobeying God. Since then, humans have been living under the curse of sin, spiritually dead. Jesus came to give mankind a way whereby they could be saved from spiritual death. Truth is actually the opposite of the lie that Satan presented to the human race. Truth is the self-expression of God.[159] Lying is Satan's nature and his primary weapon against all humans. He uses the tactic of deceit. Jesus offered Himself to God as the only way for any human being to restore the lost fellowship that mankind had with God the Father. Jesus said, "I am the way, the truth and the life . . ."

So Jesus did not only speak the truth, but He himself *is* the truth. Therefore, he was telling the Jews, "And you shall know the truth and the truth shall make you free" (John 8:32). Now the Jews took offense at that because they were proud of the fact that they were Abraham's children. They wanted to be accepted based on their father Abraham's deeds. But Jesus told them that they really were not even following Abraham's righteousness.[160]

[159.] John McArthur's Grace to You radio programs.
[160.] https://www.gty.org/library/sermons-library/43-47/false-assurance-of-the-religious

Muhammad did not choose to follow Jesus; instead, he followed the voice that spoke to him from an angel.

According to Muhammad, his Qur'an came to him as a revelation from an "angel." Muhammad said the angel squeezed him "until he could not breathe." We read in the Bible that when an angel appeared to Abraham, Zechariah, or Mary, the mother of Jesus, he greeted them and gave them a message from God, not squeezed them until they could hardly breathe. Could Muhammad's visitation have been by a different type of being? Muhammad's "angel" often caused him to forget. Several Qur'an passages talk about verses revealed to Muhammad that Allah allowed him to forget. Qur'an 87:6–7 says, "We shall make thee recite so thou shall not forget-Except what Allah please." One wonders why Allah sent his angel to give a message that he would later cause Muhammad to forget.

> And when thou see those who talk nonsense about our messages, withdraw from them until they enter into some other discourse. *And if the devil cause you to forget,* then sit not after recollection with the unjust people. (Qur'an 6:68, emphasis mine)

The above verse indicates the devil had something to do with Qur'an verses being forgotten or replaced.

Jesus, on the other hand, said, "But the Helper, the Holy Spirit, whom the Father will send in my Name, He will teach you all things and bring to your remembrance all that I said to you" (John 14:26). "For truly I say to you, until heaven and earth pass away, not the smallest letter or stroke shall pass away from the Law until all is accomplished" (Matthew 5:18).

Chapter Nineteen

The Afterlife in Islam

People everywhere all agree on one thing: death is certain! Different views surface with the question on what happens after death. Is there another life, or do we just turn into dust and are forever forgotten? Judaism, Christianity, and Islam all believe in life after death. The nature of our existence in the afterlife is where we find differences.

Judaism refers to various patriarchs as being joined to their people and the wicked as being cut off from their people in the Torah in Genesis and Deuteronomy (Genesis 25:8, 17:8; Deuteronomy 32:50). The Tanakh (Old Testament) teaches the resurrection and the rewards of righteousness and wickedness (Job 19:25–27; Daniel 12:2; Isaiah 66:5, 22–24; Malachi 3:16–18) but mostly focuses on the best way to live in this world. Religious Jews accept that when the Messiah comes, he will bring justice in the World to Come. Righteous actions can merit a good standing in the afterlife.[161]

Christians and Muslims believe in life after death but differ on the means by which one enters either heaven or hell.

[161.] http://www.jewfaq.org/olamhaba.htm

Islam and Muhammad on the Afterlife

Good and Bad Deeds

Muslims believe that they have to personally pay for each and every sin and transgression they commit toward Allah, either by good deeds that offset the bad or by punishment in the afterlife. Allah has a scale for the good and bad deeds a person does throughout his life. If the good side is heavier, the person *might* go to paradise; if the bad side is heavier, the person will suffer the consequences in hell. This punishment *begins in the grave* right after the burial of the body and before the person is sent to hell. This is called the "torment or punishment of the grave" (عَّذاب القبر). The concept of torment in the grave is very common among Muslims, causing them a lot of fear. Who are the ones to be punished in the grave? First of all, any non-Muslim; second, any person who has disobeyed Allah and his prophet and has not paid for it by good deeds. I remember once asking my Muslim taxi driver where he thought he would be going after death. He did not hesitate but quickly said, "Straight to hell." Asking him why, he told me that he drank beer and sometimes neglected to pray the five daily prayers.

A former Muslim lady who now is a Christian and has a Christian TV show shared how as a child she was terrified of the stories she was told about Munkar and Nakir, the two "angels" who torment sinners in the grave. And of course, no one knows exactly if he has paid enough for his sins or has satisfied all of Allah's commands. Muslim websites show graphic pictures of bodies that have been mutilated in the grave, claiming it was done by Munkar and Nakir for offenses they did while they were living.

Shaykh Muhammad Saalih al-Munajjid listed in the Islam Question and Answer website[162] some of the reasons for the punishment in the grave. For example, he wrote,

---

[162.] https://islamqa.info/en/45325, published November 12, 2005.

The Prophet (peace and blessings of Allah be upon him) told us about two men whom he saw being punished in their graves. One of them used to walk around spreading malicious gossip among the people, and the other failed to take precautions to avoid getting urine on himself. So the latter failed to purify himself as required (indicates one who neglects prayer, for which cleansing oneself from urine is a requirement), and the former did something that creates enmity among people by talking, even if what he says is true.

Munkar and Nakir: The Two "Angels" of the Grave[163]

Munkar and Nakir (منكر و نكير) (English translation: "The Denied and The Denier") in Islamic eschatology are angels who test the faith of the dead in their graves. (Munkar is sometimes transliterated as Monkir.)

Muslims believe that after death, a person's soul passes through a stage called *barzakh*, where it exists in the grave (even if the person's body was destroyed, the soul will still rest in the earth near their place of death). The questioning will begin when the funeral is over and the last person of the funeral congregation has stepped forty steps away from the grave. Nakir and Munkar prop the deceased soul upright in the grave and ask three questions:

1. "Who is your Lord?"
2. "Who is your prophet?"
3. "What is your religion?"

A righteous believer will respond correctly, saying that their Lord is Allah, that Muhammad is their prophet, and that their religion is Islam. If the deceased answers correctly, the time spent awaiting the resurrection

---

[163.] https://en.wikipedia.org/wiki/Munkar_and_Nakir; most of the article is quoted.

178

is pleasant. Those who do not answer as described above are chastised until the Day of Judgment.

These angels are described as having solid black eyes, having a shoulder span measured in miles, and carrying hammers "so large, that if all of mankind tried at once to move them a single inch, they would fail." When they speak, tongues of fire come from their mouths. If one answers their questions incorrectly, one is beaten every day other than Friday until Allah gives permission for the beating to stop.

Muslims believe that a person will correctly answer the questions not by remembering the answers before death, but by their faith (*iman*) and deeds, such as *salat* (prayer) and *shahadah* (the Islamic profession of faith).

The punishments of the grave are very graphic[164] and include repetitive injury to bodies that reconstitute after being torn, smashing heads, ripping faces, swimming in blood, constriction until the ribs interlock, foul smells, fire, and being burned in an oven. But this is only the physical aspect, which is compounded by the regret and longing of understanding the blessings of paradise, which are missed out on.

It is no wonder that Muslims are terrified of death and the grave with its punishment and hell.

In Qur'an 72:23, Muhammad says, "Mine is nothing but to deliver the command of Allah and his messages. And whoever disobeys Allah and his messenger, surely for him is the Fire of Hell to abide therein for ages."

The Qur'an offers scary descriptions of hell as punishment for unbelievers, but Muhammad said that not only unbelievers will go to hell, *but everyone has to go to hell*—at least for a while.

---

164. https://islamqa.info/en/8829

Qur'an 19:71 explicitly says, "And there is none of you but shall come to it. This is an unavoidable decree of thy Lord."

The above verse has been explained over and over in many ways in an attempt to negate that, according to Islam, all humans will first go to hell. However, it is evident that no one in Muhammad's time felt that he was immune from entering hell because of Muhammad's statements and Qur'an verses.

This is evidenced by Muslim traditions about Abu-Bakr, one of Muhammad's closest friends and his successor as the leader of the Muslim community. Muhammad had informed him that he was guaranteed paradise. Despite this promise, the following is reported about Abu-Bakr:

> Whenever he was reminded of his position in Allah's sight, he would say: "By Allah! I would not rest assured and feel safe from the 'makr' (scheme) of Allah even if I had one foot in paradise."[165]

This is possibly because of Muhammad's Qur'an verse saying, "They schemed and Allah schemed and Allah is the best schemer" (Qur'an 3:54), meaning that both Allah and his people schemed, but it is Allah who wins because he is a better schemer.

No One Is Immune from Entering Hell

Whenever Abu Maysarah would lie down on his bed, he would say, "I wish my mother had never bore me," and then he would begin to weep. When asked why he was

---

[165] , Khalid Muhammad Khalid, Successors of the Messenger, translated by Muhammad Mahdi Al-Sharif (Dar wl-Kotob Al-Ilmiyah, Beirut, Lebanon, 2005), cf. p. 99.

weeping, he would respond, "We were told that we would
enter Hell, but we weren't told that we would exit from it." [166]

There are also narrations of stories about people who were afraid because
of Qur'an 19:71, which says that everyone will enter hell.

It is narrated that Abdallah Ibn Rawaha wept during his illness, so his
wife wept also. He then asked her, "Why are you weeping?" She
responded, "I saw you weeping, and so I started to weep." Ibn Rawaha
said, "I know that I will enter hellfire, but I don't know whether I will
be taken out of it or not." Similarly, there are other stories of Muslims'
fear of going to hell because of what Muhammad said. When asked
about himself, Muhammad said that even he was not assured of heaven
unless Allah had mercy on him.

Muslims are very scared of hell, especially since that they are told that
even if they were to end up in paradise, they may have to first be in
hell—at least for a while.

Some Qur'an verses like 72:23 quoted above seem to say that those
going to hell stay there forever, while others say that they will be there
for a while and then will be sent to heaven.

For instance, Qur'an 6:128 says, "On the day when He will gather them
all together: O assembly of Jinn, you took away a great part of men.
And their friends from among men will say: Our Lord, some of us
profited by others and we have reached our appointed term which thou
did appoint for us. He will say: The fire is your abode—you shall abide
therein, except as Allah please. Surely thy Lord is wise and knowing."

According to this and other Qur'an verses, if Allah is willing, even the
wicked will get out of hell.

[166.] Narrated by Abu Kurayb, narrated by Ibn Yaman, narrated by Malik Ibn Maghul,
narrated by Abu Ishahaq.

According to the Qur'an and the Hadith, those who are in hell will be taken out of it. The Prophet is reported to have said, "Then Allah will say, The Angels have interceded and the prophets have interceded and the faithful have interceded and none remains but the Most Merciful of all merciful ones. So He will take a handful from the fire and bring out a people who have never done any good."

Three kinds of intercession are spoken of in this tradition: of the faithful, of the prophets, and of the angels. And the intercession of each is undoubtedly meant for people who have come in contact with them personally. The prophets will intercede for their followers. The angels, who move men to do good, will intercede for people who are not followers of a prophet but who have done some good. And the report adds that the most merciful of all (Allah) still remains, so he will bring out from fire even people who have never done any good. It follows that, thereafter, none can remain in hell; and in fact, the handful of God cannot leave anything behind.[167] This means that God's hand is so bountiful and large, that in essence, no one can remain in hell.

Allah's apostle said, "Some people who will be scorched by Hellfire as punishment for sins they have committed, and then Allah will admit them into paradise by the grant of His Mercy. These people will be called, 'Al-Jahannamiyyin' (the people of Hell)."[168]

Muhammad's Description of Hell

Various Hadith report on the size of hell. Hell is huge and immensely deep. We know this through several ways. First, innumerable people will enter hell; second, each unbeliever's molar tooth is as large as Uhud (a mountain in Medina), and the distance between the shoulders of its

---

[167.] Ali, The Religion of Islam, Chapter 6. Life after Death, Remedial Nature of Hell, pp. 233–234.

[168.] Sahih Al-Bukhari, vol. 9, book 93, number 542. Narrated by Anas.

182

inhabitants has also been described as being equivalent to three days' walk.[169] He will house all the unbelievers and sinners from the beginning of time, and there will still be room for more. Allah says, "On the day when we will say to Hell: 'Are you filled?' It will say, 'Are there any more?'" (Qur'an 50:30).

> If a stone as big as seven pregnant camels were thrown from the edge of Hell, it would fly through it for seventy years, and yet it would not reach the bottom.[170]

Stones and stubborn unbelievers make the fuel of hell, as Allah says, "O you who have believed, protect yourselves and your families from a Fire whose fuel is people and stones . . ." (Qur'an 66:6).

Muhammad also said that the majority of the people of hell were women. It was narrated that Abd-Allah ibn Abbas said, "The messenger of Allah said: 'I was shown Hell and I have never seen anything more terrifying than it. And I saw that the majority of its people are women.' They said, 'Why, O Messenger of Allah?' He said, 'Because of their ingratitude.' It was asked: 'Are they ungrateful to Allah?' He said, 'They are ungrateful to their husbands and ungrateful to good treatment. If you are kind to one of them for a lifetime, then she sees one undesirable thing in you, she will say, "I have never had anything good from you."'"[171]

Food of Hell in the Qur'an

The Qur'an gives vivid descriptions of the type of nourishment that will be offered in hell.[172]

---

[169] Sahih Muslim
[170] Sahih Al-Jami'
[171] Narrated by Al-Bukhari, 1052
[172] Islamic Religious Sources/Imam Kamil Mufti, published on May 29, 2006.

> No food will there be for them except from a bitter,
> thorny plant which neither nourishes nor avails against
> hunger. (Qur'an 88:6–7)

The food will neither nourish nor taste good. It will only serve as punishment to the people in hell. In other passages, Allah describes the tree of Zaqqum, a special food of hell. Zaqqum is a repulsive tree; its roots go deep into the bottom of hell, its branches stretching all over. Its ugly fruit is like the heads of the devils. He says the following:

> Indeed the tree of zaqqum is food for the sinful, like
> murky oil, it boils within their bellies, like the boiling
> of scalding water. Seize him, then drag him, into the
> midst of Hell. (Qur'an 44:44–47)

> Is that Paradise better as hospitality or the tree of
> zaqqum? Indeed, we have made it a torment for the
> wrongdoers. Indeed it is a tree issuing from the bottom
> of the Hellfire, its emerging fruit as if it was heads of
> the serpents. And indeed, they will eat from it and fill
> with it their bellies. Then indeed, their return will be to
> the Hellfire. (Qur'an 37:62–68)

> So no friend has he this Day, nor has he any food except
> filth from the washing of wounds which none do eat but
> those in sin. (Qur'an 69:35–37)

Mostly adulterers will be eating the pus that comes out when the wounds are washed.

> This—so let them taste it—is scalding water and foul
> purulence, and other punishments of its type in various
> kinds. (Qur'an 38:57–58)

184

This is explained as human secretion that will be offered for food to dwellers of hell.

Some Muslim biographers in the Hadith try to interpret the verse that says everyone will enter hell by saying that there will be a suspension-type bridge that extends over hell that everyone will have to cross, but only the unbelievers will fall off into hell; however, there is no mention of this bridge in the Qur'an.[173]

Because Muhammad was a man and not God, he could not forgive sins nor guarantee heaven to his followers (excepting martyrdom). He was a sinful man needing forgiveness himself. Speaking to Muhammad, Allah says, "So know that there is no God but Allah and ask forgiveness for thy sin and for the believing men and the believing women" (Qur'an 47:19).

And Allah says to Muhammad, "That Allah may cover for thee thy shortcomings in the past and those to come . . ." (Qur'an 48:2).

Islam and Paradise (*Janna*)

What is the heaven of Islam like? Muhammad gave vivid descriptions of the scary, repulsive tortures of hell in many Qur'an verses as well as in the Hadith. Contrasting this is a description of not so much what heaven looks like, but of all the bliss and enjoyment that awaits those who have fought for the cause of Allah and his prophet, Muhammad. There are many Qur'an verses that describe what Muslim men longed for here on earth but were unable to attain. These are some of the Qur'an verses describing paradise:

1. Qur'an 56:15–38 says they will be reclining "on beds inwrought, reclining on them facing each other round about them will go

---

[173.] Sahih Bukhari, vol. 9, book 93, number 532.

young boys never changing in age, with goblets, and ewers and a cup of pure drink, they are not affected with headache nor are they intoxicated, and fruits that they choose, and flesh of fowl they desire, and pure beautiful virgins (houris) with wide beautiful eyes, like hidden pearls, they are created especially for the devout. They are amid thornless lote trees, and clustered banana trees, and extensive shade, and water gushing and abundant fruit, neither intercepted nor forbidden, and exalted couches. Surely we have created them (new) creation. So we have made them virgins, loving, equal in age, for those on the right hand." (Those on the right hand are the pious.) The Prophet said, "A houri is a most beautiful young woman with a transparent body. The marrow of her bones is visible like the interior lines of pearls and rubies. She looks like red wine in a white glass. She is of white color, and free from the routine physical disabilities of an ordinary woman such as menstruation, menopause, urinal and offal discharge, child bearing and the related pollution. A houri is a girl of tender age, having large breasts which are round (pointed), and not inclined to dangle. Houris dwell in palaces of splendid surroundings" (At-Tirmizi, vol. 2, pp. 35–40).

2. Qur'an 55:54–58 says, "Reclining on beds whose inner coverings are of silk brocade. And the fruits of the two gardens are within reach . . . therein are Houris restraining their glances, (they are chaste and do not look on other men) whom no man nor Jinni (devil) has touched before them (virgins) . . . As though they were rubies and pearls."

3. Qur'an 55:66–76 says, "Therein are two springs gushing forth . . . therein are fruits and palms and pomegranates . . . therein are goodly beautiful ones pure ones confined to pavilions (means they do not go out) before them man has not touched them, (the Arabic in verse 74 يطمثهن means they have not lost the blood of their virginity) neither with man nor jinni . . . reclining on green cushions and beautiful carpets."

4. Qur'an 78:31–33 says, "(Surely for those who kept their duty) is achievement, gardens and vineyards and youthful companions the (Arabic word كواعب used here means youthful young girls whose breasts have not sagged) and a pure drink."

5. Qur'an 47:15 gives a description of gardens that the dutiful are promised: "Therein are rivers of water not changing for the worse, and rivers of milk whereof the taste changes not (stays fresh) and rivers of wine delicious to the drinkers, and rivers if honey clarified, and for them therein are all fruits and forgiveness from their Lord."

6. Qur'an 44:51–55 says, "Those who keep their duty are indeed in a secure place—in gardens and springs, wearing fine and thick silk, facing one another and we have married them with Houris. They call therein for every fruit in security."

7. Qur'an 37:40–49 says, "The servants of Allah, the purified ones, will have an apportioned sustenance: fruits. And they are honored, in gardens of delight, on thrones facing each other. A bowl of running water will be made to go around them. White, delicious to those who drink. They will not be deprived of it. And with them are those modest in gaze (houris who are submissive) having beautiful eyes as if they were the white of eggs carefully protected."

8. Qur'an 38:49–55 says, "This is a reminder and surely there is an excellent resort for the dutiful: Gardens of Eden opened for them, reclining therein calling therein for many fruits and drink. And with them there are those modest in gaze (submissive) all of them equal in age. This is what you are promised in the day of Reckoning. Surely this is our sustenance; it will never come to an end. This is for the good! And surely there is an evil resort for the inordinate."

9. Qur'an 36:55–57 says, "Surely the owners of the garden are on that day in a happy occupation; they and their wives are in the shade

reclining on raised couches. They have fruits therein and they have whatever they desire."

10. Qur'an 39:20 says, "But those who keep their duty to their Lord, for them are high places, above them higher places, built for them, wherein rivers flow. It is the promise of Allah. Allah fails not his promise."

11. Qur'an 76:10–22 says, "So Allah will ward off from them the evil of that day, and cause them to meet with splendor and happiness: and reward them for their steadfastness with a Garden and with silk, reclining therein on raised couches; they will see therein neither excessive heat of the sun nor intense cold. And close down upon them are its shadows, and its fruits are made near to them easy to reach. And round about them are made to go vessels of silver and goblets of glass, Crystal-clear, made of silver—they have measured them according to a measure. And they are made to drink therein a cup tempered with ginger—of a fountain therein called Salsabil. And around them will go young boys never changing in age; when you see them you will think them to be scattered pearls. And when you look and look there you will see blessings and a great kingdom.[174] On them are garments of fine green silk and thick brocade, and they are adorned with bracelets of silver, and their Lord makes them to drink a pure drink. Surely this is a reward for you and your striving was appreciated."

[174.] This is used in reference to the spiritual kingdom, which is granted to the faithful. They are granted blessings and a great kingdom in this life as well, to which man shuts his eyes on account of ignorance. Note, however, that the faithful followers of Muhammad were granted material blessings and a great temporal kingdom as well—a kingdom that they inherited from the Prophet himself and that subsists to this day and is indeed widening daily (Maulana Muhammad Ali explanation of verse 20).

12. Qur'an 52:22–24 says, "And we shall aid them with fruit and flesh, as they desire. They pass therein from one to another a cup wherein is neither vanity, nor sin." And round them go boys of theirs as if they were hidden pearls."

13. Qur'an 52:19–20 says, "The dutiful will be surely in Gardens and bliss, rejoicing because of what their Lord has given them, and their Lord has saved them from the chastisement of the burning fire; eat and drink with pleasure for what you did."

Again, the men are assured of virgins. The boys described above will be there just to cater to the believers. Each one will have his own job that the other boys do not do. Some will carry the cups, some will carry the goblets, and others will carry the jugs. They will look like scattered pearls. They will not go to the bathroom nor get sick nor ever die. Some commentators say that Allah created these boys especially for this task; others say they are the children of Muslims who died young, but most commentators agree that they are the children of Jews and Christians who will be serving the Muslim believers.

The Muslim heaven caters to the physical human desires of the people in Muhammad's time. Instead of the scorching desert heat, the believer is promised a heaven where water flows freely; and instead of sleeping on the sand, he sleeps on an elevated comfortable silk couch clothed in fine brocade, eating and drinking his fill of fruit, wine, milk, and honey and all kinds of fowl instead of skimpy desert food. Instead of Bedouin women, the Muslim is promised houris (beautiful wide-eyed young virgins), never aging.

When asked about the meaning of what he said about residences in the Garden of Eden, the prophet Muhammad said, "These places are built of emeralds and jewels and in each building there will be 70 rooms of red color and in each room 70 sub-rooms of green color and in each sub-room there will be one throne and over each throne 70 beds of varied colors and on each bed a hoor al-ayn (houri—a girl having wide lovely eyes with intense black irises). There will be 70 dining cloth in each room and 70 kinds of food in each dining cloth. There will be seven girls in each room. Each believer will be given such strength in the morning as he can cohabit with them."[175]

In Muhammad's heaven, man is the subject, and everything there caters to the whims and desires he had on earth. Muslims try to reach heaven through their self-effort and jihad (martyrdom for the sake of Allah and his prophet).

The messenger of Allah said, "There are six things with Allah for the martyr. He is forgiven with the first flow of blood he suffers, he is shown his place in Paradise, he is protected from punishment in the grave, secured from the greatest terror, the crown of dignity is placed upon his head—and its gems are better than the world and what is in it—he is married to seventy two wives among Al-Huril-Ayn of Paradise, and he may intercede for seventy of his close relatives."[176]

This may be why the families of suicide bombers are comforted for their departed ones. Not only is the departed assured of heaven, but can also intercede for them.

For anyone who is reading this book and speaks Arabic, I recommend you go to the Internet at Islamayat.com and watch *Daring Question*, program 444 (سؤال جرئ). The host, Rachid, is a former Muslim whose father was an imam in the mosque. Rachid studied both Islam and Christianity and chose Jesus Christ. His Arabic program deals with

---

[175] According to Al Ghazali (احياء علوم الدين), when Muhammad was asked about the beautiful mansions in the Garden of Aden. Ihya Uloom Ed-Din, vol. 4, p. 4. 428 Abu Hamid Muhammad Al-Ghazali was born in AD 1058 in Persia and was a great scholar (https://islamreligion1.wordpress.com/2011/07/15/the-hoor-al-ayn-of-jannah-paradise/).

[176] The book of virtue of jihad, Jamiat Timidhi-Sunna.com, sayings and teachings of the prophet Muhammad.

informative topics about what the Qur'an and the Hadith teach. Rachid has some English programs as well.

In his *Daring Question* TV program 444, he deals with the houris and the boys who are made to give joy to the Muslim believers in heaven. He showed videos of three different sheikhs describing the pleasures, the beautiful houris, and their beautiful attendants who will be there for the men to enjoy. One of them says, "If you are not married now, do not despair. In Janna (paradise), you will have your fill . . ." The other says, "As soon as you appear in paradise, you are given two houris as down payment until you get your seventy-plus, etc."

But nothing broke my heart like the speech of Sheikh Al-Arifi, who was telling young teenage boys about all this pleasure that awaits them. The boys' eyes grew bigger with awe and anticipation when they heard their sheikh describe how their job will be consummating their sexual desires with virgins in paradise. When a young man asked why this same privilege is not given to women, he gave them examples of how women are more interested in clothes and jewelry. The boys' looks of excitement and anticipation literally broke my heart and made me weep! It seemed to me that the cleric was enticing them to become suicide bombers so they could have unlimited sex in heaven.

While the pleasures of Muhammad's heaven mostly revolves around food, women, and sensual pleasures, Jesus speaks of a different type of heaven, which we turn to in the next chapter.

Chapter Twenty

Jesus and the Afterlife

I will share a story that happened in our family in 1945, at the time of my sister's death at age eighteen. I remember the details vividly. It was Easter Sunday when my sister and her husband, with their ten-month-old daughter, were having dinner with us. I was fourteen at the time. My sister did not feel well and lay on the couch. Later, we found out she had typhoid fever. This epidemic took the lives of many young people due to lack of antibiotics in Egypt at that time. Disturbed over her sickness, my father was trying to encourage her—or perhaps encourage himself, as well as all of us—by saying to my sister that she would soon be well. Agreeing with him, my sister replied, "I will be healed on August 6." Since it was only May, my father rebuked her, saying she would be healed much sooner. In spite of the best doctors and care, my sister and her daughter did not improve. My sister's body was wasting away because of the liquid diet the doctors were treating typhoid patients with at the time. My little niece passed away from typhoid at thirteen months of age in July, and August 6 arrived with my sister's health in total decline. She was flat on her back, unable to move. Suddenly, she pulled herself and sat up in bed, saying in French, "Jesus, Jesus!" My mother tried to help her lie back, but my sister sweetly said, "Don't you see Him, Mother? He is here to take me home!" Three hours later, she was out of her body and enjoying the presence of Jesus.

How can we be sure of this? Was my sister sinless? Of course not! But she had accepted the Lord Jesus as her personal Savior, and He came to take her to be with Him as he promises all those who believe in His saving power!

When Jesus was in the world, He said to His followers, "I am the way, the truth and the life, no one comes to the Father except through Me" (John 14:6). In His final hours on the cross, a thief who was crucified to His left began hurling insults at Jesus, saying, "You are the Messiah, aren't You? Why don't you save yourself and save us?" The other thief crucified on the right of Jesus answered him, saying, "Don't you even fear God since you are under the same sentence of condemnation? And we indeed justly, for we are receiving what we deserve for our deeds; but this man has done nothing wrong." And he said, "Jesus, remember me when you come in Your kingdom." Jesus said to him, "Truly I say to you, today you shall be with Me in Paradise" (Luke 23:39–43).

Jesus gave the assurance of heaven to the thief that trusted Him. His sins were forgiven because of his faith in Jesus even when he did not have a chance to show his change of heart by living a righteous life. Obviously, his good deeds had not exceeded his bad. It is this assurance that caused the apostle Paul to say, "We are of good cheer and prefer rather to be absent from the body, and to be at home with the Lord" (2 Corinthians 5:8). The believer can face death without fear, for he knows he will be secure in heaven in the presence of the Lord.

Once I was called by a nurse in a Middle Eastern hospital who was taking care of a young man with a terminal disease. Because I spoke Arabic, the nurse asked me if I would like to talk to her deathly ill young patient, which I did. I could tell he was very scared of dying. He was holding tightly to my hand as I talked to him about Jesus. I told him if he invited Jesus into his life, He would come in, forgive all his sins, and give him peace and that when his time to die came, He would take him to heaven to live with Him. I could tell that Muhammad (not his real name) was touched. He gripped my hand and said, "I want Jesus, but

I am scared to leave Islam, and I am also afraid to die a Muslim. I am afraid of the torture in the grave." I prayed with him, gave him my phone number, and left.

Two weeks later, on the evening before I was to return home, I got a phone call from a young man who told me he was Muhammad's friend. He informed me that Muhammad had died and that before dying, he had given him my phone number and told him to call me "because I had answers." The young man wanted to see me. Unfortunately, it was late at night, and there was no transportation available to him in his town at that hour. Because I was leaving early the following morning, I gave him a phone number of a Christian Arabic speaker, but I personally never met him. Someday I hope to meet Muhammad and his friend in heaven!

The Christian Heaven

Jesus promised His children eternal life with Him in heaven. There are many passages and verses in the Bible that speak of heaven, but there are not many physical descriptions.

At this point in my personal life, having lost my oldest son to this world, I love the verse that says, "He will wipe away every tear from their eyes, and death shall be no more, neither shall there be mourning nor crying, for the former things have passed away" (Revelation 21:4). No more tears or sorrow!

But as it is written, "What no eye has seen, nor ear has heard, nor the heart of man has imagined, God has prepared for those who love Him" (1 Corinthians 2:9). In Psalm 16:11, King David tells the Lord, "You make known to me the path of life; in your presence there is fullness of joy; at your right hand there are pleasures for evermore."

The apostle John saw a vision of the heavenly city, which was very large and very beautiful. "Having the glory of God: and her light was like a

stone most precious, like a jasper stone, clear as crystal . . . the length
and breadth and height of it are equal . . . and the city was pure gold
like clear glass. And the foundations of the wall of the city were garnished
with all manner of precious stones . . . the twelve gates were twelve
pearls; every gate was of one pearl: and the street of the city was pure
gold, as it were transparent glass" (Revelation 21:11, 16, 19, 21).

> After these things I looked, and behold, a great multitude
> which no one could number, of all nations, tribes,
> peoples, and tongues, standing before the throne and
> before the Lamb, clothed with white robes, with palm
> branches in their hands, and crying out with a loud
> voice, saying, "Salvation *belongs* to our God who sits on
> the throne, and to the Lamb!" All the angels stood
> around the throne and the elders and the four living
> creatures, and fell on their faces before the throne and
> worshipped God, saying: "Amen! Blessing and glory
> and wisdom, thanksgiving and honor and power and
> might, *be* to our God forever and ever. Amen."
> (Revelation 7:9–12)

In Revelation 22:1–5, we read, "And he showed me a pure river of water
of life, clear as crystal, coming from the throne of God and of the Lamb,
in the middle of its street and on either side of the river was the tree of
life, bearing twelve kinds of fruit, yielding its fruit every month; and
the leaves of the tree were for the healing of the nations. And there shall
no longer be any curse; and the throne of God and of the Lamb shall
be in it, and His bond-servants shall serve Him; and they shall see His
face, and His name shall be on their foreheads. And there shall no
longer be any night and they shall not have need of the light of the sun,
because the Lord God shall illumine them; and they shall reign for ever
and ever."

Jesus is the Lamb of God. John 1: 29 says, "Behold the Lamb of God
who takes away the sin of the world." Jesus is referred to as the Lamb

of God because He was offered as a sacrifice for sin, like the sacrificial lamb that was offered every year to atone for the sins of the children of Israel. But Jesus, the Son of God, died *once for all* as God's Lamb to redeem sinful man.

> But nothing unclean will ever enter it (Heaven), nor anyone who does what is detestable or false, but those who are written in the Lamb's book of life. (Revelation 21:27).

> But according to His promise we are waiting for new heavens and a new earth in which righteousness dwells. (2 Peter 3:13)

In many passages of the Bible, we read that no one can see God's face and live.[177] In heaven, not only do believers see God's face, but also they live continuously in His presence. Because the curse of sin is removed, sin—in all its hideous forms—will be entirely excluded. What was lost when Adam sinned in the Garden of Eden will be regained in paradise through Jesus, the sacrificial Lamb.

The Resurrection Body

We read in 1 Corinthians 15:42–50 that the pre- and postresurrection body possesses separate states, like a seed before and after sprouting. "So also is the resurrection of the dead. It is sown a perishable body, it is raised an imperishable body; it is sown in dishonor, it is raised in glory; it is sown in weakness, it is raised in power; it is sown a natural body, it is raised a spiritual body. If there is a natural body, there is also a spiritual body. So also it is written, 'The first man, Adam, became a living soul.' The last Adam (Jesus) became a life-giving spirit. However,

---

177. https://bible.org/question/light-gen-38-10-and-exo-3317-33-how-can-you-say-%E2%80%9Cno-man-can-see-god%E2%80%9D

the spiritual is not first, but the natural, then the spiritual. The first man (Adam) is from the earth, earthly; the second man (Jesus) is from Heaven. And as is the earthly, so also are those who are earthly. And as is the heavenly, so also are those who are heavenly. And just as we have borne the image of the earthly, we shall also bear the image of the heavenly. Now I say this, brethren, that flesh and blood cannot inherit the kingdom of God; nor does the perishable inherit the imperishable."

The Bible talks about two representative men: Adam, the first man, and Christ, the second Man. All humans are born like the first man, Adam, with a fleshly body. It is subject to sickness, weakness, sorrow, and, ultimately, death and decay. Such is the end of the bodies of all humans.

Jesus, the second Man, came to earth to begin a new race of humanity. He was also born with a human body subject to death. He too was weak and sorrowful when he faced death. He did not die an honorable death but was put to death on a cross. That is how His mortal body went to the grave. But Jesus rose from the dead; and He rose with a resurrected, transformed, glorified, immortal body equipped for eternal life in heaven! So will believers who have died in Christ—they will have real recognizable bodies like Jesus. He was recognized by the disciples. They will have extra powers. Jesus walked through closed doors and stood among His disciples. They will have no pain. They will never die again. They will retain their individuality and will recognize one another.

> At present we are men looking at puzzling reflections in a mirror. The time will come when we shall see reality whole and face to face! At present all I know is a little fraction of the truth, but the time will come when I shall know it as fully as God now knows me! (1 Corinthians 13:12, Phillips)

In the resurrection they neither marry nor are given in marriage, but are like angels in heaven. (Matthew 22:30)

Jesus said, "If anyone serves Me, he must follow Me, and where I am, there will he be also. If anyone serves Me, the Father will honor Him" (John 12:26). Jesus said, "I give them eternal life, and they will never perish, and no one will snatch them out of My hand" (John 10:28). This means that even Satan and his demons cannot pluck the believer out of the Lord's hand.

Jesus and Hell

"Do not be afraid of those who kill the body but cannot kill the soul. Rather, be afraid of the One who can destroy both soul and body in hell" (Matthew 10:28). Jesus talked more about hell than any other person in the Bible.

> The Son of Man will send his angels, and they will collect out of his kingdom all causes of sin and all evildoers, and they will throw them into the furnace of fire, where there will be weeping and gnashing of teeth. Then the righteous will shine like the sun in the kingdom of their Father. (Matthew 13:41–43)

He went on his way through cities and villages, teaching, and then traveled on to Jerusalem. One said to him, "Lord, are they few who are saved?"

He said to them, "Strive to enter in by the narrow door, for many, I tell you, will seek to enter in, and will not be able. When once the master of the house has risen up, and has shut the door, and you begin to stand outside, and to knock at the door, saying, 'Lord, Lord, open to us!' Then he will answer and tell you, 'I don't know you or where you come from.' Then you will begin to say, 'We ate and drank in your presence, and you taught in our streets.' He will say, 'I tell you, I don't know where you come from. Depart from me, all you workers of iniquity.' There will be weeping and gnashing of teeth, when you see Abraham, Isaac, Jacob, and all the prophets, in the Kingdom of God, and yourselves being thrown outside. They will come from the east, west, north, and south, and will sit down in the Kingdom of God. Behold, there are some who are last who will be first, and there are some who are first who will be last" (Luke 13:22–30).

> I promise you that on the day of judgment, everyone will have to account for every careless word they have spoken. (Matthew 12:36, CEV)

> Then He will also say to those on His left, "Depart from Me, accursed ones, into the eternal fire which has been prepared for the devil and his angels . . ." (Matthew 25:41)

Jesus told a story about Lazarus and a rich man in Luke 16: 19–31, which sounds like a parable but is not said to be one. In it, many details about hell are given:

There was a certain rich man who was clothed in purple and fine linen and fared sumptuously every day. But there was a certain beggar named Lazarus, full of sores, who was laid at his gate, desiring to be fed with the crumbs which fell from the rich man's table. Moreover the dogs came and licked his sores. So it was that the beggar died, and was carried by the angels to Abraham's bosom. The rich man also died and was buried. And being in torments in Hades, he lifted up his eyes and saw Abraham afar off, and Lazarus in his bosom.

Then he cried and said, "Father Abraham, have mercy on me, and send Lazarus that he may dip the tip of his finger in water and cool my tongue; for I am tormented in this flame." But Abraham said, "Son, remember that in your lifetime you received your good things, and likewise Lazarus evil things; but now he is comforted and you are tormented. And besides all this, between us and you there is a great gulf fixed, so that those who want to pass from here to you cannot, nor can those from there pass to us."

Then he said, "I beg you therefore, father, that you would send him to my father's house, for I have five brothers, that he may testify to them, lest they also come to this place of torment." Abraham said to him, "They have Moses and the prophets; let them hear them." And he said, "No, father Abraham; but if one goes to them from the dead, they will repent." But he said to him, "If they do not hear Moses and the prophets, neither will they be persuaded though one rise from the dead."

For the cowardly and unbelieving and abominable murderers and immoral persons and sorcerers and idolaters and all liars, their part will be in the lake that burns with fire and brimstone, which is the second death. (Revelation 21:8)

For all that is in the world, the lust of the flesh and the lust of the eyes and the boastful pride of life, is not from the Father, but is from the world. The world is passing away, and *also* its lusts; but the one who does the will of God lives forever. (1 John 2:16–17)

And I saw a great white throne, and him that sat on it, from whose face the earth and the heaven fled away; and there was found no place for them. And I saw the dead, small and great, stand before God; and the books were opened; and another book was opened, which is the book of life: and the dead were judged out of those things which were written in the books, according to their works . . . And whosoever was not found written in the book of life was cast into the lake of fire. (Revelation 20:11–12, 15)

The Way to Heaven

When He spoke of punishment and hell, Jesus offered a solution that God, according to His great love for humanity, provided. Because no human can ever atone for his own sins, God (requiring complete perfection) gave His only Son, Jesus, to die on the cross in lieu of sinful man to ransom him from hell. The Just gave His life for the unjust, the Sinless for the sinner. At the cross, God's justice was fulfilled when His only Son, Jesus, paid the penalty of man's sinfulness. And by Jesus' sacrificial love, man was rescued from eternal punishment and destruction.

> For God so loved the world that He gave His only Son,
> that whoever believes in Him will not perish but have
> everlasting life. (John 3:16)

Every sinner who puts his trust in Jesus receives forgiveness of sins. "But as many as received Him, to them He gave the right to become children of God, *even* to those who believe in His name . . ." (John 1:12). For sinners who refuse to repent and trust Jesus for their salvation, their future is eternal separation and wrath from God.

Chapter Twenty-One

Preparing to Return to Mecca: Muhammad Creates Unity

Perhaps we should make a quick review of the beginning of Muhammad's life. Muhammad was from Mecca from the Quraysh tribe. That's where he grew up and married his rich wife, Khadija. It was a good marriage; for she gave him love, encouragement, comfort, status, money, and power. As we discussed in previous chapters, without Khadija, perhaps there would have been no Islam altogether. Khadija was the one who encouraged him when he claimed that some apparition (angel) squeezed him almost to death to give him what was to be the beginning of the message of Islam. Scared, shaky, and sweaty, Muhammad ran to Khadija, who comforted him and covered his shaking body. She told him that this meant that he was to be the prophet of his time.

Based on her assessment and that of her cousin the priest Waraqa Ibn Naufal,[178] who reinforced Khadija's claim about Muhammad being a legitimate prophet, Muhammad went around Mecca, declaring Islam, which is the belief in one god, Allah, and not in the many gods that were worshiped by his countrymen. For twelve years, the Meccans did

---

[178.] Waraqa Ibn Naufal was an Ebionite priest. The Ebionite religion is a sect that acknowledges the virgin birth of Christ but denies His crucifixion.

not accept Muhammad's claim and found him to be a nuisance and a threat to their idol trade at the Kaaba,[179] which was a big source of income to them. They made and sold many idol statues of their 360 gods. He harassed them to accept his Allah and his prophethood to the point they wanted to kill him. This forced Muhammad to migrate over two hundred miles north to Al-Medina, with a very few followers. At Al-Medina and without a job to sustain them, Muhammad and his followers started raiding the caravans of the Meccans to provide for their needs as well as to retaliate against his countrymen, the Quraysh[180] Meccans.

Muhammad in Medina

Losing some raids but winning most, Muhammad attracted more followers in Medina, calling them Al-Ansar (the helpers). With the Muhajirun (the immigrants, or the ones who migrated with him from Mecca) and Al-Ansar (those who joined him in Medina), Muhammad created the ummah, which was the first Islamic state. (ISIS now is patterned after the rules that Muhammad set for the ummah.) Allegiance to the ummah became the bond that drew them together and took priority over any family, friendship, or tribal/governmental ties. With the allegiance of the ummah, Muhammad fought many battles of which the Battle of Badr decisively made him known as a successful war general. He changed the Arab religious and tribal rules of war of his people, the Quraysh, and seemed to get away with it. Muhammad still was not satisfied. His real desire was to return home to Mecca to spread Islam and conquer and subdue his Quraysh tribe.

To do so, he had to get even stronger and started attacking neighboring tribes, forcing them to join him in his Islam so he could return to Mecca

---

[179.] Al-Kaaba was and still is the center for worship in Mecca.

[180.] The Quraysh is the tribe of Muhammad who was influential in Mecca.

with power. In spite of many errors in battle, Muhammad advanced with his sword and many fortuitous circumstances.

Muhammad's Men Capture a Prize

Unbeknownst to them, Muhammad's men captured a high-ranking official, Thumamah ibn Al-Uthal from the Banu Hanifa, who lived east of Medina. Thumamah was in the business of supplying a large quantity of grain to the Meccans. While he was on his way to Mecca for a pilgrimage, he was caught in a raid by Muhammad's men. The captors did not recognize this man, nor did they know his importance; but when they brought him to Muhammad, he recognized him and knew that his men had brought him a prize! Muhammad knew this man and had tried to convince him to join his movement of Islam, but Thumamah had refused and even wanted Muhammad killed. But fate would have him accidently fall in the hands of Muhammad! When the raiders came back with their booty and the important prisoner whom they had not recognized, Muhammad was overjoyed! He had him tied to a pillar in the mosque, exposed to the elements because the mosque had no roof for the main court. He hung there for three days without food or drink. After three days, Muhammad asked him what he thought he should do to him. Thumamah answered that if the Prophet released him, he would be ever very grateful. As soon as Muhammad released him from his bonds, he converted to Islam. He went to Mecca, completed his pilgrimage, and informed the Quraysh Meccans that he would now enforce a grain embargo against them. This embargo eventually weakened the Meccans. So what was just a raid by Muhammad's men proved to pay big dividends to Muhammad and his cause by weakening the Quraysh—his biggest enemy.

From the beginning, most of those who followed Muhammad had been bandits who made their living by attacking, capturing, and killing for booty. Now under Muhammad, they gladly did their job not only to secure their livelihood, but also to contribute in the noble cause of Islam.

To attain his goal of entering Mecca, Muhammad continued to raid surrounding tribes, forcing them to enter Islam and become his allies. The neighboring tribes did not like to be constantly raided by Muhammad and his men but wanted to live in peace. The tribes had two choices: either to (1) continue fighting Muhammad's forces constantly or (2) join him in becoming Muslims and avoid being raided and killed.

Haram Blood vs. Halal Blood

Muhammad had made it clear that Muslims can only raid and kill non-Muslims because spilling the blood of Muslims is haram (forbidden), while spilling the blood of non-Muslims is halal (allowed). This means that to kill and spill the blood of a Muslim is haram (unlawful). So by joining Muhammad and Islam, the tribes became secure.

But to kill and spill the blood of a non-Muslim or a Muslim who does not practice Islam is halal (lawful) and even required. Muhammad divided human blood into two categories: (1) Muslim and (2) non-Muslim.

Muhammad gave this Qur'an verse about Muslim blood:

Qur'an 17:33 says, "And kill not the soul which Allah has forbidden except for a just cause."

According to Hadith, the word "except" allows the following:[181]

1. Killing a Muslim who murdered a Muslim
2. Killing an adulterer who is married
3. Killing a person who leaves and deserts Islam

[181.] Al-Bukhari and Muslim (the two Sahihs) on the authority of Abdullah Ibn Masud

It was reported in the two Sahihs that the messenger of Allah said,

« لَا يَحِلُّ دَمُ امْرِيءٍ مُسْلِمٍ يَشْهَدُ أَنْ لَا إِلَهَ إِلَّا اللهُ وَأَنَّ مُحَمَّدًا رَسُولُ اللهِ، إِلَّا بِإِحْدَى ثَلَاثٍ:
النَّفْسُ بِالنَّفْسِ، وَالزَّانِي الْمُحْصَنُ، وَالتَّارِكُ لِدِينِهِ الْمُفَارِعَة »

> The blood of a Muslim who bears witness to La ilaha
> illallah and that Muhammad is the Messenger of Allah,
> is not permissible (to be shed) except in three cases: a
> soul for a soul (i.e., in the case of murder), an adulterer
> who is married, and a person who leaves his religion and
> deserts the Jama'ah. ("Jama'ah" means the people of
> Islam.)

The following is recorded in the books of the Sunan. Muhammad was
reported to have said, "If the world were to be destroyed, it would be of
less importance to Allah than the killing of A Muslim."[182]

"لَزَوَالُ الدُّنْيَا عِنْدَ اللهِ أَهْون من قتل مسلم"

How about halal (allowed) blood, the blood of non-Muslims? Is it okay
for it to be spilled?

Bukhari 1:8:387 says, "Allah's Apostle said, 'I have been ordered to fight
the people till they say: "None has the right to be worshipped but
Allah." And if they say so, pray like our prayers, face our Qibla[183] and
slaughter as we slaughter, then their blood and property will be sacred
to us and we will not interfere with them except legally and their
reckoning will be with Allah.'"[184]

[182.] Al-Tirmidhi

[183.] Qibla is the direction that should be faced while praying (Mecca).

[184.] Bukhari, vol. 8 Hadith 387 (Quranexplorer.com Internet page has been removed.)

The Qur'an and Unbelievers (Non-Muslims)

The Qur'an exhorts people not to love unbelievers even if they are close relatives.

Qur'an 58:22 says, "Thou will not find a people who believe in Allah and the last day loving those who oppose Allah and his messenger, even though they be their fathers, or their sons, or their brothers or their kinsfolk. These are they into whose hearts He has impressed faith and strengthened them with a Spirit from Himself, and He will cause them to enter gardens wherein flow rivers abiding therein. Allah is well pleased with them and they are well pleased with Him. These are Allah's Party (Hezbollah) who are the successful."

The explanation of commentaries of Qur'an 58:22 is that those who follow Allah rather their unbelieving relatives, even to the point of killing them, are the ones accepted by Allah and his prophet.[185]

This, as well as other similar verses, resulted in the killing of some unbelieving relatives among Muhammad's followers. Now we see this phenomenon revamped and surfacing on some radical Islamic Internet sites reviving some parts of the "glory" of Islam that we now see in ISIS and other extremist organizations.

The following are some accounts of Muhammad's followers who killed their relatives for speaking against him:

1. Aba Kahafa insulted the Prophet. His son Abu-Bakr hit him strongly and caused him to fall to the ground. He reported the incident to the Prophet, who advised him not to do it again, to which Abu-Bakr continued, "Had my sword been near, I would have killed him."[186]

[185.] http://www.recitequran.com/en/tafsir/en.ibn-kathir/58:22
[186.] Al Kortoby

2. Omar Bin El Khattab bragged about killing his uncle. He told Saad Bin El-As, "It seems that you look like you want to say something to me. You think that it was I who killed your father. In fact if I had killed him, I would not apologize. I killed my own uncle Al-As bin Hesham for ridiculing the prophet."[187]

3. Abu Obaidah killed his father the day of Badr because he was against the Prophet.[188]

4. Hamza and Obida Bin El-Harith killed their cousins the day of Badr for not supporting the Prophet.[189]

5. A blind man killed his wife because she repeatedly reviled Muhammad. He went to Allah's apostle and told him that he had two beautiful children by her and that she took good care of him, but she would not stop ridiculing the Prophet, so he killed her. Muhammad replied that spilling her blood was halal (allowed).[190]

Ali ibn Abi Talib, the Prophet's cousin and son-in-law said, "We were with the prophet killing our fathers, our sons and our brothers, and it only increased our faith."[191]

The Prophet said, "No one of you truly believes until I am dearer to him than his father, his son, his own self and all the people."[192] Later on, we shall see how much the devotion of Muhammad's followers made an impact on his eventual success in returning to Mecca. He inspired fanatical devotion to himself and his teaching.

[187.] Al Seera al-nabawieh /Ibn Hisham Omar Ibnil Khattab 3, p. 81.

[188.] Ibn Katheer/explanation of Qur'an 58:22.

[189.] Ibn Katheer

[190.] Ibn Abbas said of Akram

[191.] Ali ibn Abi Talib became the fourth caliph after Muhammad. His followers are the Shia Muslims.

[192.] Narrated by Al-Bukhari, 15; Muslim, 44.

Muhammad's Theology Continues to Current Times

How then do ISIS and other extremists justify their killing of non-Muslims and some Muslims?

We read in Qur'an 9:29, "Fight those who believe not in Allah nor in the last day, nor forbid what Allah and his messenger have forbidden, nor follow the religion of truth (Islam)." ISIS follows the Prophet's words literally!

This and other similar verses give Islamic radicals justification for killing non-Muslims. Lately, however, we saw on the Internet horrific pictures of Muslims of ISIS killing even Muslims. How do they justify this? The justification is that they are not following Islam fully according to the prophet Muhammad and his *sahaba* (companions).

ISIS condemns any government that is ruled by a king or a president chosen by the citizens. The head of the Islamic nation has to be chosen according to the pattern of Muhammad's successors and be of Qurayshi lineage. This leader is called the khalifa, like Al Baghdadi, head of ISIS. The caliphate system was discontinued when the Ottoman Empire was abolished in 1924.

A Few Modern Examples of Radical Muslim Killings

1. On the twenty-seventh of the month of Ramadan in the year 2016, Muhammad Al-Ghamidy killed his father in Khamis Mushayt while shouting "Allahu Akbar!" because his father was not a follower of ISIS.

2. An ISIS boy killed his mother because she asked him to leave the ranks of "the Islamic nation ISIS." Therefore, he considered her not Muslim, deserving of death.

3. Sa'ad Al Ghazi killed his cousin while his brother Abd-El Aziz took the video. The cousin who was killed was raised in their home due to his mother's early death. Later, however, he had joined the Saudi army. Although Saudi Arabia is a strict Muslim country, it is a kingdom and therefore a *kafir* (infidel) government. The government should only be a caliphate, not a kingdom. While killing him, his cousin was shouting, "I am ordered to obey Allah and his prophet!"

4. An eighteen-year-old boy killed his uncle because he had been a lieutenant in the army. He went to his mother and told her, "I killed your brother because he serves in the pagan army."

Is this a new phenomenon, or was it practiced before?

Chapter Twenty-Two

Jesus and Muhammad Respond to Rejection

Muhammad gained power with his followers. They avenged him from those who disagreed with him, not even sparing the lives of their own family members.

Jesus too attracted followers; but He did not use the sword, violence, or coercion. His only weapon was the message He brought to the world and His willingness to suffer. To pursue his goal, many of Muhammad's followers had to die in battle. To accomplish His goal, Jesus accepted to die a dreadful death on the cross so that people could enjoy a life that is acceptable to God and free from the bondage and control of sin. But even then, many people still rejected Him. The Jewish leaders hated him, threatened to kill Him, and eventually did. How did Jesus respond to this rejection?

Like Muhammad, who was not welcome in Mecca, Jesus was not welcome in Jerusalem, for the religious leaders of the Jews were jealous and sought to kill Him. But how did Jesus handle this rejection? We read in Luke 9:51–56:

> And it came about, when the days were approaching for
> His ascension, that He resolutely set His face to go to
> Jerusalem; and He sent messengers on ahead of Him.

> And they went and entered a village of the Samaritans, to make arrangements for Him. And they did not receive Him because he was journeying with His face toward Jerusalem. And when His disciples James and John saw this, they said: "Lord, do you want us to command fire to come out of heaven and consume them?" But He turned and rebuked them and said: "You do not know what kind of spirit you are of; for the Son of Man did not come to destroy men's lives, but to save them." And they went on to another village.

The Lord Jesus knew that He was going to face persecution and death, yet He chose to set His eyes firmly toward Jerusalem, where His accusers and the cross awaited Him.

Why did the Samaritans refuse to welcome Jesus and his disciples? In the first place, they knew that Jesus was headed to Jerusalem, where the Jews worshipped; but the Samaritans had long since stopped worshipping in Jerusalem. In fact, there was a history of animosity between the Jews and the Samaritans that started after the conquest of Israel, which was mentioned in an earlier chapter. The original Jews hated the Samaritans as they were not a pure Jewish breed; and the Samaritans, in turn, hated the Jews. For this reason, Jews traveling between Galilee and Judea would often take a longer route around Samaria to avoid contact with the Samaritans.

However, Jesus did not have any of these animosities. He never kept grudges but told His followers they should always forgive. When He was asked how many times one should forgive, He said, "Seventy times seven," meaning an infinite number (Matthew 18:21–22).

Jesus sent His disciples to prepare lodging for Him in one of their villages, but the Samaritans refused to receive Him and His fellow Jewish travelers. How did Jesus' disciples deal with this rejection? In their zeal for their Master and with the prejudice and animosity they had toward the Samaritans, they wanted to avenge Jesus and retaliate. They knew from the Torah (the Old Testament) that God once had actually sent fire and consumed those who arrogantly rejected His representative,[193] but they failed to understand God's love as revealed in the person of Jesus Christ. Jesus had taught them not to retaliate nor return evil for evil. "You have heard that it was said, 'An eye for an eye and a tooth for a tooth' but I say to you, do not resist him who is evil; but whoever slaps you on your right cheek turn to him the other also" (Matthew 5:38–39). "For if you forgive men for their transgressions your heavenly Father will also forgive you" (Matthew 6:14). Jesus then turned to the disciples and rebuked them, saying, "You do not know what kind of spirit you are of." Did they realize what was motivating them or causing them to react in this harsh way? What kind of spirit were they exhibiting? Was it a spirit that the Lord Jesus was conveying to the people? Were they motivated by love for the salvation of these people, or were they motivated by personal anger and a spirit of vengeance? Jesus wanted them to understand that asking God to destroy people was not consistent with His character and certainly not with His mission, for Jesus came to the world to seek and to save people who have been lost because of sin.

Jesus Does Not Seek Vengeance

Jesus had the power to destroy those who rejected Him, but He did not. Instead, He had pity on them and said, "O Jerusalem, Jerusalem, who kills the prophets and stones those who are sent to her! How often I wanted to gather your children together, the way a hen gathers her chicks under her wings, and you were unwilling. Behold your house is being left to you desolate" (Matthew 23:37–38).

We sometimes feel the need to avenge ourselves from those who wrong us, forgetting God's words: "Do not be wise in your own estimation.

[193.] 2 Kings 1:10–12

Never pay back evil for evil to anyone. Respect what is right in the sight of all men. If possible, so far as it depends on you, be at peace with all men. Never take your own revenge, beloved, but leave room for the wrath *of God*, for it is written, 'VENGEANCE IS MINE, I WILL REPAY,' says the Lord" (Romans 12:16b–19, quoting Deuteronomy 32:35, NASB).

James and John, the disciples of Jesus, wanted revenge for the Samaritans; but Jesus rebuked them, showing them that retaliation is produced by the spirit of anger, not by mercy and forgiveness.

Likewise, the followers of Muhammad wanted to prove their loyalty to him by killing those who ridiculed him. Had Muhammad heard the teachings of Jesus, perhaps today we would have had a list of those forgiven by him instead of a long list of those assassinated by Muhammad and his people in revenge.

Muhammad and Revenge

Many poets were murdered for reciting poetry against Muhammad. One of the stories is about Asma bint Marwan:

Asma bint Marwan was a poetess who composed a poem blaming the people of Medina for obeying a stranger (Muhammad) and not taking the initiative to attack him by surprise. Muhammad asked, "Who will rid me of Marwan's daughter?" A member of her husband's tribe volunteered and crept into her house that night. She had five children, and the youngest was sleeping at her breast. The assassin gently removed the child, drew his sword, and plunged it into her, killing her in her sleep.[194]

[194.] Ibn Ishaq, pp. 675–76/995-96 Sirar Rasul Allah A Gillaume, Oxford University Press, 1955.

There are lists of over forty men and women who were assassinated or ordered killed by Muhammad, the prophet of Islam, for various offenses, such as writing or reciting poetry against him, or for monetary gain.[195]

Jesus said to his disciples, "Peace I leave with you. My peace I give to you. Not as the world gives do I give to you. Let not your heart be troubled, nor let it be afraid" (John 14:27).

I wonder what the world would have been like today if Muhammad had met Jesus and followed His teachings? Likewise, what if the Crusaders and other later groups also obeyed the teachings and example of Jesus?

[195] https://wikiislam.net/wiki/List_of_Killings_Ordered_or_Supported_by_Muhammad

Chapter Twenty-Three

Muhammad's Desire to Enter Mecca

Muhammad had to build much strength before he could fulfill his dream of returning to Mecca. Most of his battles were offensive, and when the enemy retaliated, Muhammad made sure to punish them severely.

Muhammad allowed his previously adopted son, Zaid, who had now lost his status as son, the privilege of leading many successive raids—a privilege he did not allow his other competent lieutenants. Zaid had good qualifications for battle, but so did a lot of his men. So why Muhammad chose to send his former son to head more battles remains unclear. Some even suggest that perhaps Muhammad saw in Zaid the danger of competition for the leadership of the newly established ummah (Islamic nation) and tried to keep him busy and out of Medina.[196] Personally, I believe Muhammad loved Zaid and wanted to compensate him for stripping him of his title of being Muhammad's son. It was reported that when Zaid later died in one of these raids, Muhammad cried and said, "Oh Zaid, my son!"

[196.] Al-Waqidi, Kitab al-Maghazi, 101.

216

The Enemy Seeks Revenge

Muhammad entrusted Zaid with the security operation of a trading caravan to Syria. When they were passing the area of the Banu Fazara, whom Zaid had previously raided, the men of Banu Fazara sought revenge by attacking the caravan, looting it and wounding Zaid and others of his men. Zaid survived; and upon their return to Medina, Muhammad decided to send a punitive expedition headed by Zaid, who had vowed not to enjoy sexual relationships until he had avenged himself.

Zaid Returns for More Revenge

Zaid and his men ambushed the Banu Fazara and captured their legendary matriarch, the elderly Umm Qirfa. They executed her by tying her legs to separate ropes, each tied to a camel. The camels were made to run in opposite directions, tearing the woman apart.[197]

Muhammad viewed the resistance of any tribe as a threat to his cause. So when the Christian tribe of Banu Kalb in Northern Arabia resisted, Muhammad attacked them and forced them either to embrace Islam or pay the jizyah or be killed by the sword. At this time, Allah gave the following Qur'an verse:

> Fight those who believe not in Allah and his messenger . . .
> until they pay the tax with humiliation recognizing
> your superiority. (Qur'an 9:29)

If they kept their religion, they had to accept their status as second-rate citizens, even bowing low as they paid the jizyah.

[197.] Al-Tabari, Tarikh al-rasul wa'l muluk, 11, 1370

The Jews were not readily willing to join Muhammad and convert to Islam, and the animosity between Muhammad and the Jews was quickly accelerating. To this day, Arabs count the Jews as their biggest enemy. Animosity started with Muhammad fourteen hundred years ago, and it continues to run even deeper today!

Killing a Prominent Jew

One particular Jew of status who lived in Khaybar[198]was Abu Rafi, a wealthy man. Muhammad's helpers, Al-Ansar, who had joined him in Medina, requested permission from the Prophet to go and kill Abu Rafi, the elderly Jew. Permission granted, Abdullah bin Unays, who spoke the local dialect of Hebrew-Aramaic, along with four others, went to Khaybar and identified Abu Rafi's castle. Abdullah followed some of his servants to the main gate and pretended to be relieving himself. Assuming him to be one of Abu Rafi's servants, the gatekeeper implored him to enter before the gate was barred. Abdullah went in and then veered off into hiding, waiting for the gatekeeper to leave. Once alone, he took the keys that were hanging on a peg and opened the door to his companions. Abu Rafi had been entertaining guests. When the party seemed to come to an end, the guests went to other rooms in the palace. Abdullah led his companions through the lower rooms of the house, closing each room behind them. Abdullah went up to a locked room and knocked on the door. Abu Rafi's wife opened the door and asked Abdullah what he needed. The men then pushed their way inside, holding a blade over her head, and called out Abu Rafi's name. Unsuspecting, he answered, and Abdullah rushed at him in the dark. It took many blows until he finally got him and heard a bone shatter in

---

[198.] At the time of Muhammad, Khaybar was a Jewish settlement ninety miles north of Al-Medina. In a future chapter (25), we will deal with the fate of the Jews of Khaybar.

218

his abdomen. The killers barely managed to exit before men with lit torches began to search for them.[199]

Apparently, the Jews of Khaybar had not yet realized the extent of the animosity of Muhammad and his men toward them, or they would have been on better guard. Abu Rafi was one of the key leaders of Khaybar, so when he died, the people appointed Usayr bin Razim as their military leader (emir).

Scheming against the New Emir

Muhammad sent a diplomatic mission to Khaybar, inviting the newly appointed leader to come to Medina to receive special recognition by the prophet Muhammad for his appointment as the new emir. Why Usayr bin Razim accepted the invitation is not clear, especially since he had been very well supported by his people. Perhaps he was pleased to be honored by a great leader such as Muhammad. He agreed to take the trip with the Muslim envoys that had come from the camp of Muhammad to escort him.

The Jewish Emir Senses Treason

Just a few miles outside of Khaybar, he realized there was treachery planned and that he had been deceived into going with the Muslims to Medina. He turned around and reached for an Arab's sword, which resulted in a fight that killed him along with his thirty Jewish companions except one who managed to escape. This incident resulted in the Muslims blaming Usayr the Jew as treacherous, but neither he nor the other thirty Jews who accompanied him were armed, and that's why he thought he was not safe in the company of the Arabs. When Usayr reached for the Arab's sword, the Arab turned his camel off the route

---

[199.] Al-Tabari, vol. 7, pp. 99–105.

and waited until he and the Jew were alone and struck the man down. It is interesting to know that the Arab was none other than Abdullah bin Unays, who had killed Abu Rafi and had stayed incognito.[200]

Muhammad Deceived

About that time, a group of eight men from the Bedouin tribe of the Hawazin came to Muhammad, wanting to embrace Islam. During their visit, they told Muhammad that the climate was not agreeing with them. Muhammad advised them to go a little south of the city where his camels were and drink some of the camel's milk and urine, which was supposed to make them feel better. They listened to him but went and killed Muhammad's herdsmen and stole the camels. When Muhammad found out, he sent his men and retrieved the camels. The Bedouin raiders were captured and brought to the Prophet, who ordered that their eyes be gouged out and their hands and feet amputated. They were left to die of exposure.[201] Some reports deny they were tortured that way. Obviously, the punishment was very severe, but Muhammad wanted to establish the severity of these two offences: (1) leaving Islam and (2) raiding a Muslim. To this day, leaving Islam is a crime punishable by death in many Muslim countries. And of course, Muhammad emphasized that raiding people of your own Muslim faith is a crime requiring death. The policy seems to have worked well, for no one dared raid Medina during Muhammad's time.

Will Muhammad Finally Reach His Goal at Mecca?

The Meccans were having food shortages because of the embargo, while Muhammad was gaining more power and felt it might be time for him to go to Mecca for a short visit. He had been fighting his Quraysh tribe

---

[200.] Ibn Sa'd Tabakat, vol. 2, pp. 66–67; Ibn Hisham, Sira, vol. 2, pp. 273–275.
[201.] Ibn Ishaq, Sirat Rasulullah, 62–63, 67.

of Mecca for almost six years but still thought his countrymen would let him in. He organized an *umrah*[202] in the month of Dhul-Qa'dah, in which no fighting was allowed among the Arab tribes. But Muhammad had previously violated this rule, claiming that Allah had allowed him to do so. Did Muhammad really want to perform the umrah, or did he view this trip as an invasion?

Muhammad, along with his party of about 1,400 armed men and four women, headed toward Mecca with the idea that even if they should be barred from entering, they would fight their way through to the Kaaba—even if they were to destroy the Quraysh. For Muhammad to think that he could simply just enter the city is ridiculous and might indicate that this trip was more than a simple umrah.

Muhammad and His People Approach Mecca

As Muhammad's force neared the city, the Quraysh were alerted and began to organize their defense with their professional force, the Ahabish.[203] Ikrimah went with five hundred men to block the Muslims and Khalid Ibnl-Waleed, who served as a mobile service with his cavalry. Muhammad had sent his spies and knew what the Quraysh were doing and changed his route to avoid them. The Quraysh were still able to block Muhammad and his men from advancing further. When Muhammad realized that it would not be an easy entry, he set up camp at al-Hudaybiyah, a well about five miles east of Mecca. The Quraysh appeared to have the upper hand at that time and could have attacked the Muslims and even perhaps killed Muhammad. They were however concerned about their reputation with the Bedouin tribes if they were to kill Muhammad. On the other hand, they did not want Muhammad

---

[202.] Pilgrimage of lesser importance than the hajj, which is observed only once a year in the month Dhul Hijja, the last month of the Islamic calendar. An umrah can take place at any time.
[203.] A mixed group of different tribal backgrounds (Ethiopian)

to push into Mecca by force. They sent several of their own men to see what Muhammad had planned to do, but one of their Quraysh leaders threatened that if they did not allow Muhammad and his company to complete their umrah, he and his troops would withdraw. Division among the Quraysh was one of the reasons that Muhammad was able to win many of his battles against them.

The Quraysh leaders indicated their willingness to negotiate some acceptable terms with the Muslim party. According to Al Tabari,[204] Khalid bin-al-Walid, the key leader of the Quraysh cavalry, might have already become a secret Muslim and was apparently helping Muhammad.[205] Eventually, he and Ikrimah, the other key person of the Quraysh, would actually join Muhammad.

Muhammad Camps Outside Mecca

Camped outside Mecca, Muhammad sent Uthman ibn Affan as his envoy to negotiate their entry into the city. The Quraysh caused Uthman to stay longer in Mecca than they originally planned, causing the Muslims to believe that he had been killed. Muhammad then gathered his *sahaba* (followers) of nearly 1,400 and called them to pledge to fight to the death and avenge the blood of Uthman. This pledge took place under a tree and is called Bay'at al-Ridwan (Oath of Divine Pleasure), or the Pledge of the Tree.

Devotion of Muhammad's Followers

The Quraysh then sent negotiators to determine what could be done. One of the negotiators, after talking to Muhammad, returned to Mecca

204. Abu Ja'far Muhammad ibn Jarir Al Tabari was a prominent and influential Persian scholar, historian, and exegete of the Qur'an.
205. Ibn Ishaq. Sirat Rasul Allah 192–93, 95–96 and Al-Tabari, Tarik al-Rusul wa'l muluk, I.I, 1207.

and informed the leaders that the Muslims were wholly devoted to their prophet and willing to die for him. He said that he had never seen a king among his people like Muhammad among his companions.

The Treaty of Hudaybiyah (صلح الحديبية)

The Quraysh Meccans then decided to negotiate a treaty with Muhammad, thinking they had better negotiate while they still had the upper hand. On the other hand, Muhammad had also made a statement, saying, "War has exhausted and harmed the Quraysh. If they wish, we will grant them a delay, and they can leave me to get stronger and deal with the Bedouin tribes."[206] Muhammad also realized that if he fought the Quraysh at that time, there was a chance he would lose; but by establishing a treaty with them, he could buy some time to subdue other neighboring tribes, forcing them to join him. He could then come back with overwhelming force, prepared to enter Mecca!

Muhammad was forced to sign the document of the Treaty of Hudaybiyah by his own name, Muhammad bin Abdullah, and not Muhammad the Prophet of Islam, as his followers had been calling him. The treaty had six provisions:

1. There would be a ten-year truce between the Muslims and Quraysh.
2. Should anyone come to Muhammad from Mecca, he would not be allowed to stay in Medina unless permission was granted by one in authority over him from his own tribe.
3. If any Muslim in Medina wished to return to Mecca and leave Islam, they should be allowed to do so without any hindrance.
4. There should be nothing accomplished by secret raids or betrayal of the treaty's terms.
5. The Muslims and Quraysh could develop any tribal alliances they wished.

206. Al-Wakidi, Kitab al-Maghazi, 212.

6. The Muslims could return a year later to engage in the umrah, remaining there for three nights, armed with sheathed swords, but no other weapons.[207]

In addition to the provisions of the agreement, it was determined that there were to be no secret agreements, bad faith, or antagonism between the parties.[208]

As soon as the treaty had been ratified, Muhammad was forced to return a Muslim back to his family after he had fled from Mecca.

This treaty was not viewed by the *sahaba* (companions of Muhammad) as a success. They were despondent, thinking that as Muslim followers of Allah and the Prophet, they deserved a better outcome; but Muhammad tried to cheer them up by getting them ready to sacrifice animals for the umrah even though they were not allowed inside Mecca. He shaved his head, as is the custom for umrah, and had the first sacrifice slaughtered and performed the umrah outside of Mecca.

Muhammad Turns the Negative to Positive

On the way back to Medina, Muhammad started reciting Qur'an 48 titled "The Victory." The chapter opens by declaring the Hudaybiyah truce to be a real victory and, after referring to the disappointment of the "idolators" (the Quraysh), concludes with a reference to the aid and allegiance that the faithful (the companions) rendered to the "holy prophet."

The second section deals with the false excuses of the hypocrites and separates them from the Muslims.

[207.] Ibn Ishaq, Sirat Rasoul Allah, 462.
[208.] Ibid., Al-Tabari Ta'rikh al-rasulwa l muluk, I.I, 1489.

The third section prophesizes more victories in battle—Khaybar[209] and the conquest of Mecca being clearly hinted at.

The fourth section brings the chapter to a close by making the important announcement that Islam will be made triumphant over all other religions of the world.[210]

All twenty-nine verses of this Qur'an chapter came as a result of the failed entry to Mecca and the Treaty of Hudaybiyah.

Indeed, Muhammad was a great man! With his determination and positive attitude, he motivated his followers and overcame what was an obvious failure in his attempt to enter Mecca. The Treaty of Hudaybiyah allowed the Muslims to be able to openly spread their belief, being now recognized as an equal partner with the already-established Quraysh tribe of Mecca.

Breaking a Treaty Rule

The rules of the treaty had to be observed; but Abu Basir, a man from the Quraysh who was held captive in jail in Mecca, ran away to Muhammad in Medina. The Quraysh sent two hunters to retrieve the man and take him back to Mecca. Muhammad complied but hoped that Abu Basir could maneuver his way back, perhaps even with others held in captivity in Mecca. Two guards were sent to bring Abu Basir back to Mecca. But it seems the guards were not careful enough, for Abu Basir killed one of the guards, and the other fled, fearing for his life! Like a lot of the people who had gone with Muhammad when he first migrated from Mecca to Medina, Basir was a bandit. It is unclear whether Muhammad helped him or just ignored reporting him, and

---

[209.] Khaybar is the Jewish tribe that Muhammad invaded. We shall deal with Khaybar in the next chapter.

[210.] Exposition of Qur'an chapter 48 by Maulana Muhammad Ali, the Qur'an, with English translation and commentary.

the man managed to flee to the coast and encouraged many who were held prisoners in Mecca to join him. Seventy other men fled from Mecca and joined him. Abu Basir and his companions started raiding the Quraysh during the time of the treaty, and Muhammad did nothing about it! The Quraysh, drained by the raids on their goods, violated their own treaty by asking Muhammad to take Abu Basir and his companions so as to stop the raids. Muhammad continued to support the raiders, if not in action, morally.

Realizing that the Quraysh were not able to force him to stick by the treaty, Muhammad allowed a few Muslim women from the Quraysh to come to Medina, further violating the treaty. But Allah gave Muhammad Qur'an 60:10, which says,

> O you who believe, when believing women come to you fleeing, examine them. Then, if you know them to be believers send them not back to the disbelievers. Neither are these women lawful for them, nor are those men lawful for them. And give them what they have spent; and there is no blame on you in marrying them, when you give them their dowries. And hold not to the ties of marriage of disbelieving women and ask for what you have spent, and let them ask for what they have spent. That is Allah's judgment; He judges between you. And Allah is knowing, wise.

This verse refers to the Arab women who were married to Arab men in Mecca; if they embraced Islam and went to Muhammad in Medina, then their marriage in Mecca was severed and considered void. They were then free to go to Medina and marry Muslim men in spite of the fact that they already had husbands in Mecca. Other than the moral issue, this was a clear violation of the treaty, for the women were supposed to be sent back. But the treaty was supplanted by Allah's intervention in the above verse. The verse deals with two issues:

1. First, believing women from Mecca should be returned to the Muslims in Medina, therefore breaking the treaty. Although the Quraysh Meccans were not Muslims, Muhammad chose to make them consent to the Qur'an verse that Allah gave him!

2. The second issue in this verse was the dowry, which is a very important part of Muslim marriages and possibly of pagan marriages before Islam. When a man marries a woman, he has to pay a dowry. This dowry belongs to the wife to protect her in case of divorce. But when the woman wants out, she has to return that dowry money.

Somehow Muhammad was able to change the treaty rules and instigated an exchange in married women; those who wanted to leave their husbands in Mecca could do so by returning the dowry money they had received when they got married. And those who wanted to leave their husbands in Medina should also do so by returning their dowry money.

Key Quraysh Men Join Muhammad

Two Quraysh men joined Muhammad in Medina. One was a previous enemy of Muhammad who had offended him but now decided to join him. Muhammad accepted him because Muhammad had a policy to accept with open arms anyone who embraced Islam. Once a Muslim, Muhammad's rules guaranteed they could not leave! The price of leaving Islam was and continues to be death, so Muhammad did not have much to lose. As for the ones who became Muslims and joined Muhammad, it was not a hard decision, for it was a choice between starvation in Mecca and financial security with Muhammad.

Muhammad's goal was to spread a new religion, Islam, and a new ideology represented by the ummah (nation) of Islam. For this, he did not spare anyone or any group of people who stood in his way. He wanted to spread Islam in the whole world. He fought and raided neighboring cities and tribes until they submitted to Islam. To do this, he had to use his sword to subdue those who resisted him and his Islam. But Muhammad's ultimate goal was to go back to Mecca and conquer those who had refused his message in the first place and caused him to flee to Al-Medina. Now six years later, with more strength and more followers, he was getting ready to go back and conquer Mecca after his first failed attempt at Hudaybiyah.

Muhammad was gaining power, and he now had a plan to go back and attack Mecca; but before doing so, he wanted to eliminate the Jews who did not join him in his Islam. So the prosperous Jewish tribe of Khaybar to the north was chosen to be attacked next.

The Treaty of Hudaybiyah reminds us of the treaty of Yasser Arafat, which he made in Oslo. When the Arab nations were mad at him for making an agreement with the Jews, all he had to tell them was one word: "Hudaybiyah." Muslims all over the world understood that Yasser Arafat was referring to Muhammad's ten-year treaty with the Meccans, which he broke after just two years. The West never understood what Yasser Arafat meant. Muhammad signed a treaty merely to give himself time to get stronger.

Chapter Twenty-Four

Jesus in the Marketplace

In this chapter, I will share a personal experience that happened to me when I was living in the Middle East. It was a Thursday afternoon, and after meeting with a friend, I thought it would be nice to stop and buy fresh vegetables and fruits. Rows of carts carrying tomatoes, cucumbers, zucchini, potatoes, eggplant, etc., were lined up—all still bearing the freshness of the fields. Other carts were loaded with overripe fruits, their peddlers proudly calling out their goods, while male customers and slender covered women tried to get their best bargain of the day. Very small shops lined around the open space with carts selling dried legumes and colorful spices.

Personally, I was always welcome in the market because of my Egyptian Arabic dialect, which many Arabs just love. This is because of Egyptian movies, which are very popular all over the Arab world, with Egypt being the major and most popular producer. So as soon as I spoke Egyptian Arabic, the merchants grinned, praising the first president of Egypt, Gamal Abdel Nasser. In fact, I've been told that my language abilities and my gray hair helped me get away with a lot, especially when my scarf would fall off my head. In Muslim countries, a woman's hair must be covered in the presence of men.

As soon as I entered the market, a handsome tall guy in his twenties dressed in a white galabia[211] approached me, saying, "Qouli Allahu Akbar (say God is Great)." I repeated after him, "Allahu Akbar," which simply means "God is greater or great." He grinned but quickly told me, "But you do not love Muhammad." I replied, "I love Jesus."

"But your Book prophesies about Muhammad." (Muslims teach that there are three verses in the Bible that speak of Muhammad.)

I said, "Oh, really? Where?" Long silence!

"I don't know. I have never seen a Bible."

"Would you like to read it?"

"I don't have one."

"Would you read it if you had one?"

"How could I get one? There are no Bibles here."

"If I gave you a Bible, would you like to read it?"

"How could you get me one? In all of this country, you cannot buy a Bible."

"I will give you one if you promise to read it and show me the passage that speaks of Muhammad."

I dug in my bag and got out a Bible I happened to have with me.

He took the Bible as if he were receiving a great treasure he never expected and began thanking me over and over. But at that very moment, another young man about his own age, also dressed in a white

---

[211.] White robe mostly worn by religious men

galabia, grabbed the Bible from his hands; and the two young men got in a fistfight, each saying, "This is mine! No, it is mine! I want it. No, I want it . . ." Worried that they might escalate in their fight, I stepped forward to where the crowd of spectators had gathered by now and said to the intruder, "Please let him have his Bible. I will get you one also." He let go and asked me, "When?" I said, "Tomorrow." "Where?" "Right here." I told him when I'd be there, but before I started to leave, a very short old man with gray hair spoke to me. "All my life, I have wanted to read this book, and now you are giving away two. But I still don't get to read it." I said, "Friend, don't worry. I will get you one too!" I turned around and headed home with one thing on my mind: tomorrow those thirsty souls will get their Bibles!

At home, excited, I started wrapping some Bibles (they are illegal). The following day, I headed to the market to give the Bibles to the two men plus any others who might want one. No sooner did I arrive than a bearded man dressed in white came toward me, screaming, "Oqtolouha! Oqtolouha! (Kill her! Kill her!)" I then went closer to the man who wanted me killed and said, "Friend, why do you want to kill me?" "Because you are distributing Bibles." "Well, do you know what the Bible says?" Total silence! By that time, a large crowd had gathered around us, so I started reciting the words of Jesus in Arabic:

> You have heard that it was said to you; You shall love your neighbor and hate your enemy, but I say to you love your enemies. Do good to those who hate you; bless those who curse you and pray for those who persecute you and despitefully use you, pray for those who mistreat you; and whoever hits you on the cheek, offer him the other also; and whoever takes away your coat give him your shirt also; be merciful just as your Father who is in heaven, is merciful.

The dead silence and peaceful looks on the listeners' faces made me think there would be great response to the words of Jesus, and maybe there was! But after I finished, the angry man dressed in white came very close to me, got his knife out of its sheath, placed the tip against my stomach, and viciously shouted "Oqtolouha!" I felt the knife and thought the time had come for me to meet Jesus whom I serve. I said this quick prayer, "Lord, if he kills me, would you please build your church here in this marketplace where my blood is spilled?" Strangely, I was not afraid!

Suddenly, a police officer appeared and grabbed the man by his two arms, saying, "Leave the lady alone." Relieved from the knife, I realized what was happening. I looked around and found the scared crowd moving away, and I too started walking away. Sad and despondent, I walked toward home. When I had walked a few blocks, I looked behind and spotted the old man who had asked for a Bible. He came nearer and in a hushed voice asked me, "Did you bring me a Bible?" I said, "Yes." He whispered, "Wrap it." I said, "It is wrapped." I got the package out and gave it to him. I will never forget how the old man hugged the wrapped Bible to his chest and kept repeating, "Thank you. Thank you. Thank you." And he walked away.

I never saw that man again, but I have often asked the Lord to let me meet him in heaven.

I do not know if the young man read the Bible or if ever he shared it with the other young man who fought him for it. I do know that they both desired to read it and learn about Jesus, and I have prayed that both would find Him throughout its pages.

From the time I had met the young man, he wanted to talk about Muhammad, repeating what he had been taught about "Muhammad in the Bible." The angry man, true to Muhammad's teachings, wanted to kill me, following the teachings of Islam and his prophet, while the teaching of Jesus also echoed in the marketplace, "Love your enemies."

The young man had challenged me, saying, "Your Bible speaks of Muhammad." That is how the story developed. This young man was actually repeating what all Muslim kids are taught in school, and they believe it. First off, they have no Bibles to read for themselves; and if they did, *Islam teaches that one should never argue about or question Allah's words.* Besides, they are told, the Christians have altered their Bible. So where do their religious leaders and scholars find Muhammad in the Bible?

They refer to two verses in the Old Testament and one in the New Testament (the Injeel).

1. Deuteronomy 18:18: "I will raise up for them a Prophet like you from among their brethren, and will put My words in His mouth. And He shall speak to them all that I command Him." Muslims believe that the *prophet spoken of was Muhammad because he was Abraham's son from Hagar,* Sarah's slave. They assume that the word "brethren" in the Bible refers to the Ishmaelites, and since Muhammad was a descendant of Ishmael, he must be the prophet referred to.

    The first two verses of chapter 18 clearly reveal that God was talking to the Israelites when He said "your brethren." "The Levitical priests, the whole tribe of Levi shall have no portion with Israel . . . the Lord is their inheritance as He promised them." Verses 1–2 clearly speak of the Levites. Their brethren are the other tribes of Israel. When Moses says that God will raise up a prophet like himself (Moses) from among the Jews, "from among their brethren" means that the prophet will be a Jew. Muhammad was not a Jew. He was born an Arab. The Arabs are not one of the tribes of Israel. Muhammad could not have been the brother of Moses.

    Who then is the prophet like Moses? Moses' prophecy in Deuteronomy, chapter 18 was fulfilled in Jesus Christ of Nazareth. Jesus said, "If you believed Moses you would believe Me; for he wrote about Me" (John 5:46–47). We also read in John 1:45, "We have found Him of whom Moses in the law, and also in the prophets, wrote—Jesus of Nazareth." Jesus was a Jew, born of the tribe of Judah through Mary, His mother. He was a Jew like Moses.[212] The apostle Peter specifically applied this verse to Jesus in his sermon in Acts 3:22.

2. Another prediction Muslims claim is about Muhammad, although less referred to, is Isaiah 29:12: "Then the book will be given to the one who is illiterate saying, 'Please read this book,' and he will say, 'I cannot read.'" Muslims insist that the book referred to in this verse must be the Qur'an, delivered to Muhammad by the angel Gabriel. They claim since Muhammad was illiterate, then the book must have been delivered to him.

    First of all, some deny Muhammad was illiterate. Second, the angel Gabriel appeared to many people and gave them messages but never squeezed them to the point they almost choked. This was the experience of Muhammad at the hands of whoever delivered the message to him. Third, this teaching misrepresents the passage in Isaiah.

    So who was the prophet Isaiah talking about? Isaiah lived in the eighth century BC and is known as the messianic prophet because he prophesied so many details about the Messiah to come. In Isaiah 29, God pronounces judgments on Judah for her sins at that time (702 BC). God's people were in deliberate spiritual blindness.

212. https://www.biblegateway.com/resources/dictionary-of-bible-themes/5104-Moses-foreshadower-Jesus. Moses foreshadows Jesus in his role as lawgiver, mediator between God and His people, and as a prophet who declared the will of God. Both were attempted to be murdered as infants and were exiles in Egypt. Supernatural miracles confirmed the callings of both Moses and Jesus. Both mediated covenants with God, Moses as servant and Jesus as Son (Hebrews 3:1–6).

"Isaiah describes the unwillingness of the people of his day to heed the truth, by comparing them to a literate person who is told to read something but refuses, excusing himself by saying the document is sealed (v. 11), and an illiterate person who excuses himself by saying he cannot read (v. 12)."[213] The point is that people in Isaiah's day refused to pay attention to God's Word as spoken through His prophets. They did not want it! Verses 13–16 explain that because of their closed minds, they will suffer for their rejection of God's Word. So these verses had to do with the children of Israel, not with Muhammad, who had not even been born.

3. The third verse Muslims claim is about Muhammad is in the New Testament. Muslims say that the prophecy in John about the "Helper," the Holy Spirit, is about Muhammad. They back this by a verse that Muhammad recited in Qur'an 61:6, which says, "And when Jesus, Son of Mary said: 'O children of Israel, surely I am the messenger of Allah to you, verifying that which is before Me of the Torah (Old Testament) and giving the good news of a messenger who will come after Me, his name being Ahmad (Muhammad),' but when he came to them with clear arguments they said: 'This is obvious enchantment (nonsense).'"

So which Bible verse are they referring to? John 14:26 says, "But the Helper, the Holy Spirit, whom the Father will send in My Name, He will teach you all things, and bring to your remembrance all that I said to you." Muslims claim that this "Helper" was Muhammad. They argue that the Greek word *Parakletos*, which is translated "Helper" should be *periklytos* (praised one), which means Ahmad or Muhammad.[214] (The Arabic root word in Ahmad and Muhammad is "praise.") They claim

[213] http://apologeticspress.org/apcontent.aspx?category=8&article=88
[214] http://www.islam101.com/religions/christianity/mBible.htm

that the Bible has been altered (changed and corrupted)[215] and that *this* particular word was changed to remove the name of Muhammad from the Bible! All of the Greek manuscripts in existence that predate Muhammad say *parakletos*; and there are numerous Greek manuscripts of the New Testament in existence today, dating from before the time of Muhammad, and not one of them uses the word *periklytos*. In fact, the word *periklytos* does not appear anywhere in the Bible.

John 14:16–20 says the following:

He will give you another Helper. Does this fit Muhammad?

Jesus is saying to his disciples, "I have been your Helper, Counselor, Comforter. I still have many things to teach you, but I will send you another Helper like Me."

He (the Father) will give you another Helper—the Spirit of Truth. The obvious thing here is that the Helper is a Spirit. Has Muhammad ever been called the Spirit of Truth?

He will abide with you forever. Muhammad was never with the disciples of Jesus. Muhammad was born in the sixth century and lived only sixty-two years and then died. He did not live with his companions forever. He was buried in Medina. Jesus said that the promised Helper would be with His disciples forever. Muhammad cannot possibly be the one referred to.

---

215. The corruption of the Bible is a big issue in Islam. It has been answered by many Christian scholars. The Bible could not have been changed or corrupted because Muhammad himself referred to the Bible. So if the Bible was corrupted, it would have had to be corrupted *after* Muhammad's time, in which case there were already translations in many languages all over the world. So to change the Bible, one would have had to collect every copy in every language and change it. This is not possible! There is a continuous chain of manuscript evidence centuries before and after Muhammad.

The Spirit of Truth whom the world cannot see. The world cannot receive the Helper because they cannot see Him. Muhammad was visible, and thousands of people saw him during his lifetime.

You know Him, for He dwells with you. Jesus is clearly talking about someone with whom the disciples were familiar. Muhammad could not have been known to them, for he was born more than five hundred years later!

He dwells in you. The Helper, the Holy Spirit, was to be in the disciples. Muhammad was a flesh and blood person who is no longer alive. He cannot dwell in humans.

Muhammad was not alive at the time of Jesus' apostles and was never called the Spirit of Truth. This prophecy cannot be about Muhammad. The Bible states the Helper is the "Holy Spirit whom the Father will send in My Name, He will teach you all things, and will bring to your remembrance all things that I said to you" (John 14:26). The Helper is indeed the Holy Spirit. He was in the disciples' hearts from the day of Pentecost and forever. He also lives in all those who have received Jesus as Savior and Lord.

You can also receive the Holy Spirit today by genuinely inviting Jesus into your life and receiving Him as your Savior.

You can explain to your Muslim friends why Muhammad was not mentioned in the Bible, but I did not have a chance to explain this to the young man to whom I gave the Bible in the marketplace. It is my prayer that he read the Bible and in it met Jesus!

Chapter Twenty-Five

Khaybar

After his failed entry into Mecca, Muhammad wanted to boost the morale of his followers and regain their respect. To placate their grumbling, he promised them that they would soon achieve big victories and an abundance of food and booty wealth. Muhammad had decided to go back to Mecca and enter it with or without the invitation or blessing of the Meccans. Allah had given him the appropriate verses (sura 48), and now he had to pursue his plan to conquer all of Arabia and subjugate the Meccans, his chief enemies. But first, he needed more strength and more wealth.

Muhammad had already invaded and conquered two of the three major Jewish tribes in Arabia. The Banu Qaynuka were allowed to leave after taking all their possessions because of the insistence of one of his most influential men. The Banu Qurayza were not so lucky. All their males were killed, the boys sold in slavery, and the women distributed among the warriors. The remaining major Jewish tribe was Khaybar, which was situated about a hundred miles to the north of Al-Medina, close to Syria. Some of the surviving Jews from previous invasions who had been allowed to leave had relocated and settled in Khaybar.

Khaybar was an agricultural oasis. The Jews were industrious, and their valley was known as the date farm of Arabia. One of their plantations reportedly had forty thousand trees, and Muhammad wanted its wealth! Khaybar consisted of a string of fortresses in several clusters spread through a long, narrow valley between ancient lava beds. Muhammad attacked the oasis not only in order to seize the wealth of the Jews, but also out of hatred for them for rejecting him and his religion and to eliminate them as a military threat.[216]

Muhammad Invades Khaybar

> When the apostle raided a people, he waited until morning. If he heard a call to prayer he held back; if he did not hear it he attacked. We came to Khaybar by night, and the apostle passed the night there; and when morning came he did not hear the call to prayer, so he rode and we rode with him.[217]

The people with Muhammad did not know why they were marching to war.

Umar ibn Khattab said, "Never did I cherish for leadership but on that day. I came before him with the hope that I may be called for this, but Allah's Messenger called Ali b Abu Talib and he conferred this honor upon him and said, 'Proceed on and do not look about until Allah grants you victory,' and Ali went a bit and then halted and did not look about and then said in a loud voice, 'Allah's Messenger, on what issue should I fight with the people?' Thereupon the prophet said, 'Fight with them until they bear testimony to the fact that there is no god but Allah and Muhammad is his Messenger.'"[218]

[216.] http www.americanthinker.com/articles. Muhammad's attack on Khaybar. Article by F. W. Burleigh, April 12, 2015.

[217.] Ibn Ishaq/Hisham 757

[218.] Sahih Muslim 2405, book 44, Hadith 52.

Muhammad conquered the tribe of Khaybar in May AD 628. The attack was a surprise for the Jews and a decisive victory for the Muslims. This is how Muslim biographers recorded it:

> The prophet offered the Fajr (Dawn) prayer near Khaybar when it was still dark and then said "Allahu Akbar! Khaybar is destroyed for whenever we approach a hostile nation to fight, then, evil will be the morning for those who had been warned."[219]

> We met the workers of Khaybar coming out in the morning with their spades and baskets. When they saw the apostle and the army they cried, "Muhammad with his force," and turned tail and fled . . . The apostle seized the property piece by piece . . .[220]

Kinana ibn al-Rabi

Khaybar had several strong forts that were eventually seized piece by piece. The last of these forts to fall to the Muslims was the fort of Al-Kamus, which was owned by Kinana ibn al-Rabi.

Ibn Ishaq writes about Kinana ibn al-Rabi:

> Kenana al-Rabi, who had the custody of the treasure of Banu Nadir, was brought to the apostle. When the apostle said to Kenana, "Do you know that if we find you have it I shall kill you?" He said "Yes." The apostle gave orders that the ruin was to be excavated and some of the treasure was found. When he asked him about the rest he refused to produce it, so the apostle gave

---

[219.] Sahih Bukhari, vol. 5, book 59, number 512.
[220.] Ibn Ishaq/Hisham, 757.

orders to al-Zubayr Al-Awwam, "Torture him until you extract what he has." So he kindled a fire with flint and steel on his chest until he was nearly dead. Then the apostle delivered him to Muhammad ibn Maslama and he struck off his head, in revenge for his brother Mahmud.[221]

In addition to Ibn Ishaq's narration, Al-Talabari writes,

The Prophet gave orders concerning Kinanah to Zubayr, saying, "Torture him until you root out and extract what he has." So Zubayr kindled a fire on Kinanah's chest, twirling it with his firestick until Kinanah was near death. Then the Messenger gave him to Maslama, who beheaded him.[222]

Safiyyah: Wife of Kinana

The following is the story of Safiyyah as told by many biographers, including Dr. Aisha Abdul-Rahman:[223]

Among the women captured in the Battle of Khaybar was Safiyyah, the beautiful wife of the slain Kinana. She was nearly seventeen at the time. Her lineage was traced back to Aaron, the brother of Moses; and her mother was Barra, daughter of Shamwal. Bilal, the prayer crier of Muhammad, led the war slaves Safiyyah and her cousin, parading them through the war zone, where the bodies of their men lay strewn on the streets. Safiyyah held her agonizing deep cry, but her cousin could not contain herself. She screamed with grief, slapped her face, and covered

[221.] Ibn Hisham. *Al-Sira al-Nabawiyya* (*The Life of the Prophet*). English translation in Guillame (1955), pp. 145–146.

[222.] Al-Tabari, vol. 8, p. 122.

[223.] Dr. Aisha, *The Wives of the Prophet*/Dar Al Maarif/ ISBN 977-02-6811-9, p. 208–222 (author's translation).

her head with dust . . . Then they were brought to Muhammad. Safiyyah hid her grief with pride while no one really knew what she felt, but her cousin stood with dust on her head and torn clothes and could not stop screaming and crying. Turning his face from her, the prophet of Allah said, "Take this devil away from me." Then he looked at Safiyyah kindly and said to Bilal, "Have you lost all compassion that you paraded two women by their dead men?" He then ordered Safiyyah to follow him, laying his mantle over her, signaling that he had chosen her for himself. He then gave her to his attendant Om Selim to prepare her to be his bride.[224]

Muhammad took Safiyyah to his house at the edge of Khaybar and had sex with her that same night. Some said he even married her, and her marriage dowry was her freedom. Outside the house where Muhammad took Safiyyah, a man from Muhammad's followers spent the night watching with his sword at his side, circling around the place where the couple slept, without the knowledge of Muhammad. When it was morning, Muhammad heard him and found where he was and asked him, "Abu Ayoub, what are you doing here?" He answered, "O prophet of Allah, I worried about you because of this woman. You have killed her father and her husband and her brother and her people and I was afraid she would hurt you." And it was said that Muhammad said to Allah, "Protect Abu Ayoub as he spent the night protecting me."

Muhammad headed back to Medina with his beautiful wife, the lady who was of the highest status among her people. Safiyyah's camel tripped, and she was thrown to the ground. Muhammad rushed to her rescue in the sight of his other wives, who said, "May Allah do away with this Jewess."[225] So the Prophet preferred not to take her in to his other seven wives, especially that all the women were looking at her, enjoying the scared look on her face.[226] Muhammad took his new bride

224. Sahih Muslim/Al Nikah.
225. Sahih Muslim 2/1048: H1365.
226. Ibn Sa'ad and Ibn Hajar/Al Isaba wa'l samt.

to the house of Al-Ansary, one of his followers. Some of his wives followed to look at her beauty—among them his favorite wife, Aisha, who also followed, all covered up, to see her new rival. Muhammad waited for her outside and caught her by her dress, laughingly asking her opinion of what she saw, to which she replied, "I saw a Jewess!" Muhammad said, "Don't say that! She has become a Muslim." Once back home, the jealous favorite wife confided in her rival and friend, Hifsa, of her fears that this beautiful new wife would probably dominate their husband. Hifsa comforted Aisha by saying that these type of women do not score well with their husbands.[227]

My Husband Is Muhammad, My Father Aaron, and My Uncle Moses

Safiyyah tried to win Aisha and her friend Hifsa to her side to avoid the unkind comments about her Jewish ancestry, for she was always reminded of the deep-seated animosity between her people and Islam. On one of Muhammad's travels, he took Safiyyah and Om Salma with him, and that day was her day. (Muhammad had appointed each of his women a day to spend with.) By mistake, Muhammad went to Safiyyah's tent and started talking to her. Angry, Om Salma confronted the prophet of Allah, telling him, "You speak to the daughter of the Jew on my day?" She then repented and told Muhammad that she just said this because she was jealous.[228] Safiyyah was facing a lot of ridicule at the hands of her rivals, and she often had to shut her ears to avoid the hurtful remarks by all the other women. She had gone the extra mile to befriend Aisha and Hifsa, but it seemed to no avail, for they too joined the others in expressing superiority over her. They were Arab Quraysh ladies, while she was the invaded Jewish stranger. It became too painful for Safiyyah; so she cried and reported it to Muhammad, who told her to answer them, saying, "How can you be better than me while my

---

[227.] Tabakat Ibn Sa'ad 8/95
[228.] Ibid.

husband is Muhammad and my father Aaron and my uncle Moses?"[229] Safiyyah was comforted by Muhammad's words, and he continued defending her.

On another of Muhammad's trips, he had taken Safiyyah and Zainab bint Jahsh (his former daughter-in-law) when Safiyyah's camel became sick. Muhammad asked Zainab if she would let Safiyyah ride with her since she had extra space. Zainab answered with pride and disgust, "You want me to give my ride to this Jewess?" Muhammad then left her in anger and did not approach her for over two months.

During Muhammad's last days when he was deathly ill, Safiyyah said to Muhammad by his bedside, "I wish I could take your pain upon myself." The other wives looked at each other, blinking their eyes in scornful disagreement, but Muhammad caught that and said, "Why do you scorn her? She is being sincere."[230]

For the rest of her life after Muhammad's death, Safiyyah remained persecuted by the Muslims for being a Jewess.

Muhammad married Safiyyah in June of 628. He was fifty-seven years old, and she was sixteen. He died four years after their marriage on June 8, 632, at the age of sixty-two. Safiyyah died around the year 650 and was buried at the same place as the other wives of the Prophet.

The conquest of Khaybar was a source of wealth for the Muslims. The Jews of Khaybar were defeated, and their fortresses and leaders were seized one by one. The surviving Jews approached Muhammad, asking him to allow them to stay in their land and continue to cultivate it. The Prophet permitted the Jews to stay on their land, whose title now passed to him by right of conquest. The Jews would stay under the protection of Muhammad, and in return, they would give him half of their crop.

[229.] Al Esaba 8/127 and Al Nakl wa'l Estiab 4/1872 wa'l Samat 121.
[230.] Ibn Sa'ad in Tabakat supported by Zayd bin Aslam.

Thus, all the Jews of the Arabian Peninsula submitted to the authority of the prophet of Islam. Muhammad benefited from this arrangement because he did not have the manpower or the know-how to continue cultivating the fertile grounds of Khaybar.

The Results of the Conquest of Khaybar

The conquest of Khaybar changed the means by which the Muslims obtained their survival. Instead of depending on caravan raiding for their sustenance, now they had a steady income from the rich crops of the fertile Jewish land of Khaybar. Muhammad divided the spoils as usual, one-fifth to the Prophet and four-fifths to the fighters. Among other historians, M. Shibli writes, "At Khaybar, the new Islamic State acquired new subjects and new territories. It was the beginning not only of the Islamic State but also of its expansion . . . Before the conquest of Khaybar, the Muslims were destitute. Khaybar suddenly made them rich. Imam Bukhary has quoted Abdullah bin Umar bin al Khattab saying, 'We were hungry at all times until the conquest of Khaybar.' And the same authority has quoted Aisha, the wife of the prophet, as saying, 'It was not until the conquest of Khaybar that I could eat dates to my heart's content.'"[231]

The story of Khaybar is not only found in history books. Today, after nearly 1,400 years, it still remains fresh in the minds of many Muslims who are proudly teaching it in their schools. What is it they are trying to remember?

---

[231] Indian historian, biography of the Prophet.

Khaybar

خيبر خيبر يا يهود

جيش محمد سوف يعود

A while ago, as I was surfing the Internet, I came across a video of a grade school in Palestine. The children of about seven to eight years old were chanting the above slogan in Arabic. It caught my attention, and I continued to watch. The teacher asked a little girl, "Do you like the Jews?" The girl responded with an emphatic "No!" The teacher asked her, "Why don't you like them?" The girl answered, "Because they are the descendants of the monkeys and the pigs." The teacher asked, "Who said that?" The girl answered, "Allah!" (There are three verses in the Qur'an that say that Allah turned the Jews to monkeys and pigs because they disobeyed him.)[232]

If you don't read Arabic, let me tell you what the slogan referenced above says, "Khaybar, Khaybar, O you Jews; Muhammad's army will be back."

How many schools are teaching children that, even though Islam is not winning right now, the day is coming when they will be like Muhammad, triumphant over the Jews? One day, I was discussing this slogan with a Palestinian Muslim. When I shared that slogan with her, she quickly responded that of course Palestinians should always remember what happened to the Jews of Khaybar and take courage that someday Muslims will have the upper hand and be the conquerors. Someday they will become victorious in their fight against the Jews and regain Palestine. Khaybar represents to them the glory days of Islam when they were victorious over their neighboring tribes.

[232.] 2:63–65; 5:59–60; 7:166

246

"I have been ordered by Allah to fight against the people until they testify that none has the right to be worshipped but Allah and that Muhammad is Allah's Apostle . . ."[233] Muhammad said to his followers, "Fighting is prescribed for you though it is disliked by you; and it may be that you dislike a thing while it is good for you . . ."[234]

---

[233] Sahih Bukhari, vol. 1, book 2, Hadith 25
[234] Qur'an 2:216

Chapter Twenty-Six

Muhammad and Jesus Deal with Adultery

Muhammad and the Adulteress

I love stories. They talk about all kinds of people. Some stories make us happy, while others make us sad and wish they were not true. In this chapter, I will share with you two stories of similar nature, but with very different outcomes. About 1,400 hundred years ago, an Arab woman from the tribe of Ghamid committed adultery. In Sahih Muslim, book 17, number 4206, we read the story of this woman:

> There came to the holy Prophet of Islam a woman from Ghamid and said, "Allah's Messenger, I have committed adultery, so purify me." He (the Holy Prophet) turned her away. On the following day she said, "Allah's Messenger, Why do you turn me away? Perhaps you turn me as you turned Ma'iz.[235] By Allah, I have become pregnant." He said, "Well, if you insist upon it, then go away until you give birth to the child." When she was

---

[235.] Ma'iz b. Malik al Aslami was a man who had also committed adultery, and the prophet Muhammad sent him away, thinking there was something wrong with his mind. When he found out that nothing was wrong with him, he pronounced judgment about him (stoning).

delivered she came with the child wrapped in a rag and said, "Here is the child whom I have given birth to." He said, "Go away and suckle him until you wean him." When she had weaned him she came to (the Holy Prophet) with the child who was holding a piece of bread in his hand. She said, "Allah's Apostle, here is he as I have weaned him and he eats food." He (the Holy Prophet) entrusted the child to one of the Muslims and then pronounced punishment. And she was put in a ditch up to her chest and He commanded people and they stoned her. Khalid ibn Walid came forward with a stone which he flung at her head and there spurted blood on the face of Khalid and so he abused her. Allah's Apostle (may peace be upon him) heard his (Khalid's) curse that he had hurried upon her. Thereupon (the holy Prophet) said, "Khalid, be gentle. By Him in Whose hand is my life,[236] she has made such a repentance that even if a wrongful tax collector[237] were to repent he should have been forgiven." Then giving command regarding her, he prayed over her body and she was buried.

The question you probably are asking is, Why did this woman choose to go to Muhammad, the prophet of Islam, and confess when she knew very well the outcome would be stoning? This would be a very painful way to die—besides the pain of leaving an innocent, helpless two-year-old alone to grow without a mother and obviously no father. The answer lies in Sharia (Islamic law). According to the Sharia, adultery has to be punished. But the punishment in the afterlife of a person who has confessed, repented, and received the punishment of stoning is less harsh than the one who dies without confession,

---

[236.] By Allah

[237.] Tax collectors who extort people were considered great sinners.

repentance, and accepting stoning as punishment. The woman from Ghamid who came to Muhammad confessing was seeking a lighter punishment.

Islamic Ruling concerning the Criminal Act of *Zina* (Adultery)

Punishing of *Zina* in the Hereafter

The punishment of those who die without repenting from *zina* begins in the grave. In a long Hadith,[238] Allah's Messenger related a dream in which he saw two men (Jibreel and Maalik) accompanying him,[239] showing him how a number of sinners were being punished in al-Barzakh (life between death and Judgment Day). The Prophet said, "We proceeded until we came across a hole in the ground that resembled a baking pit, narrow at the top and wide at the bottom. Babbling and voices were issuing from it. We looked in and saw naked men and women. Underneath the pit was a raging fire; whenever it flared up the men and women screamed and rose with it until they almost fell out of the pit. As it subsided, they returned to the bottom. I said, 'Who are these?' They said . . . 'As for the naked men and women who were in the pit, they are men and women who indulge in zina.'"[240] In a similar narration, Allah's Messenger said, "We moved on until I saw people who were awfully swollen, and had the most foul stench, like that of the sewers. I asked, 'Who are these?' They replied, 'Those are the male and female adulterers.'"[241] As for punishment in the hereafter, Allah the Most High says, "And they (the servants of Allah) do not commit zina, and whoever does this shall meet a full penalty. The torment will be

---

[238] Sayings of the prophet Muhammad
[239] Angels
[240] Sahih Bukhari
[241] Ibn Khuzayma and Ibn Hibbaan

doubled to him in the Day of Resurrection, and he will abide therein in disgrace."[242]

The present-day Qur'an does not explicitly mention adultery, but according to Hadith, Qur'anic verses of stoning were written on a piece of paper and were lost when a goat ate it.

Umar said, "I am afraid that after a long time has passed people may say we do not find the verses of Rajam (stoning to death) in the holy book and consequently they may go astray by leaving an obligation that Allah has revealed . . . surely Allah's Apostle carried out the penalty of Rajam, and so did we after him" (Sahih Bukhari 8:82:816).

Ali said, "I have stoned her according to the tradition of Allah's Apostle (Muhammad)" (Sahih Bukhari 8:82:803).

Jesus and the Adulterous Woman

The other story that I will share with you happened in Jerusalem nearly two thousand years ago. It is found in the Bible in John 8:1–11: "Jesus went to the Mount of Olives. And early in the morning He came again into the temple and all the people were coming to Him; and he sat down and began to teach them. And the scribes and the Pharisees brought a woman caught in adultery; and having set her in the midst, they said to Him, 'Teacher, this woman has been caught in adultery, in the very act. Now in the Law, Moses commanded us to stone such women; what do you say?' And they were saying this, testing Him in order that they might have grounds for accusing Him. But Jesus sat down and with His finger wrote on the ground. But when they persisted in asking Him, He straightened up, and said to them, 'He who is without sin among you, let him be the first to throw a stone at her.' And again He stooped down and wrote on the ground. And when they heard it, they began to go out

---

[242.] Al Furqaan, 25:68–69

one by one, beginning with the older ones, and He was left alone, and the woman where she had been in the midst. And straightening up, Jesus said to her, 'Woman, where are they? Did no one condemn you?' and she said, 'No one, Lord.' And Jesus said, 'Neither do I condemn you; go your way. From now on sin no more.'"

Two women, similar acts, different outcomes. Why?

In the account of Muhammad and the woman from Ghamid, the woman had probably repented of her adulterous action but was so scared of the punishment she would receive after death that she chose to partially pay for her sin by submitting to be stoned. The compassionate prophet of Islam stood helpless to save the woman. This woman needed something the prophet Muhammad could not give her. She asked him to purify her, but he could not.

Jesus had to answer the Jewish religious leaders about what to do with the woman caught in adultery. They were trying to trap Him. If he agreed with them and allowed them to prevail in their unfair treatment of this woman and stone her according to the law of Moses,[243] he opened Himself up to trouble from the Roman government. He would be held responsible if the stoning proceeded because the Romans did not allow the Jews to execute the death sentence without their permission. On the other hand, if He was lax with the woman, then He would be condemned for not upholding the law of Moses. The religious leaders waited for Jesus' answer to their question. "What do You say we should do to the woman?" Jesus did not answer right away, but began to write in the sand. We are not told what Jesus wrote. Perhaps Jesus wrote commands He knew them to be guilty of breaking. So when He called the one without sin to cast the first stone, He knew there would be no stoning, but rather each of them would reflect on his own sinfulness before God. One by one, they left, starting with the elders, who perhaps had a longer account of wrongdoing before God. Those who came to condemn, went

---

[243.] Leviticus 20:10; Deuteronomy 22:22. Both of the guilty parties were condemned.

252

away condemning themselves, and the woman was left alone with Jesus, the only sinless Man who had the right to execute punishment. But He did not! As Augustine says, "The two were left alone, Misera and Misericordia (Misery and Mercy)."[244] He asked the woman, "Where are they? Did no one condemn you?" She said, "No one, Lord." Jesus said to her, "Neither do I condemn you; go your way. From now on sin no more."

Did Jesus then compromise God's law given by Moses to punish sin? Absolutely not! The penalty for this woman's sin had to be paid in full; otherwise, she could never be forgiven. *God's holiness demands that justice be executed, and the penalty for sin be enacted*—mine, yours, and the woman from Ghamid's.

Punishment is what we sinful humans deserve before our Holy God. In our own natural state, hopeless and helpless, we stand before God, unable to satisfy His law. But Jesus did! He was able to tell the adulterous woman, "Neither do I condemn you. He had the right to forgive because He chose to pay for all sins. He gave His life to ransom not only the adulterous woman but all sinners who accept His forgiveness. And you know that He appeared in order to take away sins; and in Him there is no sin" (1 John 3:5). At the cross, He paid the price to redeem us from God's law that we could not fulfill. At the cross, God's justice and mercy were displayed. Grace was offered to all mankind.

[244.] http://jonlemmond.blogspot.com/2014/01/when-misery-and-mercy-meet-story-that.html

Chapter Twenty-Seven

Events before Mecca

War Is Deceit

When the Prophet, peace and blessings be upon him, intended to go to an expedition, he would pretend to go somewhere else and he would say, "War is deception."[245]

After the Conquest of Khaybar

When Khaybar had been conquered, Al Hajjaj ibn al-Sulami of the tribe of al-Bahz, who had converted to Islam, asked permission of Muhammad to go to Mecca. He wanted to collect money owed to him that he had invested in various business projects with the Meccan merchants. He also had money with his wife in Mecca. His wife did not know that her husband had become a Muslim and a follower of Muhammad. To get the money, Al Hajjaj knew he had to lie to the Quraysh people in Mecca, and he asked permission of Muhammad. Muhammad said, "Say what you want to say." So Al Hajjaj went to Mecca and found some men of Quraysh trying to get news about how Muhammad fared because they had heard he had gone to

---

[245] Sunan Abu Dawud 2637 Sahih.

Khaybar, and they knew it was the most fortified town in Hejaz. They did not know that Hajjaj had become Muslim when they asked him to tell them the news. He said, "I have very good news for you. Muhammad has suffered defeat and has been captured, and many of his companions have been killed." The men of Khaybar want to bring him to Mecca and have him killed by the Meccans in revenge for their men whom he has killed. As the Meccans rejoiced over the news of Muhammad's defeat, Al Hajjaj told them that he had come to collect the money from the merchants so that he could quickly go back and purchase some of the captured Muslims in Khaybar before the merchants beat him to it. He asked the Meccans to help him collect his money quickly and they helped him recover all of it. He also deceived his wife and had her give him their money, telling her the same story he told the men. Muhammad's uncle was living in Mecca, and when he heard the news about his nephew being captured, he went to Al Hajjaj to inquire. Al Hajjaj met secretly with him and asked if he could keep a secret. He then told him the truth about Muhammad conquering Khaybar and that the Jews had been captured and the town plundered. He also told him that he had become a secret Muslim and that Muhammad was well and actually married Safiyyah, the daughter of the chief and wife of the owner of the fort of Al-Kamus. He asked the uncle not to reveal any of this for three nights, allowing him enough time to return to Medina. After the three nights, the uncle wore his robe, perfumed himself, and went walking around the Kaaba. The Quraysh people were surprised about the attitude of Muhammad's uncle after having heard the terrible stories of his defeat. Al-Abbas, the uncle, then told them the truth and that Al Hajjaj was the one who told him. The Quraysh were devastated to hear about Khaybar's fate and to find out that they had just had a big-time traitor among them—Al Hajjaj. Muhammad's conquest of Khaybar meant that that their old enemy was gaining more power!

Poison

But all did not go well for Muhammad, for soon after celebrating his victory over Khaybar, he encountered treason!

When the apostle of Allah conquered Khaybar and he had peace of mind, Zainab Bint al-Harith, the Jewish spouse of Sallam Ibn Mishkam, inquired about which part of the goat Muhammad liked. She was told "the foreleg." Then she slaughtered one from her goats and poisoned it with potent poison, especially the foreleg, and roasted it and offered it to Muhammad. Muhammad took a piece of the foreleg and put it in his mouth. Bishr, who was eating with him, took another piece and put it in his mouth. When the apostle of Allah ate one morsel of it, Bishr ate his, and other people also ate from it. Then the apostle of Allah said, "Hold back your hands because this foreleg informed me that it is poisoned." Thereupon, Bishr said, "By him who has made you great, I discovered it from the morsel I took. Nothing prevented me from emitting it out, but the idea that I did not like to make your food unrelishing. When you had eaten what was in your mouth, I did not like to save my life after yours, and I also thought you would not have eaten it if there were something wrong." Bishr did not rise from his seat, but his color changed to that of a green cloth, and he died.

The apostle of Allah sent for Zainab and said to her, "What induced you to do what you have done?" She replied, "You have done to my people what you have done. You have killed my father, my uncle, and my husband. So I said to myself, if you are a prophet, the foreleg will inform you; and others have said, if you are a king, we will get rid of you . . ."[246]

The apostle of Allah lived after this for three years till, as a consequence of his pain, he passed away. During his illness, he used to say, "I did not

---

[246.] Some reporters say that the Jewish woman was killed by Muhammad, while others prefer to say she was forgiven.

256

cease to find the effect of the poisoned morsel I took at Khaybar and I suffered several times from its effects but now I feel the hour has come of the cutting of my jugular vein."[247]

During the illness from which he died, the mother of Bishr had come in to visit him. He said, "Umm Bishr, at this very moment I feel my aorta being severed because of the food I ate with your son at Khaybar."[248] So during the last three years of his life, Muhammad lived with pain, but this did not deter him from sending raiding parties to neighboring tribes that had refused to join him and become Muslim. On the whole, he was successful; but he still had three particular key tribes on his agenda: the Ghatafan, the Hawazin, and the Sulaym.

Muhammad Fulfills the Umrah

By now, the Hudaybiyah agreement between Muhammad and the Quraysh in Mecca had lasted a year, and he was accordingly allowed to go for an umrah (pilgrimage). Muhammad headed to Mecca with almost two thousand men armed with swords, coats of mail, and spears, all loaded on camels along with at least one hundred horsemen. This was obviously a violation of the treaty that stipulated that Muhammad would be allowed to enter Mecca peacefully with only sheathed swords for self-protection. The Quraysh were terrified to see Muhammad with an invading army approaching, but Muhammad did not proceed with his weapons. He left the weapons outside Mecca guarded by some of his men while he advanced to Mecca. As they entered, one of the Prophet's companions was holding the halter of the Prophet's camel while reciting the following poetic verse:

[247.] Ibn Sa'd, pp. 251–252.
[248.] From Al-Tabari, vol. 8, p. 124 (different narrator).

Get out of his way, you unbelievers make way.

Every good thing goes with His Apostle.

O Lord I believe in his word.

I know God's truth in accepting it.

We will fight you about its interpretation.

As we have fought you about its revelation.

With strokes that will remove heads from shoulders.

And make friend unmindful of friend.[249]

Another Marriage for Muhammad[250]

While in Mecca, a twenty-six-old widow desired to marry Muhammad. Some reports say that the widow told her sister, whose husband then arranged for Muhammad to marry her. Other reports say that she gave herself to the Prophet. At any rate, he consented to marry her, and Allah gave him a verse regarding this matter: "And a believing woman if she gives herself to the prophet if the prophet desires to marry her, (it is especially for you) not for the believers . . ." (Qur'an 33:50).

The agreed-upon three-day stay for the umrah was up, with Muhammad still in Mecca. The Meccans then sent him two messengers reminding him that he had to leave. Muhammad, wanting to stay longer, told them

---

249. Rodgers, The Generalship of Muhammad, p. 205; quoting Ibn Ishaq. Sirat Rasul Allah, 450 and Ibn Sa'ad Kitab al Tabakat al-Kabir 2:80.

250 This part is taken from the book *The Wives of the Prophet* by Aisha Abdul-Rahman, pp. 246–250, author's translation.

that he had married a new wife and would like to invite them for a wedding feast. The Quraysh were afraid to open wide their city to Muhammad and rudely answered that they did not want his food and asked him to leave. Muhammad consented, and leaving his new wife there in the custody of one of his followers, he and his companions returned to Medina.

Jealousy in Muhammad's House

Aisha, Muhammad's youngest wife and his favorite, is reported to have said, "I was jealous of women who 'gave themselves' to the prophet of Allah and would always say, 'Does a woman give herself?' but when the verse came I said to Muhammad, 'I find that your god is always swift to fulfill your wishes.'" Aisha was not the only jealous wife, for when the new bride eventually joined Muhammad's household, she realized that Aisha was indeed the favorite wife and that Maria the Coptic had her special place because she was the only wife who had given him a son.

After Muhammad's Successful Umrah

Muhammad returned to Medina triumphant after his successful umrah. Encouraged by his success and now having subdued the Jews for the most part, he also wanted to bring the Christian world to Islam. Muhammad sent letters to heads of states asking them to embrace Islam, but his emissary carrying a letter to the Byzantine emperor was captured and killed in the village of Mu'tah by members of the Christians of Banu Ghassan, who were allies of the Byzantine emperor.[251]

---

[251] Sayed Ali Asgher Razwy, A Restatement of the History of Islam and Muslims, The Battle of Mutah, ISBN0-9509879-1-3

Fighting the Christians: The Battle of Mu'tah

In retaliation for the killing of his messenger, Muhammad sent his biggest army. According to later Muslim historians, Muhammad sent three thousand to attack and punish the tribes. The army was led by Zaid ibn Haritha (who was previously his adopted son). When they arrived at the area of the east Jordan and realized the size of the Byzantine army, Zaid wanted to wait and call for reinforcements from Medina; but when they considered their desire and goal for victory or martyrdom, they continued to march and fought the Byzantines in the Battle of Mu'tah. The two armies fought a very fierce battle.

Death of Zaid and the Two Other Leaders

Zaid fell wounded with missiles and bled to death. When the next two in command also fell, Khalid ibn al-Walid was asked to assume command, and he continued the fight. The fighting was so intense that Khalid used nine swords, which broke in battle. Seeing that the situation was hopeless, he continued to engage the Byzantines in skirmishes but avoided formal battles. It is said that Khalid killed at least one identified Arab Christian commander named Malik.[252]

When the Muslim force returned to Medina, they were berated for apparently withdrawing and were accused of fleeing from the enemy. Muhammad ordered the talk to stop, saying that they would return to fight the Byzantines again and win, and he bestowed upon Khalid the title of Saifullah al Maslool, meaning "the Sharpened Sword of Allah." Some Muslims claim that this was a successful battle since the Muslims challenged the Byzantines and made their presence felt among the Arab Bedouin tribes in the region. A mausoleum was later built at Mu'tah over their grave.[253]

[252.] https://en.wikipedia.org/wiki/Battle_of_Mu%27tah
[253.] http://islamichistory.org/khalid-ibn-al-waleed/

Chapter Twenty-Eight

Mecca: Muhammad's Ultimate Dream

After his major success in Khaybar, Muhammad was closer to fulfilling his long-held desire of returning to Mecca, where he was born and raised. But he needed more power and more support to ensure a successful entry. It takes a great man to keep focused on his goal and not allow hindrances and discouragements—no matter how hard—to deter him. It was his determination and charisma that attracted so many followers who were willing to even die for his cause.

It had now been seven-plus years since the day Muhammad was forced to escape from Mecca, leaving his tribe, the Quraysh, who had refused to hear about his new religion. He migrated north to Al-Medina, where he was able to establish and spread Islam. After Muhammad's death, his successors designated the day of his migration, Muharram 1, AH 1,[254] as the beginning of the Islamic calendar year. This corresponds

---

[254.] Muharram is the first month of the Islamic year. AH, or *Anno Hegirae*, is how it is referred to in Latin texts. Arabic texts can say H, or year of the Hijri. It refers to the year of Muhammad's migration. The year is however a lunar month of 29.53 days. There is dispute about the exact day because of lunar to solar conversion. April 19, July 16, and September 24 are various proposed dates. *Anno Domini* (the year of our Lord) is the basis of Western civilization's beginning (or CE, common era).

with AD 622. Muhammad's goal had always been to go back and subdue Mecca and bring the Quraysh under the banner of Islam. Now that he was getting stronger, he was looking for a good reason to attack, although he had signed the Hudaybiyah agreement, which called for a ten-year peace treaty between him and the Quraysh of Mecca.

Khaybar was won in May/June of the year 628, and this made him much stronger, but Muhammad was still waiting for the opportune time to enter Mecca. During this waiting period, he sent his men to engage in sixteen expeditions to ensure additional support of neighboring clans.

Expeditions of Muhammad before Mecca

The total number of conquests and expeditions that Muhammad was involved with during his life was sixty-four, according to Richard Gabriel.[255] We have already mentioned some of the details of the bigger ones in earlier chapters; but the last sixteen were fought after Khaybar, between May 628 and January of 630, when Mecca was conquered.

Generally, his expeditions were offensive, aiming at ensuring safety against the enemies of Islam and increasing the number of Muslims. The following are a few examples of what took place:

In October 629, Muhammad sent Abu Ubaidh ibn al-Jarrah, along with three hundred men, to attack and chastise the tribe Juhaynah on the

---

[255.] Listed expeditions vary from sixty-four to ninety-six. https://en.wikipedia.org/wiki/Book:Military_career_of_Muhammad. The list of expeditions numbers twenty-eight, followed by links to ninety-six expeditions in chronological order (April 2017). Richard Gabriel, a military historian and author of a book on Muhammad, lists sixty-four campaigns: eight major battles, eighteen raids personally led, and planning for an additional thirty-eight raids. Muhammad invented insurgency warfare and was the first successful practitioner of it (http://www.historynet.com/muhammad-the-warrior-prophet.htm).

seacoast. There was no fighting as the enemy fled after they heard of their arrival.[256]

Hadrad al-Aslami raided the camp of Rifa'ah bin Qays for reportedly enticing the people against Muslims. He beheaded him and ran across the camp shouting, "Allahu Akbar!"[257]

In November 629, Abu Qatadah ibn Rab'i al Ansari attacked the Ghatafan tribe because they heard they were amassing troops to fight against them and were still outside the domain of Islam.[258]

Muhammad had some defeats but mostly victories. These victories were steps leading to the goal he had in mind all along. The ten-year Hudaybiyah agreement of peace between the Muslims and the Quraysh Meccans had not yet lasted two years, but Muhammad was now powerful enough and ready for an early entry to Mecca to claim it for Islam.

Reasons for the Early Conquest of Mecca

Before Islam, there had been animosity between the Banu Bakr and the Banu Khuza'ah;[259] but when the treaty of Hudaybiyah was drawn, the two clans had to choose either between Muhammad and the Muslims or between the Quraysh of Mecca. Banu Bakr chose the Quraysh, and Banu Khuza'ah chose the Muslims. With the treaty in place, some of the Banu Bakr decided to use the period of peace to take revenge against the now-Muslim Banu Khuza'ah for a past killing of one of their men. They attacked some of the Muslim men and killed one, reigniting a

---

[256.] Sahih al-Bukhari, 3:44:663.

[257.] Tabari, vol. 8, History of Islam.

[258.] Ibn Sa'd Kitab al-Tabakat al-Kabir, vol. 2.

[259.] The Banu Khuza'ah's roots date back in and around Mecca several years before Islam.

small war. They secretly received arms and help from the Quraysh.[260] The Banu Bakr fought the Khuza'ah (Muslim followers) at night and pushed them into the sacred area surrounding Mecca where no fighting was allowed to take place and massacred them. When Muhammad's followers complained, the leader of the Bakr party reminded them that Muhammad and his men used to steal in this area, so why could they not fight in it now?[261]

This fight was in violation of the rules of the treaty, but it had not been the first time that the treaty had been broken by either Muhammad's party or the Quraysh party. This time, however, turned to be significant because it provided Muhammad with an opportunity for the conquest of Mecca.

The following events helped shape the final plan of Muhammad's big conquest. When the Khuza'ah were attacked by the Bakr and Quraysh, some of the Khuza'ah men, headed by Budayl, went from Mecca to Medina to complain to Muhammad about the way they had been attacked by the Quraysh in Mecca. With Muhammad's promise to support them, they turned back and headed to Mecca. At the same time, Abu Sufyan, who ranked high among the Quraysh leaders, was sent as a delegate from Mecca to Medina to try and reach a settlement in order to avoid conquest. On his way to Muhammad, he ran into Budayl and his company, who had gone complaining to Muhammad. When Abu Sufyan asked Budayl where he had been, he concealed the fact that he had gone to see Muhammad and instead said that he had come from the seacoast for a business matter. When they separated, Abu Sufyan suspected that he probably had gone to see Muhammad. He thought to himself that if they had been to Medina to speak to Muhammad, they probably fed their camels on dates. (Recall that since the conquest of Khaybar, Muhammad had a good supply of dates.) Abu Sufyan

---

[260.] Al-Wakidi-Al Maghazi, vol. 2, p. 742.
[261.] Ibn Ishaq Sirat Rasoul Allah 541.

opened the droppings of the camels and found date pits, which indicated that they had indeed gone to see Muhammad.[262]

Abu Sufyan hurried to Muhammad, trying to negotiate peace. He first stopped to see his daughter, who was married to Muhammad, his enemy. His daughter treated him coldly and told him she would not intercede between him and her husband, who always made his own decisions. At this, Abu Sufyan appealed to Muhammad, who told him that he was not willing to make any alterations to the treaty.[263] Bewildered, Abu Sufyan went to Muhammad's next in command, but again to no avail, and so on to the next until he was told that when Muhammad decided on something, no one could make him change his mind. Finally, Abu Sufyan was told that when he went back to Mecca, he had better declare himself a protector of those who wanted to stay neutral to avoid being killed. Abu Sufyan returned to Mecca with the bad news, and the people were furious. They told him, "You bring us neither war that we may be warned, nor peace that we may feel safe."[264]

Muhammad had been planning to enter Mecca, and now that he had a good excuse, he seized that opportunity. He wanted this operation to be of ultimate secrecy to the point that even those close to him did not know about it. His youngest and favorite wife, Aisha, was preparing her husband's clothes for travel when her father Abu-Bakr, who was next in command to Muhammad, came in. He asked his daughter if Muhammad was planning a trip, to which she replied that her husband did not disclose his plans to anyone. At that time, even Abu-Bakr did not know of Muhammad's intention. The two men then met secretly to discuss Muhammad's plan to go to Mecca. To divert attention from his plan to attack Mecca, Muhammad dispatched a raid to attack a

---

[262.] Ibn Ishaq, Sirat Rasul Allah, 543.

[263.] Al Wakidi, Kitab al-Maghazi, 323.

[264.] Al-Baladhuri, Kitab Futuh al-Buldan, part 1, 37, 62.

caravan passing through Edam, which is nowhere in the direction of Mecca. During this battle, one Muslim was killed by another Muslim.[265]

Muhammad moved quickly to organize his men for the attack on Mecca. He sent messages to the surrounding tribes, asking them to join him in the attack, and began marching south to Mecca, with some joining him along the way.[266]

Muhammad did not want the Quraysh to have time to prepare for defense. Some of his intelligence found out that Hatib, a Muslim living in Medina, had sent a letter with a woman to Mecca. This was alarming since the plan had been to totally surprise the Meccans with the attack. They caught up with the woman and asked her to produce the letter, which she denied having until she was threatened with death. She then removed it from her hair and handed it to them.[267] The letter was to be given to people Hatib knew in Mecca, asking them to look after his property when Muhammad's army invaded Mecca.[268] Muhammad's followers wanted to cut off Hatib's head for leaking information, but because he was a Muslim and had fought with Muhammad at the Battle of Badr, Muhammad asked them to spare his life. When asked why he had done this, he said that he had no Quraysh family in Mecca and no one to watch out for his property there when Mecca fell to the Prophet.

In his book *The Generalship of Muhammad*,[269] author Russ Rodgers explains that many of the people who went to Medina with Muhammad as well as Muhammad himself had families still residing in Mecca. These family members took steps to watch out for their families who had gone to Medina to be with the Prophet. Essentially, these family members became part of a loosely organized group to undermine Mecca

---

[265.] Sahih Muslim, 43:7176.

[266.] Ibn Sa'd, Kitab al Tabakat al-Kabir 2:166.

[267.] Sahih-al Bukhari, vol. 4, 251.

[268.] Al Tabari, Tarikh al-Rusul wa'l muluk, LI, 1626.

[269.] Rodgers, The Generalship of Muhammad, pp. 214–215.

266

and support the property claims of their relatives now living in Medina. Some were more active in supporting Muhammad's cause, possibly sending intelligence and other resources to the Prophet. Some would indirectly sabotage the efforts of their Qurayshi leaders who tried to hinder Muhammad's claims to the city, while some were active agents focused on bringing down the current Quraysh regime. The Quraysh failed not only in defeating Muhammad in the field or destroying his base in Medina, but also in suppressing or eliminating the subversive element within their own city, Mecca.

By the time Muhammad was near Mecca, he had a force of ten thousand men and one thousand horsemen. After accomplishing many triumphant battles, he was now finally reaching his longtime dream of entering Mecca. Muhammad had been estranged from Mecca and the Quraysh for over seven years, and now he was seizing the opportunity to reenter and build the Islamic ummah.[270]

A Plan for a Peaceful Entry

There were four entry routes to the city; and Muhammad divided his army into four divisions, each headed by one of his leading fighters, to advance through each pass. Muhammad was in the main division headed by Ubaidah ibn al-Jarrah, which was to enter Mecca through the Medina route. The strategy was to advance simultaneously from all sides, meeting inside Mecca. This would divide the enemy forces and prevent them from helping each other. Additionally, if any of the Muslim forces faced resistance and were unable to break through, the attack could continue from the other fronts; and all the escape routes would be blocked. Having been thus prepared, Muhammad emphasized to his men that no fighting was to take place unless the Quraysh attacked.[271]

[270.] Islamic nation, regardless of geographic location
[271.] https://en.wikipedia.org/wiki/Conquest_of_Mecca

Abu Sufyan

The Quraysh of Mecca were taken by surprise. They knew that Muhammad and his forces had moved toward them, but they had no idea where he was at that point. Meanwhile, Abu Sufyan—still trying to reach an agreement between the Quraysh of Mecca and Muhammad—was trying to find the location of Muhammad's camp. He ran into Budayl, one of Muhammad's agents, who volunteered to take Abu Sufyan to Muhammad. Muhammad had asked all his men to each build an individual fire, giving the impression to the Quraysh that his forces numbered much more than their actual count. Muhammad's tactic had always been to plant fear in the enemy before attacking. Seeing this at a far distance, Abu Sufyan was overwhelmed. At that time, Al-Abbas, Muhammad's uncle who had decided to leave Mecca and join Muhammad, met Abu Sufyan and told him that he was concerned that if the Prophet conquered Mecca, the Quraysh would be slaughtered, and Abu Sufyan would be beheaded.[272] Al-Abbas agreed to take Abu Sufyan to Muhammad's camp and meet with the Prophet. Abu Sufyan met with Muhammad and quickly agreed to join him. He embraced Islam and recited the Shahada (witness). The Shahada is one of the five pillars of Islam and is required to become a Muslim. It is the following statement: "I declare that there is no other God but Allah, and Muhammad is his prophet." At this point, Muhammad asked Abu Sufyan to provide protection for the people of Mecca when Muhammad's army entered. Muhammad sent him back to Mecca to declare that anyone who would not oppose Muhammad and sought protection with Abu Sufyan would be safe.

[272.] Muhammad had pointed out to Abu-Bakr that if he saw Abu Sufyan, he was to be beheaded. Al-Waqid, Kitab al-Maghazy, 330.

The Triumphant Entry to Mecca

Now that Muhammad had Abu Sufyan spread fear and offer protection to the Quraysh, he knew that his long-term goal of ruling the Quraysh and dominating Arabia was now within reach. He did not need to attack and shed blood; rather, he could enter Mecca peacefully. His struggle with the Meccans would now be over, and he was ready to forgive those who would surrender.

A "bloodless" coup would help ensure his success, and Muhammad wanted to extend mercy to his tribe and win them to Islam. Although some refer to the entry of Mecca as a bloodless coup, records show there were a number of casualties. In addition, there were ten people Muhammad did not want to forgive and had ordered his followers to track down and kill once he had taken over Mecca. These were personal enemies of Muhammad who had committed various offenses against him.

Muhammad and his army entered Mecca peacefully on the twentieth day of Ramadan in the eighth year of the hijra (Monday, January 11 of AD 630). Muhammad was riding his favorite camel, Al Kaswa, having Usama Ibn Zaid (Zaid's son) sitting behind him. On his way, he was reciting the previously given victory verses of Qur'an 48:1–2: "Surely we have granted thee a clear victory. That Allah may cover for thee thy sins in the past and those to come and complete his favor to thee and guide thee on a right path."

Once in Mecca, Muhammad declared, "Even he who enters the house of Abu Sufyan will be safe, he who lays down arms will be safe, he who locks his door will be safe."[273]

[273.] Al Kamil fi Al-Tarikh by Ibn al-Athir (Arabic), p. 329.

Muhammad then entered al-Kaaba,[274] along with some of his companions and started smashing all the idols while reciting Qur'an 17:81.

ظهر الحق و زهق الباطل ان الباطل كان زهوقا

> Truth has come and falsehood vanished. Surely falsehood is bound to vanish.

The prayer caller Bilal climbed on top of the Kaaba and recited the call to prayer there for the very first time.[275]

On this very important day, Muhammad fulfilled his life calling of eradicating polytheism in Mecca and instituting the worship of the one

---

[274.] The place in Mecca where people worshiped different gods is now where Muslims go for their pilgrimage, the hajj. "Kaaba" means "cube" in Arabic. It is located inside the Grand Mosque in Mecca, Saudi Arabia. The Kaaba is considered the center of the Muslim world and is a unifying focal point for Islamic worship.

[275.] Bilal was the slave of an important Quraysh chief named Umayyah bin Khalaf. Bilal rebelled against his master by joining Islam. When Bilal's master, Umayyah found out, he began to violently torture Bilal. Umayyah tied Bilal up and had him dragged around Mecca as a means to break Bilal's faith. In addition, children mocked Bilal for disobeying his master....Bilal never renounced Islam even when the torture was taken to an extreme. Frustrated with Bilal's refusal to renounce Islam, his master became more angry and ordered Bilal's limbs stretched out and tied to stakes on the desert sand, so that he could feel the intensity of the sun and the Arabian heat. Whipped and beaten while tied to the stakes, he still remained firm in his belief. After such punishments, news of this slave reached Muhammad. Muhammad then sent Abu Bakr, who negotiated a deal with Umayyah to purchase Bilal in exchange for three of Abu Bakr's slaves (a pagan male slave and his wife and daughter) and he emancipated Bilal from his slavery. Bilal became the one who eventually was in charge of the Muslim *adhaan* (call to prayer). The happiest moment of his life was when Muhammad conquered Mecca. Bilal ascended to the top of the Kaaba, the house of Allah, to call the Muslims to prayer. This was the first time the call to prayer was heard in Islam's holiest city of Mecca. Wikipedia, Ibn Hisham, Sirah, Vol. 1, pp. 339-340; Ibn Sa'd Tabaqat Vol. 3, p. 232.

true Allah. Ten years before, Muhammad had tried to bring his people, the Quraysh of Mecca, to give up idol worship. He told them that there was only one god, Allah, and that he was his messenger. No one wanted to listen to him and scorned him, saying he was mad. As he persisted in his claim and continued to harass them, they tried to get rid of him. He escaped from Mecca and went to Medina where he established Islam and the Muslim ummah. With his sword, he conquered and subdued all who would oppose him in his religion, Islam. His ultimate desire was to go back and subdue those who had scorned and opposed him. Ten years later, he had enough power to accomplish his goal.

Muhammad Extends Mercy

Muhammad was prepared to use force against the Quraysh, who opposed him; however, he did not have to, for they surrendered unconditionally. Some Quraysh resisted and attacked Khalid's division. The Muslims fought back and subdued them. The Quraysh retreated after losing twelve men, and the Muslims had two losses. Muhammad's followers tracked down the ten people he wanted executed. Eventually, all were found, but only six of them were killed. The others became Muslims and were pardoned.

Those Muhammad Wanted Killed

Abdullah bin Sa'd Abu Sarh had become a Muslim and migrated to Medina. He became one of Muhammad's scribes because he could read and write. When Muhammad recited Qur'an verses, he used to write them down, then read them back to him. He sometimes made changes to Muhammad's verses on purpose, and when he read them back to him, Muhammad did not notice the changes and agreed with Abdullah. As a result, Abdullah became disillusioned with Muhammad's claim to be a prophet, left Islam, and fled back to Mecca.[276] When Muhammad conquered Mecca, he was scared and went into hiding; but because he was a foster brother of Uthman ibn Affan, later to become the third caliph, he was able to go to Muhammad and ask forgiveness, which was granted begrudgingly.

> Uthman hid him at first, and when the atmosphere at
> Mecca had subsided after the conquest, brought him to
> Muhammad and pleaded for mercy. It was only after
> some time had lapsed, while all sat in tense silence, that
> Muhammad pardoned the offender. Throughout his
> lifetime Muhammad was always very sensitive to anyone
> who challenged his claim to be receiving revelations
> from above . . . He was clearly unwilling to spare
> Abdullah and patiently waited for one of his companions
> to strike his neck. They obviously did not read his
> mind . . . When Uthman had left he said to his
> companions who were sitting around him, "I kept silent
> so that one of you might get up and strike off his head!"
> One of the Ansar said, "Then why didn't you give me a
> sign, O Apostle of God?" He answered that a prophet
> does not kill by pointing. (Ibn Ishaq, *Sirat Rasulullah*,
> p. 550)

Abdullah bin Khatal used to recite poetry insulting Muhammad and had also earlier killed a slave of his. When Muhammad entered Mecca, Abdullah was scared and went hiding in the Kaaba. Muhammad's

---

[276.] http://answering-islam.org/Gilchrist/Vol1/1d.html. The alleged fabrication of the revelation centers on Surah 23.12–14. In the Tafsir-i-Husaini (vol. 2, p. 80), we are told that when the description of the creation of man in these verses was ended, this same Abdullah, recording the verses as Muhammad's amanuensis, exclaimed "Fatabaarakallahu-ahsanul-khaaliqlin" (Blessed be Allah, the best of Creators). Muhammad promptly told him to record his ejaculation in the passage as part of the revelation. Abdullah forsook Islam, claiming that if Muhammad was inspired, so was he! (The words are duly recorded at the end of Surah 23.14).

followers found him taking refuge under the curtains of the Kaaba and told Muhammad. The Prophet said, "Kill him."[277] He was killed.

Fortana and *Quraybah* were two of the singing girls Abdullah bin Khatal used to have. They used to recite derogatory poems against Muhammad. Muhammad ordered both of them killed, but only Fortana was executed. Quraybah ran away and later embraced Islam and obtained forgiveness from Muhammad.[278]

Huwayrith ibn Nafidh was an enemy of Muhammad who stabbed the camel that Muhammad's daughters were riding when they were fleeing out of Mecca to Medina. After Muhammad's triumphant entry to Mecca, he was not forgiven and was killed.[279]

Miqyas was a Muslim who asked Muhammad to give him permission to kill his brother's killer. After killing him, he went to Mecca and left Islam. He was killed after Muhammad's entry to Mecca[280] for leaving Islam and running away from the Prophet in Medina.

Sarah was killed because Muhammad claimed that she used to molest him when he was in Mecca.[281]

Ikrimah ibn Abu Jahl was hostile to Muhammad, like his father, who was killed by two young boys of Muhammad's followers. Ikrimah also tried to resist Muhammad's entrance to Mecca. Ibn Ishaq says his wife became a Muslim and asked for his immunity, and Muhammad gave it, but Tabari says he was eliminated.[282]

[277] Sahih Bukhari, 5:59:582; and 3:29:72.
[278] Ibn Sa'd, Kitab al-Tabaqat al-Kabir, vol. 2, 84.
[279] Ibn Hisham and Ibn Ishaq, Sirat Rasul Allah, 83.
[280] Ibn Hisham and Ibn Ishaq Sirat Rasul Allah, 83.
[281] Tabari, vol. 8, History of Islam.
[282] Ibn Hisham and Ibn Ishaq, Sirar Rasoul Allah, 83; Tabari, vol. 8, History of Islam, 93.

Hind Bint Utbah mutilated the body of Muhammad's uncle after he died in the Battle of Uhud. She then became a Muslim and was pardoned.[283]

Habbar Ibn al-Aswad bin Ka'b al-Ansi was killed because he was a liar; he claimed he was a prophet.[284]

Muhammad had left Mecca a fugitive, mocked by his countrymen in the year AD 622; now at the beginning of the year 630, he was back as the unchallenged ruler. He was now in charge and took total control of the administration of Mecca, along with some of his capable key men. For the first time in history, Mecca became the central governmental location for Islamic rule from where he could run the ummah. To secure and solidify the ummah, he had to draw the neighboring tribes who had not yet embraced Islam and could become a threat to the newly founded Islamic state in Mecca. Muhammad decided that for the safety of the ummah, neighboring tribes had to join in to ensure Arab solidarity and security.

[283.] Tabari, vol. 8, History of Islam 100.
[284.] Tabari, vol. 9, The Last Years of the Prophet, 90.

Chapter Twenty-Nine

Muhammad in Charge of Mecca

With Muhammad now in control, many of the Meccans embraced Islam mostly to be safe (remain alive), and there was relative peace among the people in Mecca. But there were some tribes living in the east and southeast of Mecca who did not want to become Muslims. They knew that should Muhammad decide to attack them, their options would be to either convert to Islam or be killed. Muhammad also knew that in order to maintain the peace, he had to make sure that Islam continued to dominate not only Mecca but all neighboring Arab tribes as well.

The Last Two and a Half Years of Muhammad's Life

How did Muhammad spend the last two and a half years of his life? Just as a quick review, Muhammad was born in the year AD 570 in Mecca. He migrated to Medina in the year 622 at the age of fifty-two. In the beginning of the year 630, he was able to conquer and control Mecca at the age of sixty. Muhammad died on June 8, 632, at the age of sixty-two. So if you do the math, it took this great man only ten years to establish a new religion that today is followed by nearly 25 percent of the world's population.

We have walked you through only some of Muhammad's raids, invasions, and battles as well as his famous conquest of Mecca. But what really sealed Muhammad's triumph after the invasion of Mecca was the submission of the neighboring tribes. Because even after he subdued the Meccans, Islam may not have survived without the rest of Arabia following along.

Some tribes, in particular the Hawazin and Thaqif, were upset at the spread of Islam. They wanted to continue in their idol worship and did not want to be dominated by Muhammad and his forces. They planned to stop the Muslims by attacking Mecca; however, Muhammad didn't give them a chance.

Now Muhammad's army had become even larger, for after controlling Mecca, two thousand fighters from the Meccans were added to the existing ten thousand who had come with him from Medina. The Muslims were proud of their huge army, and Abu-Bakr said, "We shall not be defeated because our soldiers far outnumber those of the enemy."[285] Very soon, however, Abu-Bakr was proven overly confident in his estimation because at the beginning of the next battle, the Muslims were losing even though their number was three times that of the enemy.[286]

The Battle of Hunayn

It had only been two weeks since Muhammad had conquered Mecca; however, he knew of the enemy plan to attack, and he did not want to fight inside Mecca. So Muhammad put on two coats of mail and a helmet on his head, mounted his white mule, and moved on behind his

---

285. Tabakat-il Kubra, vol. 2, p. 150.
286. "Allah has helped you on many occasions including the day of Hunayn. When you were happy with the number of your men who proved to be of no help to you and the whole vast earth seemed to have no place to hide you (from your enemies) and you turned back in retreat" (Surah al-Tawbah, 9:25).

army of Islam, which now numbered twelve thousand fighters.[287] There, Muhammad's men met with the Bedouin tribe of the Hawazin in the Battle of Hunayn.

Before the battle began, the chief commander of the Hawazin and the other tribes ordered that the women and children should march behind the army who was going to battle. A retired senior officer protested about including the women and children, but the chief insisted and gave his reasoning: "The soldiers would continue to push on toward the enemy and win because of the moral support of the family's presence."[288] The retired general's advice against family involvement was later proven prudent and correct.

A sudden attack by the enemy terrified the Muslims so much that they began to flee, creating disruption among their ranks. This caused some of the Muslims in Muhammad's army, who were called the Hypocrites, to reject Islam. The Hypocrites didn't really believe but converted out of self-interest. Why should they die for a cause they weren't fully convinced of? They even wanted to kill the Prophet and destroy Islam. Muhammad knew that if he did not turn the battle around very soon, the forces of polytheism would overcome the army of Islam. He cried loudly, "O supporters of Allah and his prophet. I am Muhammad ibn Abdullah." Muhammad's uncle with his very loud voice called back the Muslims, saying, "O Ansar (friends), who helped the prophet! O you who took the oath of allegiance to the prophet under the tree of Paradise! Where are you going? The prophet is here!"[289]

[287.] Chapter 49: "The Battle of Hunayn"/The Message/Books on Islam and Muslims (https://www.al-islam.org/the-message-ayatullah-jafar-subhani/chapter-49-battle-hunayn).
[288.] Mughazi il-Wakidi, vol. 3, p. 897.
[289.] In Mughazi (vol. 111, p. 602), Waqidi has mentioned some feats of valor of the commander of the faithful at that critical juncture.

The fleeing men returned in compliance with the orders of the Prophet, who was saying, "I am the prophet of Allah and never tell a lie, and Allah has promised me victory." After praying to Allah, Muhammad picked a handful of sand and threw it toward the enemy soldiers, saying, "May their faces be black."[290] At that moment, as if a miracle, all of the enemy soldiers' eyes were filled with sand. Muhammad was known to be very superstitious, and "may their faces be black" meant "may they be disgraced." The Muslims fought fiercely and attacked the enemy, causing them to retreat.

It is worth mentioning here that Muhammad always assured his men of victory. They would either crush the enemy and win or be crushed by the enemy and die as martyrs, which meant endless heavenly rewards. Many Qur'an verses and Hadith assure the Muslim warrior.

Qur'an 4:74 promises, "Let those fight in the way of Allah who sell the life of this world for the Hereafter. Whoso fighteth in the way of Allah, be he slain or be he victorious, on him we shall bestow a vast reward."

In his Hadith, Bukhari says in 52:46, "Allah guarantees that He will admit the Mujahid (one who dies a martyr) in His cause into Paradise if he is killed, otherwise he will return him to his home safely with rewards and war booty."

Many Muslims were killed, but the enemy warriors of the Hawazin ran away to Taif, leaving behind their women and children and those killed in the battle. Muhammad wanted to have a definitive victory, but the fighting in Hunayn was not completed because the enemy took refuge in Taif. The Hawazin fled, leaving behind six thousand captives, twenty-four thousand camels, forty thousand sheep, and approximately four thousand *waqih*[291] of silver. Some of the Muslims started killing the

---

[290.] Ibn Sa'ad, vol. 2, p. 151; Sahih Muslim, vol. 3, p. 402.

[291.] A *waqih* is 213 grams, or 27,395 troy ounces today (https://www.al-islam.org/the-message-ayatullah-jafar-subhani/chapter-49-battle-hunayn).

captive children, but when Muhammad found out, he stopped them. At that point, Muhammad's goal was not to acquire war booty but rather to bring all Arabia to submit to Islam. Now having won the Battle of Hunayn, the Prophet sent the booty and captives obtained in the battle to the place called Ji'ranah. He ordered the companions he sent there to keep them until his return from Taif, when he would distribute booty.[292]

Taif

Taif is one of the fertile country towns of Hijaz, the western region of Arabia. It is situated to the southeast of Mecca, one thousand meters above sea level. On account of its fine weather, gardens, and palm groves, the town of Taif provided a very comfortable life. It was inhabited by the tribe of Saqif, who fought against the Muslims in the Battle of Hunayn. Muhammad proceeded to Taif because he did not want to leave any refuge that could serve as an asylum to his enemies. The army of Islam proceeded to besiege the fort of Taif but was met with a shower of arrows that killed some of them in the very first moment.[293] It was very difficult for the Muslim army to conquer Taif, so when a number of Muslims were wounded and killed, they abandoned their attempt.[294]

The inhabitants of Taif were keenly interested in their safety and shut themselves in their fort to avoid the Muslim invasion. Muhammad announced that if they continued to resist, he would order their vineyards and orchards to be destroyed. When the people saw that their orchards, which were their only source of income, were being destroyed, they said to the Prophet, "O Muhammad! Why are you cutting off our plants? If you defeat us, you will take them. Otherwise, leave them to

---

[292] Ibn Hisham, vol. 4, p. 101.
[293] Seerah-i-Halabi, vol. 3, p. 132.
[294] Mughazi-i-Waqidi, vol. 3, p. 928.

us by considering the consent of God and the rights of kinship."[295] The people of Taif did not want to surrender. Some slaves who had run away from Taif were also saying that the people were prepared to hold out in a siege up to a year because they had plenty of provisions. Muhammad decided to stop the fighting because he realized it would not be an easy surrender, and the month when fighting was not allowed among the Arabs was also approaching. He wanted to avoid criticism but vowed to come back.

Qur'an 9:5 says, "So when the sacred months have passed, slay the idolaters, wherever you find them, and take them captive and besiege them and lie in wait for them in every ambush. But if they repent and keep up prayer and pay the poor-rate leave their way free. Surely Allah is Forgiving, Merciful."

Moreover, the hajj season was near; and the supervision of hajj ceremonies was now the responsibility of the Muslims, whereas before the conquest of Mecca, the hajj ceremonies were performed by the polytheists of Mecca.

Muhammad gave up on the siege. He destroyed the vineyards and orchards around Taif[296] and retreated, but he vowed to resume his war with Taif after the sacred months were over and proceeded with his soldiers to Ji'ranah to distribute the booty of the Battle of Hunayn.

The Booty of the Battle of Hunayn

A lot is written about the booty of Hunayn because it consisted of many hostages as well as a wealth of goods. But what makes this stand out is Muhammad's generosity. In the past, Muhammad depended on caravan

---

[295.] One of the great-grandmothers of Muhammad was from there (Wakidi, Maghazi, vol. 3, p. 928).

[296] Haykal, Muhammad, Hassanein, Life of Muhammad.

280

and war booties for survival for himself, his family, his army, and their families. Neither Muhammad nor his followers had been gainfully employed. Since the conquest of Khaybar, his material needs were amply supplied. But Muhammad continued his raids to further his growing movement until he could accomplish his goal of returning to Mecca. By conquering Mecca, he regained his prestige, which was once lost to the Quraysh Meccans, and gained control of its resources. As a result, Muhammad was able to act more generously than he had in his prior conquests.

Hawazin Captives Liberated and Returned to Their Tribe[297]

The Muslims returned to Ji'ranah to divide their booty and captives. Muhammad took his fifth and distributed the rest among the companions. Before they finished, a newly converted delegation from the Hawazin tribe came to appeal for the return of their family and property. Muhammad listened as the tribe pointed out the captives contained relatives of his and that if other kings had done what Muhammad had done, they would have granted their request for mercy. Among the captives, an older-looking woman whom the soldiers had treated roughly shouted in their faces, "Woe to you! Learn that I am the sister of your leader by virtue of having had the same wet nurse as he." The soldiers did not believe her and brought her to Muhammad to verify her story. The Prophet immediately recognized her. She was al Shayma', daughter of al Harith ibn 'Abd al 'Uzza. Muhammad went out to meet her and spread out his mantle for her to sit on. After reassuring her of his devotion and respect, Muhammad asked the old lady whether she chose to stay in his camp or to return to her people. When she chose to return, Muhammad gave her some gifts and returned her to her people unharmed.

---

[297] http://www.islam4theworld.net/sirah/LifeMuhammadS/30.%20hunayn%20Alta.htm. Quotes in the next three titled sections are from this website.

Muhammad asked the tribe, "Which are more precious to you, your women and children or your property?" They answered, "O Prophet of God, if you are giving us a choice between our relatives and our property, we take the former." Muhammad told the tribe he was willing to give up his share of the booty to them. He then coached them on how to appeal to him publicly after the noon prayer. After the appeal, Muhammad announced he was giving up his share. The Muhajirun and the Ansar quickly followed his lead. To the few who didn't agree, Muhammad promised to make up their losses sixfold in the next campaign. In this way, the captives of Hawazin were returned, and the whole tribe converted to Islam.

The People's Fear of Losing Their Booty

Muhammad sent an offer through the Hawazin delegation to Malik, their leader, that if he would convert, Muhammad would return his family and property and make him a gift of one hundred camels. Malik was happy to announce his conversion and collect his prize. Muhammad also gave one hundred camels to half a dozen people as well as to the nobles and chieftains of the tribes which he had won over after the conquest of Mecca. He gave fifty camels to less important leaders.

Some grumbling among the rank and file began to spread, fearing that after the giveaways, little of the booty would be left for them. Word of this reached Muhammad.

> He pulled out a hair of the camel nearest him, lifted it up for his people to see and said, "O Men! By God, no part of your booty shall come to me that exceeds my legitimate share by as much as this hair, and this very share of mine I hereby return to you." The Prophet then asked everyone to return what he had taken that Muhammad might redistribute it to each according to his due. The Prophet proclaimed that anyone unjustly

taking anything, however little, would be guilty of eternal shame and hellfire.

Muhammad made this proclamation while enraged against those of his followers who had picked up his mantle thinking that it was part of the spoils of war. However, they returned it to him after he called out to them, "Return my mantle to me, O Men. By God, even if your cattle were as numerous as the trees of Tihamah, I would still divide it all among you in absolute fairness and justice, without avarice, fear, or deception. That which I have given away belongs to the fifth which is my due."

Al-Ansar and the Reconciliatory Gratuities

When the Ansar heard what Muhammad had given away, they were angry and accused him of favoring his own tribesmen. Sa'd ibn Ubadah reported this to Muhammad but sided with the people. Muhammad instructed him to bring everyone together and made a speech.

"O Ansar! It has been reported to me that you were personally angry, that you do not approve of my distribution of the booty. Do tell me, when I came to you, did I not find you languishing in misguidance and error and did not God guide you to the truth through me? Did I not find you in a state of need and did not God make you affluent? Did I not find you enemies of one another and did not God reconcile your hearts?" Confused, al Ansar answered, "Indeed! God and his Prophet have been very generous and very loving," and they fell into silence. Muhammad continued, "Will you not then say more than this, O Ansar? By God, had you replied, 'Rather, it was you Muhammad, who were under our obligation. Did you not come to us belied by your fellow men and did we not believe in you? Did you not come to us vanquished and defeated and did we not come to your rescue? Did you not come to us banished and repulsed and did we not give you shelter? Did you not come to us in want and need and did we not give you of our bounty?' Had you replied to me in this vein you would have said nothing but the truth and I would have had to agree. O Ansar, are you angry because I have given away some goods to those whom I sought to win to Islam? Because I deemed their faith confirmable by material goods whereas I deemed yours to be based on solid conviction, to be candid beyond all dissuasion? Are you not satisfied, O Ansar, that all the people return from this conquest loaded with goods and camels whereas you return with the Prophet of God? By Him who dominates Muhammad's soul, except for the fact of my birth, there is no people to whom I love to belong beside al Ansar. If all mankind went one way, and al Ansar went another, I would certainly choose the way of al Ansar. O God, bless al Ansar, their children, and their grandchildren. Show Your mercy to them and keep them under Your protection.'" Indeed, he was so moved by his feelings for them that he cried. The Ansar cried with him and declared their contentment.

Muhammad left Ji'ranah to perform the umrah, or lesser pilgrimage, at Mecca. He appointed Attab ibn Usayd governor of Mecca and Mu'adh ibn Jabal to teach religion and the Qur'an. Then he returned with his followers to Medina to await the birth of his son Ibrahim and prepare for the next expedition to Tabuk.[298]

[298.] There were rumors of a Byzantine invasion at Tabuk. Muhammad and his men went to Tabuk and stayed for twenty days. The enemy did not show up, and Muhammad's army retreated back to Medina. No battle took place. Tabuk was

Meanwhile, the residents of Taif, the Banu Thaqif, were sending delegations to Muhammad, seeking to make peace with him. But Muhammad did not accept peace until they agreed to accept Islam and destroy the temple of the goddess Allat. The Banu Thaqif "worshipped the goddess Allat and had a great bejeweled statue of her. The goddess of Allat had been worshipped in Arabia for at least 1,000 years. We know this because Herodotus mentions her as an Arabian goddess back in the 5th century BC.[299] Although Muhammad was becoming more and more powerful, it was not easy for him to persuade the Arabs to give up belief systems that had become so steeped in tradition."[300]

The Banu Thaqif were willing to accept Islam but asked that they be allowed to keep their temple of Allat for three years. Muhammad rejected this condition. Then they reduced the period to two years, one year, and, finally, one month.[301] Muhammad is reported to have replied, "You accept Islam, or else I shall send one to you who is from me. He will cut your necks and enslave your women and children and confiscate your wealth and property."[302]

> The Banu Thaqif finally consented on the condition that they themselves would not have to be the ones to destroy their temple. This Muhammad could agree to. He appointed Abu Sufyan (his former enemy who had adopted Islam to avoid a battle during the conquest of Mecca) to go to Taif and destroy the idol. Abu Sufyan and his men destroyed the temple while the women of

---

the last battle the apostle of Islam attempted.

[299] Herodotus-Histories 1:131

[300] http://explorethemed.com/mohammed.asp?c=1 from Historical Atlas of the Mediterranean, The Birth of Islam in Arabia.

[301] Muhammad Husayn Haykal, p. 280. http://explorethemed.com/mohammed.asp?c=1

[302] Al-Istiab, vol. 2, p. 477, cited in Husayn Haykal, p. 289. http://explorethemed.com/mohammed.asp?c=1.

Banu Thaqif watched moaning and crying, but no one dared to stop the Muslims.[303]

Muhammad sent Khalid (whom he had named the Sword of Allah) to destroy the temple of the goddess Al-Uzza.[304] Khalid ransacked the temple, killing a man and an Ethiopian woman there.

Muhammad did not go to any more battles after the rumored attempt of the Byzantines of Syria at Tabuk, which never materialized. He continued to live in Medina, enjoying his son Ibrahim, who was born to him by the freed slave Mariam the Coptic. It is interesting that none of his other wives bore him any children except, of course, the first wife, Khadija, who was fifteen years his senior. His two sons by Khadija had died in infancy, so Ibrahim was very special to him, and he spent most of his time with him until he too died before his second birthday.

Muhammad's Pilgrimage and Farewell Sermon

It was now the year AH 10 (Hijri), or AD 632, ten years after Muhammad's migration from Mecca to Medina. After he conquered Mecca, Muhammad appointed his men to run the affairs of Mecca, but he himself had been living in Medina with his wives. Now Muhammad wanted to perform his first hajj in Mecca, which also was his last! His farewell pilgrimage to Mecca is one of the most significant historical events in the minds of Muslims, for it was the first and last pilgrimage made by the prophet Muhammad and was the model of performing the fifth pillar of Islam, the hajj.

[303.] Haykal and Ibn Ishaq, pp. 916–918, http://explorethemed.com/mohammed.asp?c=1.
[304.] Hisham Ibn Al Kalbi

Farewell Sermon Delivered by Muhammad
on March 6 of AD 632

After performing the rituals of the hajj, Muhammad addressed the numerous people who were gathered on Mount Arafat. His speech is quite lengthy, so the main points are summarized:

1. O people, just as you regard this month, this day, this city, as Sacred, so regard the life and property of every Muslim as sacred trust.
2. Allah has forbidden you to take usury (interest).
3. Beware of Satan for the safety of your religion.
4. Rights of wives to be fed and clothed in kindness. They are your partners.
5. Husbands' rights that wives make no friends with anyone of whom you do not approve, as well as never to be unchaste (unsubmissive).
6. Say your five daily prayers (*salah*), fast during the month of Ramadan, and give your wealth in alms (*zakat*), and perform hajj if you can afford it.
7. Every Muslim is a brother to every Muslim and the Muslims constitute one brotherhood.
8. Nothing shall be legitimate to a fellow Muslim unless it was given freely and willingly.
9. O People, No Prophet or Apostle will come after me and no new faith will be born.

10. All those who listen to me shall pass on my words to others again.

11. Be my witness O Allah, that I have conveyed your message to your people.[305]

[305.] Al-Bukhari, Hadith 1623, 1626, 6361. Sahih of Imam Muslim also refers to this sermon in Hadith number 98. Imam al-Tirmidhi has mentioned this sermon in Hadith numbers 1628, 3046, 2085. ImamAhmad bin Hanbal has given us the longest and perhaps the most complete version of this sermon in his Masnud (Hadith number 19774).

Chapter Thirty

The Death of Muhammad

After Muhammad delivered his farewell sermon in Mecca, he went back to Medina to be with his wives. His health was starting to decline, and he was experiencing a lot of headaches and pain in the aorta. He would tell Aisha that after he ate the bite of the poisoned goat, which the Jewish woman in Khaybar had given him, he never felt well. Biographers, for the most part, uphold that poison was the probable cause for his death.

Muhammad's Final Days

During his final days, Muhammad suffered from a very high fever and headache and was mostly bedbound. When he felt a little better and well enough to go to the mosque, he was led by Ali, his cousin and son-in-law, and Fadhl, his cousin.

He entered it with his head wrapped with a band. Then he sat on the pulpit and made a speech to the people who were gathered together around him. He said, "The curse of Allah falls upon the Jews and

Christians for they have made their Prophets' tombs places of worship." [306] Then he said, "Do not make my tomb a worshipped idol."[307]

Muhammad also reminded the people to be kind to the Ansar (the helpers), who came to his side in Medina and fought his battles with him.

Then he said, "O people! The time has arrived when I should leave you. If I have made a promise with anyone I am prepared to fulfill it." A man stood up and said, "You promised me some time back that if I married, you would help me with the money." The Prophet ordered the money to be paid to him.[308]

Muhammad also said, "Whoever has any right over me should mention it, for punishment in this world is lighter than the punishment on the Day of Judgment." Muhammad had no assurance that he was forgiven and was afraid to die and face God's punishment without making amends because God's punishment would be much heavier than man's.

Sawadah bin Qays also stood up and said, "At the time of return from Taif, you raised your scourge to hit your animal, but by chance it struck my belly. I now want revenge." Muhammad ordered the same scourge to be brought from his house and pulled his shirt so that Sawadah could actually take revenge. Instead, Sawadah kissed the belly and the chest of Muhammad. At this point, Muhammad prayed, "O Allah! Forgive Sawadah in the same manner in which he has forgiven the Prophet of Islam."

[306.] Sahih al-Bukhari, 1/62; Muwatta' Imam Malik, p. 360.
[307.] Muwatta' Imam Malik, p. 65.
[308.] Manaqib-Ali-ibn Abi Talib, vol. 1, p. 164.

Muhammad's Final Words

One of Muhammad's final words that all accounts agree on is "O Allah, with the highest companions."[309] The story around this is that the angel Jibreel gave Muhammad the choice to be healed and live or to die, but Muhammad chose to go and be with his departed companions. Aisha said that he looked to the ceiling and chose to go in reference to the following verse:

> These are with those upon whom Allah has bestowed favors from among the Prophets and the truthful and the martyrs and they are the best friends that one can have. (Qur'an 4:69) O Allah! (with) the highest companions.

There is a report narrated by Ahmad (no. 1691) from the Hadith of Abu Ubaydah, who said that the last words that the Prophet (peace and blessings of Allah be upon him) spoke were, "Expel the Jews of the Hijaaz and Najraan from the Arabian Peninsula, and know that the most evil of people are those who took the graves of their Prophets as places of worship." This was classed as Sahih[310] by al-Albaani in al-Sahihah, no. 1.

And Abu Dawoo (5156) and Ibn Maajah (2698) narrated that Ali (may Allah be pleased with him) said that the last words that the messenger of Allah, PBUH (peace and blessings of Allah be upon him) spoke were, "The prayer, the prayer! And fear Allah with regard to those whom your right hands possess." This was classed as Sahih by al-Albaani in Sahih Abi Dawood.

---

309. This is the title that al-Bukhari gave to a chapter in Kitaab al-Maghaazi in his Sahih. Narrated by al-Bukhari, 4463; Muslim, 2444.

310. The sayings of the Prophet have been quoted by many people. They are classified as either correct or trustworthy (Sahih); good (Hasan), which is also acceptable; and weak (Da'if), which is doubtful.

"The prayer, the prayer" was Muhammad's command to his followers to uphold the five times daily prayer, which remains one of the most important pillars.[311] "Your right hand possesses" refers to women whom the companions acquired and lived with, but who did not have the same rights as the wives (whose number could not exceed four) as in Qur'an 4:3.

When it was daytime, the Prophet (sallallahu 'alayhi wa sallam)[312] called his daughter Fatimah and told her something in a secret voice that made her cry. Then he whispered to her something else that made her laugh. Aisha inquired from her after the Prophet's death as to this weeping and laughing, to which Fatimah replied, "The first time he disclosed to me that he would not recover from his illness and I wept. Then he told me that I would be the first of his family to join him, so I laughed" (Sahih Bukhari, 2/638).

He gave Fatimah glad tidings that she would become the lady of all women of the world (Rahmatul li'l-Alamin, 1/282). Fatimah witnessed the great pain that afflicted her father. So she said, "What great pain my father is in!" To these words, the Prophet remarked, "He will not suffer any more when today is over" (Sahih Bukhari, 2/641).

Muhammad asked that al-Hassan and al-Hussein, Fatimah's sons, be brought to him. He kissed them and recommended that they be looked after. He asked to see his wives. They were brought to him. He preached to them and told them to remember Allah. Pain grew so severe that the trace of poison he had at Khaybar came to light. It was so sore that he said to Aisha, "I still feel the painful effect of that food I tasted at Khaybar. I feel as if death is approaching" (ibid., 2/637). He ordered the people to perform the prayers and be attentive to slaves. He repeated it several times (ibid.).

[311.] The five pillars of Islam are the Shahada (I declare there is no God but Allah, and Mohammad is his prophet), prayer, fasting, almsgiving, and pilgrimage to Mecca.
[312.] Peace be upon him.

The Prophet Breathes His Last

When the pangs of death started, Aisha leaned him against her. She used to say, "One of Allah's bounties upon me is that the Messenger of Allah died in my house while I am still alive. He died between my chest and neck while he was leaning against me. Allah has mixed his saliva with mine at his death. For Abdur-Rahman, the son of Abu-Bakr, came in with a *siwak* (the root of a desert plant used for brushing teeth) in his hand while I was leaning the Messenger of Allah against me. I noticed that he was looking at the *siwak*, so I asked him, for I knew that he wanted it, 'Would you like me to take it for you?' He nodded in agreement. I took it and gave it to him. As it was too hard for him, I asked him, 'Shall I soften it for you?' He nodded in agreement. So I softened it with my saliva, and he passed it (on his teeth)."

In another version, it is said, "So he brushed his teeth as nice as he could. There was a water container available at his hand with some water in. He put his hand in it and wiped his face with it and said, 'There is no god but Allah. Death is full of agonies'" Sahih Bukhari, 2/640).

"As soon as he had finished his *siwak* brushing, he raised his hand or finger up, looked upwards to the ceiling and moved his lips. So Aisha listened to him. She heard him say, 'With those on whom You have bestowed Your Grace with the Prophets and the Truthful (as-Siddiqin), the martyrs and the good doers. O Allah, forgive me and have mercy upon me and join me to the Companionship on high'" (ibid, 2/638–641). Then at intervals, he uttered these words, "The most exalted companionship on high. To Allah we turn, and to him we turn back for help and last abode." This event took place at high morning time on Monday, the twelfth of Rabi' al-Awwal in the eleventh year of hijra. He was sixty-three years and four days old when he died.

The Companions' Concern over the Prophet's Death

The great loss was soon known by everybody in Medina. Dark grief spread over all areas. Anas said, "I have never witnessed a day better or brighter than that day on which the Messenger of Allah came to us; and I have never witnessed a more awful or darker day than that one on which the Messenger of Allah died."[313]

When he died, Fatimah said, "O Father, whom his Lord responded to his supplication! O Father, whose abode is Paradise. O Father, whom I announce his death to Gabriel."[314]

Abu-Bakr's Attitude

Abu-Bakr (Aisha's father) left his house and came forth to the mosque on a mare's back. At the mosque, he dismounted and entered. He talked to nobody but went on till he entered Aisha's abode and went directly to where the messenger of Allah was. The Prophet was covered with a Yemeni mantle. He uncovered his face and bended down, kissed him, and cried. Then he said, "I sacrifice my father and mother for your sake (meaning that Muhammad is more precious to him than his father and mother). Allah, verily, will not cause you to die twice. You have just experienced the death that Allah had ordained."

Then he went out and found Umar talking to the people. Umar had not told them that Muhammad had died. He said, "Umar, be seated." Umar refused to do so. People parted from Umar and came toward Abu-Bakr, who started a speech, saying,

> And now, he who worships Muhammad, *sallallahu ʿalayhi wa sallam* (lit. "God prayed-upon him-and-bestowed

---

[313.] Mishkat al-Masabih, 2/547.
[314.] Sahih al-Bukhari, 2/641.

peace" translated as "blessings of God be upon him"*)*, Muhammad is dead now. But he who worships Allah, He is Ever Living and He never dies. Allah says, "Muhammad is no more than a Messenger, and indeed (many) Messengers have passed away before him. If he dies or is killed, will you then turn back on your heels (as disbelievers)? And he who turns back on his heels, not the least harm will he do to Allah, and Allah will give reward to those who are grateful." (Qur'an 3:144)

Ibn Abbas said, "By Allah, it sounded as if people had never heard such a Qur'anic verse till Abu-Bakr recited it as a reminder. So people started reciting it till there was no man who did not recite it."

Ibn al-Musayyab said that Umar had said, "By Allah, as soon as I heard Abu-Bakr say it, I fell down to the ground. I felt as if my legs had been unable to carry me, so I collapsed when I heard him say it. Only then did I realize that Muhammad *sallallahu 'alayhi wa sallam* had really died."[315]

Burial and Farewell Preparations

Dispute about who would succeed him broke out even before the messenger of Allah's body was prepared for burial. Lots of arguments, discussions, and dialogues took place between the helpers and immigrants in the roofed passage of Banu Sa'ida. Finally, they acknowledged Abu-Bakr as a caliph. They spent the whole Monday there till it was night. People were so busy with their arguments that it was late night, nearly dawn of Tuesday, yet his body was still lying on his bed covered with a garment. He was locked in the room.

[315.] Sahih al-Bukhari, 2/640,641.

295

On Tuesday, his body was washed with his clothes on. He was washed by Al-Abbas, Ali, and al-Fadl and Qathm (the two sons of Al-Abbas), as well as Shaqran (the messenger's freed slave), Usamah ibn Zayd, and Aws ibn Khawli. Al-Abbas, al-Fadl, and Qathm turned his body around while Usamah and Shaqran poured out water. Ali washed him, and Aws leaned him against his chest.

They shrouded him in three white Sahuli cotton cloths, which had neither a headcloth nor a casing, and inserted him in.[316]

A sort of disagreement arose with regard to the burial place. Abu-Bakr said, "I heard the Messenger of Allah say, 'A dead Prophet is buried where he dies.'" So Abu Talhah lifted the bed on which he died, dug underneath, and cut the ground to make the tomb.

People entered the room ten by ten. They prayed for the Prophet "Sallallahu 'alayhi wa sallam." The first to pray for him were people of his clan, then the immigrants, then the helpers. Women prayed for him after men. The young were the last to pray.

This process took all day Tuesday and into the early hours of Wednesday morning. Aisha said, "We did not know that the Prophet . . . was being buried till we heard the sound of tools digging the ground . . ."[317]

From Ar-Rahiq al-Makhtoum[318]

According to most accounts, the Prophet breathed his last in the house of Aisha, with his head leaning on her chest.

[316.] Sahih al-Bukhari, 1/169, Sahih Muslim, 1/306.

[317.] Mukhtasar Sirat ar-Rasul, p. 471; Ibn Hisham, 2/649–665; Talqih Fuhum Ahlul-Athar, pp. 38–39; Rahmatul li'l-Alamin 1/277–286.

[318.] *Ar-Rahiq al-Makhtoum* (The Sealed Nectar) is a reference book by Safiur Mubarakpuri, a twentieth-century Indian man who wrote this biography of the prophet Muhammad.

According to Shia Muslims, Muhammad breathed his last while his head was in the lap of Ali, but that Aisha claims he was on her chest.[319]

He was buried under the house he shared with Aisha.

Disagreement regarding Muhammad's Successor

Islam has two major sects: Sunni and Shiite. Sunnis are a majority in the Arab world, China, Southeast Asia, and Africa. Meanwhile, Shiites are a majority in Iran, Iraq, Azerbaijan, and Bahrain.

The Origin of the Two Sects

The controversy between Sunni and Shiite Muslims had its beginnings toward the end of Muhammad's life, intensified after his death, and continues to this day. It started with the selection of Abu-Bakr as the first khalifa (successor) to Muhammad. After some dispute, most Muslims accepted the selection of Abu-Bakr. However, a small group of Muslims, who became the Shiite, opposed the selection. They wanted Ali, not Abu-Bakr, to be the first khalifa since Ali was a blood relative of Muhammad.

Now who was Abu-Bakr, and who was Ali?

Abu-Bakr was a close friend of Muhammad, and was two years younger. Muhammad married Abu-Bakr's daughter Aisha when she was six years of age. He became the successor of Muhammad, the first khalifa.

Ali ibn Abi Talib was the cousin of Muhammad. He was married to Fatima, Muhammad's daughter by Khadija, his first wife. Fatima was the only daughter who survived Muhammad but died shortly after. She was very loved by her father and was at his bedside when he died. Ali

---

[319.] Tabaqat, vol. 2, p. 263.

and all his followers felt that he was cheated of becoming Muhammad's successor. He eventually became the fourth khalifa, but the relationship between Ali and Aisha had not been a cordial one and ended up in a big war between them after Muhammad's death. When Aisha had been accused of having an affair, Ali had advised Muhammad to divorce her.

A Will That Was Not Written[320]

According to the Shia, Muhammad wanted to affirm Imam Ali as the khalifa after his death. "Bring me a sheet of paper and an inkpot so I may write something for you, after which you will never be misguided." At this moment, Umar bin Khattab, who later became the second khalifa, broke the silence and said, "Sickness has overpowered the Prophet. The Qur'an is with you. The divine book is sufficient for us." But others said, "The orders of the Prophet must be obeyed." Muhammad was extremely annoyed on account of the dispute and presumptuous words and said to everyone, "Get up and leave the house."

After narrating this incident, Ibn Abbas said, "The greatest calamity for Islam was that the discord and dispute of some companions prevented the Prophet from writing the deed which he intended to write."[321] The Shiite refer to that day as a painful Thursday because they claim that Muhammad wanted to appoint Ali as his successor but was not given the opportunity.

A lot has been written from both Sunni and Shiite sides; but as it turns out, Abu-Bakr, not Ali, became the first khalifa.

---

[320] The Message, Ayatullah-jafar-subhani, chapter 62.
[321] Sahih Bukhari, Kitabul'lIlm, vol. 1, p. 22, and vol. 2, p. 14; Sahih Muslim, vol. 2, p. 14.

Chapter Thirty-One

The Death of Jesus

Last Thursday in the Life of Jesus on Earth

The last Thursday in the life of Muhammad and his followers had been indeed a very sad one. He was not only suffering from the pains of death, but he was also grieved over his followers' discord and disagreements about who would be his successor.

The last Thursday in the life of Jesus was spent commemorating the Passover feast with His disciples.

Passover Feast

Passover is a major religious feast in Israel, celebrated each year in remembrance of how God sent Moses and delivered them from slavery in the land of Egypt. God had sent nine plagues of increasing severity on the land of Egypt to force Pharaoh to allow the children of Israel to go free, yet he would not. The tenth and final punishment was the death of every firstborn, man and beast, in all the land of Egypt. Only those homes that were sprinkled by a lamb's blood painted on the sides and tops of the doorframes were "passed over" by the angel of death, and their firstborn was spared.

That evening, under the direction of Moses, the children of Israel were commanded to sacrifice a lamb and sprinkle its blood on their doorposts. They were to roast the lamb and eat it standing up and dressed for travel.

The firstborn in every Egyptian house died because their homes were not covered with the blood of the lamb, but the angel of death passed over the houses of the children of Israel when he saw the blood, and the firstborn was spared. This is the origin of the Passover feast, which the Jews still celebrate today.[322]

It was not a coincidence Jesus wanted to celebrate this Passover feast with His disciples just before His death. He knew it would be the last time His followers would celebrate Passover where a lamb had to be sacrificed for the forgiveness of sins. Jesus Himself was going to be the final sacrificial lamb, for He was going to the cross to die and by His blood obtain forgiveness for all who would accept His free gift of salvation.

The Passover Supper

Judas: The Disciple Who Betrayed Jesus

Jesus and His disciples gathered in an upper room to celebrate the feast. "Now when evening had come, Jesus was reclining at the table with the twelve disciples and as they were eating He said, 'Truly I say to you that one of you will betray Me.' And they were deeply grieved and began to say to Him, 'Surely not I, Lord?' And He answered and said, 'He who dipped his hand with Me in the bowl is the one who will betray Me. The Son of Man (Jesus) is to go, just as it is written of Him; but woe to that man by whom the Son of Man is betrayed! It would have been good for that man if he had not been born.' And Judas, who was

---

[322.] For a complete account of the first Passover, see Exodus, chapter 12.

betraying Him, answered and said to Him, 'Surely it is not I Rabbi?'
Jesus said to him, 'You have said it yourself'" (Matthew 26:21–25).

The New Covenant: First Communion

> And while they were eating, Jesus said to them, "I have
> earnestly desired to eat this Passover with you before I
> suffer; for I say to you I shall never again eat it until it
> is fulfilled in the kingdom of God." And when He had
> taken some bread, and given thanks, He broke it and
> gave it to the disciples, and said, "Take, eat, this is My
> body which is given for you; do this in remembrance of
> Me." And in the same way He took the cup after they
> had eaten saying, "Drink from it all of you; for this is
> My blood of the covenant, which is poured out for
> many for forgiveness of sins." (Luke 22:15–20)

Jesus offered the bread and wine of the Passover to His disciples as a
symbol for His body, which was to be broken, and His blood, which
was to be shed at the cross for the salvation of mankind. No more lambs
to be killed, no more blood to be spilled. Christians all over the world
do this in memory of the death and resurrection of Jesus. It is the
communion of which believers partake, remembering Jesus Christ's
"New Covenant."

Jesus Teaches Humility

After this last supper together on Thursday, "Jesus rose from supper and
laid aside His garments and took a towel and girded Himself. Then he
poured water into the basin and began to wash the disciples' feet and
wipe them with the towel. Peter said to Jesus, 'Never shall you wash my
feet.' But Jesus answered him, 'If I do not wash you, you have no part
with Me.' Peter then said, 'Lord not my feet only, but also my hands
and my head.' Jesus replied, 'He who has bathed needs only to wash his

feet, but is completely clean, but not all of you are clean [meaning Judas]'" (John 13:4–16). Jesus pointed out to the disciples that even though He was their teacher and Lord, He was demonstrating humility to them, and they should follow His example. Jesus had told them before, "Just as the Son of man did not come to this world to be served, but to serve and give His life a ransom for many" (Matthew 20:28).

Besides teaching His disciples to be humble, Jesus was saying that in the natural life, a man who has bathed only needs to wash the dust off his feet when he goes out. Likewise, in the spiritual life, a man who has been cleansed from his sin, if he sins again, need only confess to restore fellowship with God.

The Betrayal

After singing a hymn, they went out to the Mount of Olives to a place called Gethsemane. Then Jesus said to them, "You will all fall away because of Me this night, for it is written 'I will strike down the Shepherd (Jesus) and the sheep of the flock shall be scattered.' But after I have been raised, I will go before you to Galilee" (Matthew 26:31–32, quoting Zechariah 13:7).

Peter Protests

Peter said, "Even if all may fall away because of You, I will never fall away." Jesus said to him, "Truly I say to you that this very night before a cock crows, you shall deny Me three times" (Matthew 26:33–34).

Jesus Betrayed by Judas

Jesus knew the time of His painful death on the cross was quickly approaching, and He was sorrowful and heavy. He came to Gethsemane and asked His disciples to wait there while he went a little beyond them to pray. He fell on His face in the darkness of night, praying, "My Father, if this cannot pass away unless I drink it, Thy will be done." Then He came to the disciples and said to them, "Arise, let us be going, behold, the one who betrays Me is coming." While He was still speaking, Judas, one of His disciples, came accompanied by a great multitude with torches, swords, and clubs from the chief priests and elders of the people. Judas came to Jesus and said, "Hail, Rabbi," and kissed Him, for he had given them a sign that the one he kissed would be Jesus. So they came and laid hands on Jesus and seized Him. And Jesus said to them, "Have you come out with swords and clubs to arrest Me as a robber? Every day I was with you in the temple teaching and you did not seize Me. But this has happened that the Scriptures might be fulfilled." Having a sword, Simon Peter, therefore, drew it and struck the high priest's slave and cut off his right ear; the slave's name was Malchus. But Jesus said to Peter, "Put the sword back into its place. For all those who take up the sword, shall perish by the sword. Or do you think that I cannot appeal to my Father, and He will at once put at My disposal more than twelve legions of angels?" And He touched the slave's ear and healed it (Matthew 26:36–56, Luke 22:52–53, John 18:10).

Peter Denies Even Knowing Jesus

After Jesus was arrested, he was taken to face interrogation before the high priest Caiaphas. Peter followed from a distance. Now Peter was sitting outside in the courtyard, and a certain servant girl came to him and said, "You too were with Jesus the Galilean." But he denied it before them all, saying, "I do not know what you are talking about." And when he had gone out, another servant girl saw him and said to those who were there, "This man was with Jesus of Nazareth." And again, Peter denied it and said, "I do not know the man." And a little while later, bystanders came up and said to Peter, "Surely you too are one of them, for the way you talk gives you away." Then Peter began to curse and swear, "I do not know the man!" And immediately, a cock crowed. And Peter remembered the word that Jesus had said, "Before a cock crows, you will deny Me three times." Peter went out and wept bitterly (Matthew 26:69–75).

Jesus Questioned by the Jewish Leaders

When it was day, the council of the elders of the people assembled both chief priests and scribes and began asking Him if He were the Christ. He answered, "If I tell you, you will not believe Me, but from now on, the Son of Man will be seated at the Right Hand of the power of God." Then they all said, "Are you the Son of God, then?" And He said, "Yes, I am." They said, "We need no further proof, we've heard it ourselves" (Luke 22:66–71).

Jesus before the Roman Governor

Then they led Jesus from Caiaphas into the Praetorium, and it was early; and they themselves did not enter into the Praetorium so that they would not be defiled, but might eat the Passover. Therefore Pilate went out to them and said, "What accusation do you bring against this Man?" They answered and said to him, "If this Man were not an evildoer, we would not have delivered Him to you." So Pilate said to them, "Take Him yourselves, and judge Him according to your law." The Jews said to him, "We are not permitted to put anyone to death," to fulfill the word of Jesus which He spoke, signifying by what kind of death He was about to die.

Therefore Pilate entered again into the Praetorium, and summoned Jesus and said to Him, "Are You the King of the Jews?" Jesus answered, "Are you saying this on your own initiative, or did others tell you about Me?" Pilate answered, "I am not a Jew, am I? Your own nation and the chief priests delivered You to me; what have You done?" Jesus answered, "My kingdom is not of this world. If My kingdom were of this world, then My servants would be fighting so that I would not be handed over to the Jews; but as it is, My kingdom is not of this realm." Therefore Pilate said to Him, "So You are a king?" Jesus answered, "You say *correctly* that I am a king. For this I have been born, and for this I have come into the world, to testify to the truth. Everyone who is of the truth hears My voice." Pilate said to Him, "What is truth?"

And when he had said this, he went out again to the Jews and said to them, "I find no guilt in Him." (John 18:28–38, NASB)

At the feast, the governor was accustomed to release to the Jews any one prisoner whom they wanted. And they were holding at that time a notorious prisoner called Barabas. When they were gathered together Pilate said to them, "I do not see in Jesus anything worthy of death. Whom do you want me to release for you? Barabas, or Jesus who is called Christ?" For he knew, that because of envy they delivered Him up. (Matthew 27:11–18, Luke 23:1–24, John 18:28–40)

The Roman Governor's Wife Has a Dream

And while he was sitting on the judgment seat, his wife sent to him, saying, "Have nothing to do with that righteous Man, for last night I suffered greatly in a dream because of Him." But the chief priests and the elders persuaded the multitude to release Barabas. The governor then said to them, "Then what shall I do with Jesus?" They shouted, "Crucify Him, Crucify Him." When Pilate saw that a riot was rising, he took water and washed his hands in front of the multitude and said, "I am innocent of this Man's blood, see to it yourselves." And all the people answered and said, "His blood be on us and on our children!" Pilate then released Barabas and delivered Jesus to be crucified. (Matthew 27:19–26)

The Crucifixion

The Roman soldiers of Pilate took Jesus and dressed Him up in a purple robe, weaved a crown of thorns, put it on His head, and began mocking

Him, saying, "Hail, King of the Jews!" The soldiers beat Him and spit on him. They took the purple robe off Him and scourged Him. (The Roman scourge was designed to quickly shred the skin off the body and bring the victim close to death.)[323] Then they put His garments on Him and led him to be crucified in a place called Golgotha, which means "place of the skull." There, they crucified Jesus along with two criminals, one on His right and one on His left. They gave Him wine to drink mixed with gall, and after tasting it, He was unwilling to drink. And when they had crucified Him, they divided His garments among them, casting lots; and sitting down, they began to keep watch over Him. And they put up above His head the charge against Him, which read, "THIS IS JESUS, KING OF THE JEWS." And the chief priests and the scribes along with the elders were mocking Him, saying, "He saved others. He cannot save Himself. He trusts in God. Let Him deliver Him now, for He said, 'I am the Son of God'" (Matthew 27:27–44; Luke 23:26–43; John 19:17–27).

The Seven Last Sayings of Jesus on the Cross

1. And about the ninth hour Jesus cried out with a loud voice saying: "Eloi, Eloi, Lama sabachthani," which means, *"My God, My God, why have you forsaken Me?"* (Matthew 27:46). Jesus was expressing His feelings of abandonment by His Father, for God placed the sins of the world on His only Son; and because of the sin of the world laid on Jesus, God had to turn away from Him. As Jesus was feeling the weight of sin, He was experiencing a separation from God for the only time in all eternity. This was also a fulfillment of the prophetic statement of David, "My God my God, why hast Thou forsaken Me?" (Psalm 22:1).

2. On the cross, in His agony, Jesus responded to His tormentors and to all who had ridiculed and rejected Him by saying, *"Father, forgive*

[323.] http://www.bible-history.com/past/flagrum.html

them, for they do not know what they are doing" (Luke 23:34). Those who crucified Jesus were not aware of the full extent of what they were doing because they did not recognize Him as the Messiah. Christ's prayer in the midst of their mocking expresses the limitless scope of His compassion and divine grace.

3. The criminal who was hanging on the left was hurling abuse at Jesus, saying, "Are you not the Christ? Save yourself and save us!" The thief on the other side answered, "Do you not fear God? We indeed deserve our punishment, but this Man has done nothing wrong." And he said to Jesus, "Remember me when You come into your kingdom." Jesus answered and said to him, "*Truly I say to you, today you shall be with Me in Paradise*" (Luke 23:43). The thief was granted pardon because he expressed his faith in Jesus, recognizing Him to be the Son of God.

4. When Jesus saw His mother and the disciple John whom He loved standing nearby, He said to His mother, "*Behold Your Son*," and He said to the disciple, "*Behold Your Mother*." And from that time the disciple took her into his own household. Jesus, the compassionate Son, made sure His earthly mother was cared for after His death (John 19:26–27).

5. Jesus cried out and said, "*I am thirsty!*" (John 19:26). By saying He was thirsty, Jesus prompted the Roman guards to give Him vinegar, which was customary at a crucifixion. In this, Jesus fulfilled the prophecy: "They put gall in My food and gave Me vinegar for My thirst" (Psalm 69:21).

6. Jesus cried out in a loud voice and said, "*It is finished*" (John 19:30). Jesus' last words meant that His suffering was over, and the whole work His Father had given Him to do was accomplished. He preached the gospel, fulfilled the law, worked miracles, and obtained eternal salvation for His followers. All was done, accomplished, and fulfilled. The debt of sin was paid in full.

7. *"Father, into Your hands I commit my spirit"* (Luke 23:46). Here, Jesus is willingly giving up His soul into the Father's hands, indicating that He was about to die and that God had accepted His sacrifice. And Jesus cried out again with a loud voice and yielded up His spirit.

> And behold the veil of the temple was torn in two from top to bottom, and the earth shook . . . and the tombs were open . . . (Matthew 27:51–52)

Why Was the Curtain Torn?

Jack Wellman gives a brief explanation of why the curtain was torn. Jesus died at the exact moment that the sacrifice for Passover was held. At the same time that Jesus breathed His last, the temple veil was rent. The veil's being torn by God Himself symbolized the fact that mankind's separation from God had been removed by Jesus' supreme sacrifice at the cross. Since Jesus was without blemish, without sin, and kept the law perfectly for us, His death was the propitiation or satisfaction of the wrath of God against our sins. Isaiah 59:2 declares that *"your iniquities* [or sins] *have separated you from your God; your sins have hidden his face from you, so that he will not hear you."* Now that Jesus' once-for-all sacrifice has been completed, we have access to the very throne of God.

Why Was It Torn from Top to Bottom?

The veil was not a small curtain like you see in some movies. The veil was sixty feet tall and thirty feet wide, and it was thick. The veil was so massive and heavy that it took three hundred priests to manipulate it.[324]

[324.] The Bible does not specify the size or thickness of the veil in Herod's temple. Josephus says it was 82' x 42' but doesn't specify the thickness. Early rabbinic literature said it was as thick as a man's hand, later labeled hyperbolic by later rabbinicliterature(https://cbumgardner.wordpress.com/2010/04/06/the-thickness-of-the-temple-veil/).

An important point here is that no one could simply tear the veil themselves. It would take more than human strength to tear it. The analogy is that it took the mighty hand of God Himself to tear it supernaturally; and this tearing, which represents the removal of the separation between God and man, could not be done by humans. It had to be done by God alone, and that's the point. No one can remove our separation from God but God Himself (Isaiah 59:2). 1 John 2:2 says, *"He [Jesus] is the atoning sacrifice for our sins, and not only for ours but also for the sins of the whole world."* Since Jesus' death atoned for our sins, Jesus' sacrifice allowed for the veil to be torn and the separation between God and man to be removed.

The fact that the veil was torn from the top down, some sixty feet above the floor (where humans could not reach it), shows that God was the One that caused the veil to be torn. He is the initiator of the veil being rent. He is the cause of the tearing. He, in Jesus Christ, is the reason it was torn.[325]

Now when the centurion and those who were with him keeping guard over Jesus saw the earthquake and the things that were happening, they became frightened and said, "Truly, this was the Son of God" (Matthew 27:54).

The Burial of Jesus

When it was evening, Joseph of Arimathea went to Pilate and asked for the body of Jesus. He wrapped the body in a clean linen cloth and laid it in his own new tomb. Then he laid a large stone against the entrance of the tomb and went away. Now the chief priests and Pharisees gathered

---

The gospel writers use the motif of tearing as a literary device, framing the tearing of the heavens at Jesus' baptism with the tearing of the veil at His death. *Journal of the Evangelical Society*, Daniel Gurtner, 49/1, (March 2006), 97–114.

[325] http://www.whatchristianswanttoknow.com/tearing-of-the-temple-curtain-why-was-this-significant/

together with Pilate and said, "Sir, we remember that this deceiver, when He was still alive, said, 'After three days I will rise again.' Therefore give orders for the grave to be made secure until the third day, lest the disciples come and steal Him away and say to the people, 'He has risen from the dead.'" Pilate said, "You have a guard, go make it as secure as you know how." And they went and made the grave secure, and along with the guard they set a seal on the stone[326] (Matthew 27:57–66).

The Empty Tomb

Jews and Gentiles had both agreed to crucify Jesus, the Son of God; and they both agreed to seal the tomb to make sure no one stole the body. But God wanted them to become witnesses to the strangest and most important miracle in all human history.

On the first day of the week, early at dawn, Mary Magdalene and the other women went to the tomb[327] but found the stone rolled away and an angel sitting on it who said to them, "I know you are looking for Jesus who has been crucified. He is not here, for He has risen!" (Matthew 28:5–6).

[326.] The Roman seal was also placed over the tomb. The seal was sign of authentication that the tomb was occupied and the power and authority of Rome stood behind the seal. Anyone found breaking the Roman seal would suffer the punishment of an unpleasant death. There is a question as to which one of two groups was watching over it. The context seems to favor the Roman guard over the temple police. The Roman guard was a sixteen-man unit that was governed by very strict rules. Each member was responsible for six square feet of space. The guard members could not sit down or lean against anything while they were on duty. If a guard member fell asleep, he was beaten and burned with his own clothes. But he was not the only one executed; the entire sixteen-man guard unit was executed if only one of the members fell asleep while on duty (https://www.blueletterbible.org/faq/don_stewart/don_stewart_247.cfm)

[327.] https://blogs.thegospelcoalition.org/justintaylor/2008/07/24/what-did-jesus-tomb-look-like-interview/

What an amazing scene it must have been to find the stone rolled away and an angel simply sitting on it. Jesus abolished what both the Jews and the Roman Empire had done and forever displayed the new heavenly seal on the open empty tomb. "He is not here, for He has risen!" (Matthew 28:6).

Chapter Thirty-Two

The Legacy of Jesus

Jesus said, "Peace I leave with you. My peace I give to you; not as the world gives do I give to you. Let not your heart be troubled, nor let it be fearful" (John 14:27).

Jesus also said, "These things I have spoken to you, that in Me you may have peace. In the world you may have tribulation, but take courage, I have overcome the world" (John 16:33).

"Let not your heart be troubled; you believe in God, believe also in Me. In My Father's house are many dwelling places; if it were not so, I would have told you; for I go to prepare a place for you. And if I go and prepare a place for you, I will come again, and receive you to Myself; that where I am there you may be also" (John 14:1–3).

From the words of Jesus, we see that He promises His followers peace that is very unique—even peace in the face of hardship and persecution. It is not a peace that they would achieve by conquering and subduing others, gaining their land and their wealth. He promises them a place in His Father's house, where they would live forever with Him in perfect peace.

Who Is Jesus?

The Bible speaks clearly of the identity of Jesus, beginning with His miraculous birth by a virgin called Mary. We also read about Jesus in the gospel of John: "In the beginning was the Word, and the Word was with God, and the Word was God" (John 1:1). This means that in the beginning, before time began, Jesus the Messiah was already in existence with God. "The Word" here refers to Jesus, who is all that God is and the expression of Him.

"He was in the beginning with God. All things came into being by Him, and apart from Him nothing came into being that has come into being" (John 1:2–3). This means that Jesus (the Word) was actively involved in the Creation. No creation took place without His involvement with God the Father. Then we are told that Jesus—the Word of God, who was from the beginning with God the Father—left His home in heaven and came to the world in human form. We read in John 1:14, "And the Word became flesh, and dwelt among us, and we beheld His glory, glory as of the only begotten[328] from the Father full of grace and truth."

[328.] "Begotten" is the English translation of the Greek word *monogenes*. So what does *monogenes* mean? According to the *Greek-English Lexicon* . . . (BAGD, 3rd ed.), *monogenes* has two primary definitions. The first definition is "pertaining to *being the only one of its kind within a specific relationship.*" This is its meaning in Hebrews 11:17 when the writer refers to Isaac as Abraham's "only begotten son" (KJV). Abraham had more than one son, but Isaac was the only son he had by Sarah and the only son of the covenant. Therefore, it is the uniqueness of Isaac among the other sons that allows for the use of *monogenes* in that context.

The second definition is "pertaining to *being the only one of its kind or class, unique in kind.*" This is the meaning that is implied in John 3:16 (see also John 1:14, 18; 3:18; 1 John 4:9). John was primarily concerned with demonstrating that Jesus is the Son of God (John 20:31), and he uses *monogenes* to highlight Jesus as uniquely God's Son—sharing the same divine nature as God—as opposed to believers who are God's sons and daughters by adoption (Ephesians 1:5). Jesus is God's "one and only" son.

The bottom line is that terms such as "Father" and "Son," descriptive of God and Jesus, are human terms that help us understand the relationship between the

The question to be asked is, Why did Jesus leave the glory of heaven and choose to become human like us? For this, we have to go back in time to the Creation.

Adam and Eve: The Creation

The triune God—Father, Son, and Holy Spirit—created man to love Him and have fellowship with Him. But in order for Holy God to fellowship with man, man had to also be holy, which means to be without sin. So God created Adam in His image, pure and holy. He also created a partner for him to enjoy and placed them in the Garden of Eden with the animals He also created. He told Adam and Eve that they could enjoy all the fruit of the garden except one tree: the tree of the knowledge of good and evil. God did enjoy the man and his wife and fellowshipped with them, walking with them in the Garden of Eden. Here we have to remember that before creating man, God had created heavenly beings, angels. We also have to remember that God never usurps from His creatures their freedom. God created them with a free will—free to love and obey Him or free to walk away from Him. The Bible tells us how Lucifer, with all his splendor and beauty, did not last in heaven forever. He became a prideful being who wanted to become equal with God! Instead of being God's archangel, he fell from grace and became God's enemy, Satan. He and his followers, the demons, became God's enemies, having one thing in mind: to attack His creation and take away man's devotion to Him. Satan and his fallen host of angels will do anything to prevent people from loving and obeying God.

---

different Persons of the Trinity. If you can understand the relationship between a human father and a human son, then you can understand, in part, the relationship between the First and Second Persons of the Trinity. The analogy breaks down if you try to take it too far and teach, as some Christian cults, that Jesus was literally "begotten" as in "produced" or "created" by God the Father (https://www.gotquestions.org/only-begotten-son.html).

The Saddest Day in the History of Man

Satan came to the Garden of Eden in the form of a serpent and approached Eve, saying,

> "Indeed, has God said, You shall not eat from any tree of the garden?'" And the woman said to the serpent, "From the fruit of the trees of the garden we may eat; but from the fruit of the tree which is in the middle of the garden, God said, 'You shall not eat from it or touch it, lest you die.'" And the serpent said to the woman, "You surely shall not die. For God knows that in the day you eat from it your eyes will be opened and you will be like God, knowing good and evil." When the woman saw that the tree was good for food, and that it was a delight to the eyes, and that the tree was desirable to make one wise, she took from its fruit and ate; and she gave also to her husband with her and he ate! (Genesis 3:1–6).

Something Gained, Something Lost

Satan succeeded in turning the first of God's creation against Him. Whereas Adam and Eve had been living in harmony with their Creator, they disobeyed God and, as a result of their disobedience, lost fellowship with Him. Since they chose to follow Satan's directions instead of God's, they could no longer be part of God's family and came under Satan's control. In an instant, they fell from God's grace and became subject to His enemy! Oh yes, something was gained that day! Adam and Eve gained their independence from God, their Creator. Now they did not have to follow Him nor obey Him in all that He said. They exercised the free will they were given by their Creator, and chose it to undermine God's command! They could do what they wanted when they wanted, and they chose to listen to another voice—that of God's enemy! They gained independence from God but lost their connection to Him. He would no longer be their Guide in all they did. They used their free will, and they chose to disobey God and go after a quick pleasure; and now they became subject to Satan, the enemy of their soul.

Consequences of Disobedience to God

God had said to Adam and Eve that the day they ate from the forbidden fruit they would die. Was God serious? Did they really die? Adam and Eve died immediately—*spiritually*! What is spiritual death? To be spiritually dead is to be separated from communion with God, our Creator. Adam and Eve could no longer live in the presence of God, nor fellowship with Him. They were permanently separated from God because they no longer were holy and blameless—not fit to live in God's presence and be part of His family. They now became disobedient sinners in the family of Satan! Something was lost! They lost their intended identity in God, their Creator! Gaining their independence from God, they came under the dominion of their new master, Satan! They were like so many people today who pride themselves in being self-sufficient but have no power to resist Satan and his demons, seeking pleasures that never fully satisfy and wondering why life sometimes is so hard!

But Adam and Eve not only faced spiritual death (separation from God); they also came under the curse of physical death. Now as fallen creatures, their bodies would have to die. As soon as Adam and Eve had disobeyed God and eaten of what He forbade, their eyes were opened, and they knew that they were naked. They sewed fig leaves together to make themselves aprons. "And they heard the sound of the Lord walking in the garden in the cool of the day, and the man and his wife hid themselves from the presence of the Lord God, among the trees of the garden. Then God called to Adam and said, 'Where are you?' Adam said to God that he was hiding because he was naked. And God asked Adam, 'Have you eaten from the tree of which I commanded you not to eat?' Adam replied, 'The woman whom you gave me, she gave me and I ate.'" And the woman said it was the serpent who gave her, and she ate. Neither Adam nor Eve acknowledged their disobedience but blamed their failure on someone else. Does this sound familiar? It is always somebody else's fault, or it is the circumstances we find ourselves in that are to be blamed.

God cursed Satan, who had come in the form of a snake and said to him, "I will put enmity between you and the woman, and between your seed and her seed; He shall bruise you on the head, and you shall bruise him on the heel" (Genesis 3:15). This prophecy refers to the enmity between the spiritual descendants of Satan and the seed of the woman, explicitly Jesus. Jesus Christ would deal a deathblow to Satan's head at the cross. Satan would bruise Christ's heel, meaning causing Him to suffer on the cross.

Who Can Reconcile the Human Race with God?

In his fallen state, man needs an intercessor to reconcile him with his heavenly Father. But is there a mediator who qualifies to reach both God and man at the same time?

The story of Job is very familiar to most Jews, Christians, and Muslims. We read in the Bible in the book of Job that Job was a righteous man and blameless before God, but God allowed Satan to test him. He lost his children, his wealth, and even his health. When friends came to comfort him, they soon started hinting that perhaps what happened to him was a result of hidden sin in his life. Job had had it with his friends, and he felt that even God was far from him, detached from His creation. In his helplessness, he cried out for an umpire or arbitrator, someone who understands both God and man and can bring them together in harmony. He complained, "There is no Umpire (judge; arbitrator) between us, who may lay his hand on us both" (Job 9:33). Later, Job would say, "I know that my Redeemer lives . . . and though worms destroy this body, yet in my flesh shall I see God, Whom I shall see for myself . . ." (Job 19:25–27).

Sin Separated Mankind from God

So why do we need someone to intercede between us and God, our Creator? The answer is that we are sinners, and our sins have separated us from God. Adam disobeyed God, and his sin separated him from God. So did every person who was born from the seed of Adam. That is me and you and everybody because we are all descendants of our father, Adam. So when Adam sinned, we sinned because we were *in* him; our seed was in him. Our spiritual *and* physical ancestry goes back to Adam, for if our father or grandfather had died before siring us, we would not have been born. So in Adam, we were born sinners before we ever committed any sin. In other words, we sin because we were born sinners; we do not become sinners because we sin. And as sinners, we are separated from God because He is Holy and will not fellowship with sinners. That is the reason why Adam could no longer live in the Garden of Eden in the presence of the Lord after he sinned. But God still loved Adam, and He continues to love all His creation and desires to have fellowship with them.

Jesus: The Mediator between God and Man

Remember in his frustration, Job said, "There is no umpire between us who may lay his hand upon us both." We need a mediator between us and God. Thanks be to God, for He provided a mediator for us! He says in His word, "There is one God and one Mediator between God and men, the Man Jesus Christ" (1 Timothy 2:5). So Jesus is the Mediator between God and man. A mediator is a reconciler. He stands between two parties that differ and are separated and seeks to bring them together in reconciliation. Sin has separated us from God. The Bible says, "But your iniquities have separated between you and your God, and your sins have hidden His face from you so that He does not hear" (Isaiah 59:2). Jesus is the only One who can stand in the gap between sinful man and God, the Judge.

One God, One Mediator

Whoever is mediator between God and man must *be* both God and man. He must be deity to be in the presence of God, being God, knowing God, understanding God; yet he must also be a man, relating to man, sympathizing with man, holding man and God together. With one hand, he must touch God and hold God; and with the other hand, he must touch humanity in understanding and in sympathy. But he should also be without sin—sinless. The Bible tells us, "For we do not have a high priest who cannot sympathize with our weakness, but One who has been tempted in all things as we are, yet without sin" (Hebrews 4:15).

Why did God send a mediator to the world? God loves us and wants to fellowship with us. The Bible says, "For God so loved the world that He gave His only begotten Son, that whoever believes in Him should not perish, but have eternal life. For God, did not send His Son into the world to condemn the world, but that the world should be saved through Him. He who believes in Him is not judged; he who does not believe has been judged already, because he has not believed in the name of the only begotten Son of God" (John 3:16–18).

Jesus Promises Christians Heaven

Jesus said to His followers, "My sheep hear My voice, and I know them, and they follow Me; and I give eternal life to them, and they shall never perish; and no one shall snatch them out of My hand. My Father who has given them to Me, is greater than all; and no one is able to snatch them out of the Father's hand" (John 10:27–29).

Jesus is able to give His followers the assurance that they will be in heaven with Him and His Father. No one—even Satan, God's enemy—has the power to take God's children away and send them to hell. What joy and relief for the followers of Jesus! But God is Holy and cannot nor will not accept sinners in His heaven, just as He did not allow Adam to remain in His presence after he sinned. The Bible says, "For all have sinned and fall short of the glory of God" (Romans 3:23). God also said, "The soul that sins, it shall die" (Ezekiel 18:20). We read in the Bible, "For the wages of sin is death, but the free gift of God is eternal life in Jesus Christ our Lord" (Romans 6:23). Sin has to be punished, and God says the punishment for sin is death. Through the sin of Adam, death passed to all mankind; and through the sacrificial death of Jesus Christ, the price for man's sin was fully paid. The Bible says, "But God demonstrated His own love toward us, in that while we were yet sinners, Christ died for us" (Romans 5:8). Jesus—being fully human, born of a woman, and fully God, born in the world by the Holy Spirit—was the only One who could satisfy the death penalty for man, the sinner. We read in the Bible, "Therefore, just as through one man (Adam) sin entered into the world, and death through sin, and so death spread to all men because all sinned . . . that as sin reigned in death, even so grace might reign through righteousness to eternal life through Jesus Christ our Lord" (Romans 5:12, 21).

Through all the verses referenced above, we see that you and I sinned against God and are born spiritually dead, separated from God. We also see that Jesus Christ offered Himself as mediator to pay for the penalty of our sin and make us once again accepted by God the Father. Jesus said, "I am the way, and the truth and the life; no one comes to the Father but through Me" (John 14:6). What was the way that Jesus paid to rescue us and save us from the penalty of sin? Jesus accepted to die on the cross and become the bridge between sinful man and Holy God. First, Jesus accepted to leave His heavenly home and become man and live among men. He was tempted in everything like us, yet He never sinned. He was condemned to die on the cross like a criminal because He said he was the Son of God. As a human, He felt humiliation and torture at the hands of His accusers. At the cross, even God the Father turned His face away from Jesus because on Him lay all the sins of mankind. Through His death on the cross, Jesus fulfilled God's required law for the payment of man's sin. Through His resurrection, we know that God accepted His sacrifice as redemption for mankind.

In the person of Jesus hanging on the cross, grace met with justice. Grace expressed compassion and forgiveness, while justice demanded full payment. There, in the broken body of Jesus, God's love for humans met with His hatred for sin; and love won, and sin was forgiven.

One day, I was discussing with a Muslim woman what Jesus has done for us. Her response was that she could not accept anyone to pay for her sins. This is a clear teaching of Islam. Muslims believe that they should offset bad deeds with good ones, and just maybe they can make it to heaven. In spite of the clear teaching of the Bible that no one can ever pay for their sins, some Christians who know about grace still try to partially depend on their good works to obtain God's forgiveness. But how could we, sinful as we are, satisfy a Holy God? The prophet Isaiah says, "All our righteousnesses are as filthy rags (menstrual cloths)" (Isaiah 64:6). Our offenses toward God are forgiven only by grace through the Son of God.

We are told in the Bible, "For by grace you have been saved through faith; and that not of yourselves, it is the gift of God. Not as a result of works, that no one should boast" (Ephesians 2:8–9). *God does offer free and unconditional forgiveness through the blood of Jesus, but we must ask for it individually.* We have to acknowledge that we have sinned, and our sin is offensive to God and separates us from Him. We also have to acknowledge that Jesus is the only One who can reconcile us with God. Then we must individually ask Jesus to come into our lives and redeem us. Jesus says to everyone, "Behold I stand at the door and knock; if anyone hears My voice and opens the door, I will come in to him, and will dine with him, and he with Me" (Revelation 3:20).

The invitation to follow Jesus is open to all. The Bible says, "He came to His own (the Jewish nation), and those who were His own did not receive Him. But as many as received Him, to them He gave the right to become children of God, even to those who believe in His name" (John 1:11–12).

Dear reader, if you were born in a Christian home but have never individually come to Jesus, He is calling you. If you were born in a Muslim home and did not know of his grace, Jesus is calling you. If you were born in a Jewish or Buddhist home and did not know He made a way for you to go to heaven, He is calling you. If you were born in a Hindu belief or no belief, Jesus came for you!

Jesus said, "I am the good shepherd; and I know My own, and My own know Me, even as the Father knows Me and I know the Father; and I lay down My life for the sheep. And I have other sheep that are not of this fold; I must bring them also, and they shall hear My voice; and they shall become one flock with one shepherd" (John 10:14–16). "After these things I looked, and behold, a great multitude which no one could number, of all nations, tribes, peoples, and tongues, standing before the throne and before the Lamb, clothed with white robes, with palm branches in their hands . . ." (Revelation 7:9).

Dear Lord Jesus, I have heard Your call to me, and I want to follow You. I believe that You are the Son of God and that You came into the world to save me, a sinner. I believe that You died on the cross, You were buried, and on the third day, You rose from the dead. I believe that because of Your death, all my sins are forgiven. I believe that because of Your resurrection, I have a new life. I invite You to be the Master of my life. Lead me, Lord, in everything I do. Thank you, Lord, for saving me. Amen.

Chapter Thirty-Three

The First Followers of Muhammad

Muhammad was the author and first leader of Islam. He was a religious as well as a military and political leader. Under his leadership, Islam spread and stretched across Arabia. How did Islam expand into a great empire after the death of Muhammad? In this chapter, we shall explore how Islam survived and spread after his death, especially through his first four successors.

The First Four Khalifas

The Arabic word "caliph," or "khalifa," means "successor." The first four are known as "the rightly guided caliphs" and were chosen by a vote of the followers.

As discussed in chapter 30, Muhammad did not appoint a successor. Apparently, on his death bed, Muhammad wanted to write a document that would guide his followers; but Umar Ibn Al Khattab interrupted by saying that the Prophet was deeply inflicted with pain. He said that the Qur'an was sufficient, while others insisted on bringing him material to write with. As the dispute between those present accelerated, Muhammad became upset and said, "Get up and go away."[329]

The two logical people to be successors were Ali ibn Abi Talib, Muhammad's cousin and son-in-Law, and Abu-Bakr, Muhammad's close friend and father-in-law. Ali was married to Muhammad's daughter Fatima by his first wife, Khadija. Abu-Bakr was the father of Aisha, his favorite wife.

The split in the Muslim community grew wider after Abu-Bakr was chosen as the first khalifa. The followers of Ali never abandoned the belief that he, not Abu-Bakr, should have succeeded Muhammad and thus began the division between Sunni Muslims (Abu-Bakr) and Shia Muslims (Ali), which continues to this present time.

First Khalifa (Two Years)

Abu-Bakr and the Ridda Wars[330]

Troubles began soon after Abu-Bakr took over. The unity and stability of the new community state of Islam was threatened. Various Arab tribes of Hijaz and Nejd rebelled against the new caliph and his system. Some tribes would not pay the Zakat[331] even though they did not challenge the prophethood of Muhammad. Many other tribes, however, returned to their pre-Islamic religion and traditions, which Muhammad and his followers considered idolatry. The tribes claimed that their submission was to Muhammad and that after his death, they were again free to do what seemed best to them. Abu-Bakr insisted that they had not just submitted to a leader, but had actually joined the Muslim religious community of which he now was the new head. Abu-Bakr

---

[329.] Sahih Muslim.

[330.] Ridda ("reverted") wars are Wars of Apostasy.

[331.] Zakat is 2.5% of disposable income to be paid into the treasury as alms tax

considered their rebellion to be apostasy, which is a capital offense under Islam. Abu-Bakr began the Ridda wars, or the Wars of Apostasy.

Abu-Bakr, Muhammad's closest companion, explained in a letter at the time that Muhammad "struck whoever turned his back to him until he came to Islam, willingly or grudgingly." Thus, Abu-Bakr promised to "burn them with fire, slaughter them by any means, and take women and children captive" of any who left Islam.[332]

The most severe struggle against the apostates was the war against the self-declared prophet Ibn Habib Al Hanafi, known as Musaylimah.[333] He was from the Christian tribe of Banu Hanifa, which was an independent tribe before Islam. Musaylimah had declared himself to be a prophet, but Muhammad had refused to acknowledge him as such and named him Musaylimah Al Kathab (Musaylimah the Liar). After Muhammad's death, Musaylimah claimed to be Muhammad's successor as a prophet.

The caliph Abu-Bakr gave Khalid bin al-Walid the mission to destroy the forces of Musaylimah at Yamamah. Musaylimah was encamped in the plain of Aqraba with an army of forty thousand warriors to defend his prophethood and the right not to be Muslim.[334] The Muslim army advanced and launched three attacks against Musaylimah, of which the most dreadful became known as the Gulley of Blood.

After more than a year of fighting, Musaylimah, along with his remaining army of seven thousand, took shelter in a walled garden and closed the gate. A Muslim soldier jumped into the garden, killed the guards, and opened the gate. All the Muslims poured in. All

---

[332.] Al-Tabari, vol. 10, pp. 55–57.

[333.] Some Christian Copts believe that Muhammad learned some of the Bible from him.

[334.] A. I. Akram, the Sword of Allah: Khalid bin al-Waleed, His life and Campaigns, Nat. Publishing House, Rawalpindi 1970, ISBN 0-7101-0140-X

Musaylimah's men were killed as well as thousands of Muslims in what was to be known as the Garden of Death. With this, the biggest opposition to Abu-Bakr was defeated. Islam survived and advanced because Abu-Bakr dealt harshly with any who would dare denounce Islam.

The Battle of Yamamah played a major role in motivating Abu-Bakr to complete the compilation of the Qur'an. During the life of Muhammad, many parts of the Qur'an were scattered among his companions, much of them as private possession. However, seven hundred hafizes (Muslims who had memorized the Qur'an) were killed at Yamamah. Consequently, upon the insistence of his future successor Umar, Abu-Bakr ordered the collection of the pieces of the Qur'an into one copy.[335]

Does Islam Condone Beheading, Torture, and Burning?

One of the most respected Sunni scholars, Yusuf al-Qaradawi, admitted in 2012 that "if Muslims had gotten rid of the apostasy punishment, Islam wouldn't exist today."[336] He did not however apologize for the beheading, torture, burning, and murder of millions, but rather tried to rationalize it.

The world was aghast about the burning in a cage of the Jordanian pilot Lieutenant Kasasbeh on February 3, 2016. Most Muslims abhor killing and would certainly oppose burning someone alive. But how did ISIS justify this punishment?

Muhammad was quoted to have said that burning belongs to Allah alone. However, other sayings seem to justify these actions. The Prophet said, "No prayer is harder for the hypocrites than the Fajr (dawn) and

[335.] Hasan, Sayyid Siddi; Nadwi, Abul Hassan Ali; Kidwai, A. R. (translator) 2000, The Collection of the Qur'an. Karachi: Qur'anic Arabic Foundation, pp. 34–35.
[336.] https://www.youtube.com/watch?v=huMu8ihDlVA "Yusuf al-Qaradawi: Killing Of Apostates Is Essential For Islam To Survive"

Isha (night prayer). And if they knew the reward for these prayers at their respective times, they would certainly present themselves in the mosques even if they had to crawl." The Prophet added, "Certainly I decided to order Mu'adh-dhin (one who calls for prayer) and then take a fire flame to burn all those who had not left their houses (to go to the mosque for prayer) . . . along with their houses."[337]

Abu-Bakr also set the example when a captive who had fought against the Muslims was brought to him. Abu-Bakr ordered a fire to be kindled with much firewood in the prayer yard of Medina and threw him into it with arms and legs bound.[338] Abu-Bakr said, "I shall not sheathe a sword that Allah had unsheathed against the unbelievers."[339] Khalid ibn al-Walid took Abu-Bakr's admonishment to heart and was known for burning many captives alive. After two years as khalifa, Abu-Bakr died after a high fever and an illness. Some say he was poisoned. He was buried next to Muhammad and chose Umar as the next successor.[340]

Second Khalifa (Ten Years)

Umar ibn al-Khattab was the father of Hifsa, one of Muhammad's wives. Hifsa, you will remember, along with Aisha, had caused the Prophet so much trouble that he threatened to divorce them all. Umar was the chief advisor to the first khalifa and became the second khalifa of Islam. During his caliphate rule, Islam expanded to the empires of Persia and the Byzantine. Egypt, which had been part of the Byzantine/ Eastern Roman Empire, fell to the Muslims after a long period of struggle. Islam continued to invade countries and expand. The Islamic invasions that took place during the four caliphs are called الفتوحات,

---

[337.] Sahih Bukhari, vol. 1, book 2, number 626.

[338.] The History of al-Tabari, The Conquest of Arabia, p. 80.

[339.] The Origins of the Islamic State, Abu Al-Abbas Ahmad Bin Jab Al-Baladhuri, translated by Philip Hitti, p. 148.

[340.] https://en.wikipedia.org/wiki/Abu_Bakr

which means "the Openings." Muslims believe that due to these invasions, the peoples' hearts were opened to Islam.

Umar was stabbed six times by a slave as he was leading prayers in the mosque. Many were killed in the mosque, and the assassin ended up committing suicide.

Third Khalifa (Twelve Years)

Uthman ibn Affan was chosen as the third successor even though some people still thought that it should have been Ali. Uthman was from the rich Ummayad clan of Mecca and was a very wealthy man. He was married to two of Muhammad's daughters by Khadija: Ruqqayyah and, after she died, Umm Kulthum, her sister. He was very devoted to Islam. During the invasions and conquests of Islam, there were many different versions of the Qur'an. One of these versions was compiled by Ali but was not accepted. Uthman ordered all manuscripts to be burned except his and compiled only one version to be distributed to all provinces.

There was a lot of antigovernment propaganda, so Uthman called all the governors of his twelve provinces to Medina to discuss the problem. The rebels called for Uthman to step down, but Muhammad's words to him kept ringing in his ears. "Perhaps Allah will clothe you with a shirt, Uthman, and if the people want you to take it off, do not take it off for them." Uthman did not step down in spite of his many enemies.

Eventually, rebels were sent to assassinate him. Uthman's enemies surrounded his house and eventually snuck in and murdered him. The Shia versions of why and how Uthman was murdered differ from those of the Sunnis. At any rate, Uthman too was murdered.

Fourth Khalifa (Six Years)

Finally, Ali was appointed the fourth khalifa, but not with the consent of everyone. Many of Uthman's followers wanted revenge for his murder, but Ali did not act upon it. During his rule of six years, Ali had to deal with the prevalent corruption, rebellion of his governors, and treachery by his own followers. He also fought several wars, including a war against Aisha, the widow of Muhammad.

Battle of the Camel

Aisha, along with her two brothers-in-law and the Ummayads (who were believed to be the instigators of Uthman's death), wanted Ali to avenge the blood of the third khalifa, Uthman. Ali thought it would not be wise to shed blood between the Muslims since there were many Muslim factions fighting one another. On her side, Aisha never did like Ali, the husband of Fatima, who was Muhammad's favorite daughter. In fact, when the scandal of the *ifk* had spread in Medina about Aisha's possible affair, Ali had advised Muhammad to replace Aisha with other better wives.

When Ali became the fourth khalifa, Aisha was hoping that her two brothers-in-law would become governors under him; but when this did not materialize, Aisha's animosity toward Ali grew even more. Soon, she decided to go to war against him for not avenging the blood of Uthman, the third khalifa.

So Aisha mounted her camel from Mecca at the head of one thousand men and her two brothers-in-law, and headed to Basra (southern Iraq), where Ali's caliphate was. On the way, many more followed her, and the numbers became three thousand. Ali did not want to fight Aisha, ام المؤمنين (the mother of believers),[341] and tried to persuade her not to

---

[341.] The wives of the prophet Muhammad were called "the mothers of the believers."

fight. But Aisha did not accept any negotiations and ignored Ali's many pleas and his letter that stated,

> In the name of Allah who is most Beneficent and most Merciful. You have left your home in direct contravention of the commandments of Allah and his messenger, and now you are sowing seeds of civil war among the Muslims. Just pause for a moment and think about this. What do you have to do with armies and wars? Is it your job to fight? And fight against whom? Against the Muslims? Your place is in your home. God has commanded you to stay in your home. Therefore, fear Him, and do not disobey Him and return immediately to Medina.

Aisha refused all Ali's suggestions, mounted her camel, and urged her troops to prepare for battle. Thus began the Battle of Jamal (Camel), where Muslims fought against Muslims. Although outnumbered, Ali and his soldiers were too skilled to be defeated. Soon, victory was on Ali's side. Aisha's camel was brought down, and Ali ordered Aisha's brother Muhammad bin Abu-Bakr to take care of his sister.

Aisha's plans had come to nothing, but ten thousand men lay dead as a result of the Battle of the Camel.

Ali restrained his men from taking any booty, and all property found on the battleground was gathered in the mosque of Basra, from where the owners could claim their possessions.

After this success by Ali, Mu'awiya, a Meccan stationed as the governor of Syria, waged a prolonged war against Ali to avenge the murder of the khalifa Uthman, his kinsman. They wanted Uthman's death to be avenged, but Ali didn't avenge his death.

In the Islamic year AH 40, year AD 661, while praying in the Great Mosque of Kufa, Ali was stabbed by Abd-al-Rahman Ibn Muljam. He was wounded by Ibn Muljam's poison-coated sword while prostrating in the Fajr prayer. He was taken to his home, where he died from his wounds two days later. His two sons al-Hassan and al-Hussein washed his body and buried him. They also put to death the killers of their father.

Ali's death marked the end of the four "rightly guided caliphs" (الخلفاء الرشيدون) and widened the gap between the Sunnis and Shia.

After Ali's death, the Shias of that area (Iraq) declared Ali's eldest son, Hassan, the successor to Ali, pronouncing him their new khalifa; but this was disputed by many. To avoid further bloodshed, Hassan abdicated and signed a treaty with Mu'awiya, who then became the first khalifa of the Umayyad caliphate. In this treaty, Hassan handed over power on the condition that Mu'awiya not establish a dynasty.[342] Hassan was poisoned to death in 670.[343]

The Umayyad Caliphate

Upon Ali's death, Mu'awiya, the leader of the struggle against Ali and his supporters, established himself as the undisputed khalifa. Mu'awiya was a member of one of the most prominent families in Mecca. Against a lot of opposition, he established a new rule that the caliphate would become hereditary rather than elected by the people. The Umayyad caliphate continued to rule for the next century from Damascus.

The late Sunni theologian Maududi[344] wrote that the establishment of the caliphate as a monarchy began with the caliphate of Mu'awiya. It

---

[342] https://en.wikipedia.org/wiki/Battle_of_Karbala

[343] https://www.al-islam.org/articles/karbala-the-chain-of-events-ramzan-sabir#the%20battle

[344] Maududi, Sayyid Abul A'la, Khilafat Wa Mulukiyat (Caliphate and the Monarchy), chapter 5, pp. 158–159.

was not the choice of the people, but he fought in order to obtain the caliphate by force. Consequently, the people had no choice but to give him their allegiance and put an end to civil war. As Maududi pointed out, Mu'awiya's own speech during the initial days of his caliphate expressed his own awareness of this. He said,

> By Allah, while taking charge of your government I was not unaware of the fact that you are unhappy over my taking over government and you people don't like it . . . but still I have taken it from you on the basis of my sword . . . now if you see that I am not fulfilling your rights, then you should be happy with me with whatever is there [meaning tough luck].

The Gap between Shia and Sunni Widens

The Shia's cause did not die with the death of Ali but was taken up by his second son, Hussein. When Mu'awiya I died, Hussein refused to give allegiance to his son Yazid I, who succeeded him because this was against the treaty. Yazid instructed the governor of Mecca to secure Hussein's loyalty or his head. There were plans to assassinate him. Supporters of Ali in the city of Kufa, which is in present-day Iraq, invited Ḥussein to take refuge with them, promising to have him proclaimed caliph there. Hussein sent his cousin as an ambassador to scope out the situation.[345] His cousin found favorable opinion and was working to generate support, and so Hussein started toward Kufa. On the way, he was met by a famous poet, Al-Farazdaq, who told him that while the people were sympathetic to him, they would never fight for him. Meanwhile, Yazid replaced the governor of the area. The new governor, Ubaidullah Ibn Ziyad, captured Hussein's cousin and his host and chopped their heads off. He had an army intercept Hussein on the

[345.] https://www.al-islam.org/articles/karbala-the-chain-of-events-ramzan-sabir#the%20battle

second of Muharram and put him under siege without food or water. Hussein negotiated with the general in charge, Umar Ibn Sa'ad, to lift the siege and let him return. Governor Ziyad initially agreed but was then convinced by Shimr Bin Dhil-Jawshan to send a letter to General Sa'ad stating his position would be given to Shimr and his head on a stick if he did not kill Hussein. Meanwhile, the seventy-two people with Hussein, including women and children, were suffering greatly from lack of water. They fought bravely, with some warriors on the other side even switching sides to help them, but the opposing force was thousands. Finally, only Hussein of the warriors was left alive, holding his infant son, who was crying out of thirst. The enemy shot an arrow into the child and then injured Hussein by sword blows. Shimr's mother delivered the final decapitating blow, and then his head was put on a spear to be carried back to Yazid. The bodies of the dead were mutilated, and a few remaining women were taken to Yazid and to prison. The Battle of Karbala secured the position of the Sunni Umayyad dynasty, but for Shiite Muslims, the tenth of Muharram became an annual holy day of public mourning.

Battle of Karbala, oil on canvas by Abbas Al-Musavi, Brooklyn Museum/Corbis

Pilgrims worshipping at the tomb of Hussein ibn Ali, Karbala[346]

The spread of Islam began by the sword and continues to this day between various factions of Islam and the rest of world.

---

346. https://www.britannica.com/event/Battle-of-Karbala

Chapter Thirty-Four

The First Followers of Jesus

Jesus entrusted His mission to His disciples. He told them at His ascension to wait in Jerusalem until they received the promised power from the Father (the Holy Spirit), after which they would be His witnesses and preach repentance for the forgiveness of sins to all nations. He showed them how to interpret the Old Testament. "And He opened their understanding, that they might comprehend the Scriptures. Then He said to them, 'Thus it is written, and thus it was necessary for the Christ to suffer and to rise from the dead the third day, and that repentance and remission of sins should be preached in His name to all nations, beginning at Jerusalem. And you are witnesses of these things. Behold, I send the Promise of My Father upon you; but tarry in the city of Jerusalem until you are endued with power from on high'" (Luke 24:45–49, NKJV).

Before leaving the world, Jesus had asked Peter, "Do you love me?" When Peter answered in the affirmative, Jesus said to him, "Feed My sheep" (John 21:16). How was Peter to feed the followers of Jesus? He was to teach and carry on the legacy of Jesus, spreading the message of redemption available to all through the death, burial, and resurrection of Jesus. But how could Peter or any human follow in the footsteps of Jesus, who was the Son of God Almighty appearing in the flesh?

Before He ascended to heaven, Jesus gave His disciples His last words on earth, His commission: "All authority has been given to Me in heaven and on earth. Go therefore and make disciples of all the nations, baptizing them in the name of the Father and the Son and the Holy Spirit, teaching them to observe all that I commanded you; and lo, I am with you always, even to the end of the age" (Matthew 28:18–20).

> But you shall receive power when the Holy Spirit has come upon you; and you shall be My witnesses both in Jerusalem, and Samaria, and even to the remotest part of the earth (Acts 1:8).

Jesus was not going to leave them powerless. He sent the Holy Spirit to empower them to speak the truth boldly. "And when the day of Pentecost had come, they were all together in one place. And suddenly there came from heaven a noise like a violent, rushing wind, and it filled the whole house where they were sitting. And there appeared to them tongues as of fire distributing themselves, and they rested on each one of them. And they were all filled with the Holy Spirit and began to speak with other tongues as the Holy Spirit was giving them utterance" (Acts 2:1–4). Word of this event spread; and the diaspora pilgrims in Jerusalem were amazed that Galileans, who were looked down upon as unsophisticated country people, were now speaking in multiple languages. Filled with the Holy Spirit of God, the disciples were able to witness and spread the gospel of Jesus into their world!

Handling Opposition

Jesus knew that this gospel message would generate opposition and division within families and even nations. Before His crucifixion, he warned the disciples,

> Do not think that I came to bring peace on earth. I did
> not come to bring peace but a sword, for I came to set
> a man against his father, and a daughter against her
> mother, and a daughter-in-law against her mother-in-
> law. And a man's foes shall be those of his own
> household. He who loves father or mother more than
> Me is not worthy of Me . . . (Matthew 10:34–36)

This would mark the division between those who accept Christ and those who don't. The sword that Jesus brought was not made of metal to cut flesh but was the gospel message, which requires a decision of each person and thus divides.

Jesus told a story about a farmer (Jesus) whose enemy (Satan) planted weeds in the farmer's wheat field (the earth). The farm hands (angels) wanted to know if they should rip out the weeds. The farmer told them to allow both to grow together in this age, until the time of the harvest (judgment). Matthew 13:24-30; 36-43 Jesus' followers were not given the task of weeding.

Jesus instructed His disciples to go to all the world and give people the good news, but He knew there would be many who would refuse to accept His message. Then what? He said, "And whoever does not receive you nor heed your words, as you go out of that house or that city, shake off the dust of your feet. Truly I say to you, it will be more tolerable for the land of Sodom and Gomorrah in the day of judgment than for that city" (Matthew 10:14–15). This rejection is the sword of division between believers and nonbelievers. But when Peter wanted to use his sword to defend Him, Jesus ordered him, saying, "Put your sword back into its place; for all those who take up the sword shall perish by the sword" (Matthew 26:52).

Finally, our real enemies are not other human beings, but demonic powers. The apostle Paul says in Ephesians 6:11–12, "Put on the whole armor of God, that you may be able to stand against the wiles of the devil. For we do not wrestle against flesh and blood, but against principalities, against powers, against the rulers of the darkness of this age, against spiritual *hosts* of wickedness in the heavenly *places.*"

Some New Testament writers refer to the word of Jesus as a sword that comes from His mouth and pierces. The sword of Jesus slices the spirit open. It penetrates the conscience. In Ephesians 6:17, Paul refers to the "Sword of the (Holy) Spirit, which is the word of God." Hebrews 4:12–13 states that the "word of God is living and powerful, and sharper than any two-edged sword, piercing even to the division of soul and spirit, and of joints and marrow, and is a discerner of the thoughts and intents of the heart. And there is no creature hidden from His sight, but all things are naked and open to the eyes of Him to whom we must give account" (NKJV). In Revelation 1:16, the apostle John had a vision of the risen Christ, and "out of His mouth went a sharp two-edged sword." Jesus will fight "with the sword of My mouth" those who promote false teaching (Revelation 2:16).

Without a weapon but empowered by the Holy Spirit, the followers of Jesus went out to tell the whole world about Jesus.

Stephen: The First Martyr

The first follower of Jesus to be martyred was Stephen, whose story is recorded in Acts 6 and 7. He was not one of the twelve apostles but was a follower of Jesus and one of the leaders of the first church in Jerusalem.

Stephen was described as a wise man filled with faith and the Holy Spirit. In public debates, he again and again emphasized that the Torah had predicted the coming of Jesus and His death and resurrection.

Losing the debates, his opponents persuaded some men to make false charges that they had heard him speaking blasphemies against Moses and God. The high priest asked if this were true, and Stephen addressed the people. He began, "Hear me brethren and fathers," and he gave them a detailed history of how the Jewish people had disobeyed God and rejected and killed the prophets that testified of the coming of Jesus. He said to them, "You men who are stiff-necked and uncircumcised in heart and ears are always resisting the Holy Spirit; you are doing just as your fathers did."

Now when they heard this, they began gnashing their teeth at him. But Stephen, full of the Holy Spirit, gazed intently into heaven and saw the glory of God and Jesus standing at the right hand of God; and he said, "Behold, I see the heavens opened up and the Son of Man standing at the right hand of God." But they cried out with a loud voice, and they rushed upon him with impulse. And when they had driven him out of the city, they began stoning him, and the witnesses laid aside their robes at the feet of a young man named Saul.[347]

And they went on stoning Stephen as he called upon the Lord and said, "Lord Jesus, receive my spirit." And falling on his knees, he cried out with a loud voice, "Lord, do not hold this sin against them." And having said this, he fell asleep.

The Story of Saul

Saul, who later became the apostle Paul and wrote half of the New Testament, was a zealous Jewish Pharisee who was well versed in the Scriptures and possessed a top-notch religious education. His conversion story is repeated in Acts 9, 22, and 26. He was very much against the followers of Jesus and wanted to destroy their religious movement, which he thought was a heresy. "At that time a great persecution arose against the church which was at Jerusalem; and they were all scattered throughout the regions of Judea and Samaria, except the apostles . . . As for Saul, he made havoc of the church, entering every house, and

---

[347.] Saul was a witness to the stoning but later became Paul, a believer in Christ who was later martyred.

dragging off men and women, committing *them* to prison" (Acts 8:1, 2, NKJV).

> Then Saul, still breathing threats and murder against the disciples of the Lord, went to the high priest and asked letters from him to the synagogues of Damascus, so that if he found any who were of the Way, whether men or women, he might bring them bound to Jerusalem. As he journeyed he came near Damascus, and suddenly a light shone around him from heaven. Then he fell to the ground, and heard a voice saying to him, "Saul, Saul, why are you persecuting Me?" And he said, "Who are You, Lord?" Then the Lord said, "I am Jesus, whom you are persecuting. It *is* hard for you to kick against the goads." So he, trembling and astonished, said, "Lord, what do You want me to do?" Then the Lord *said* to him, "Arise and go into the city, and you will be told what you must do." (Acts 9:1–6, NKJV)

Paul states what Jesus told him: "But rise and stand on your feet; for I have appeared to you for this purpose, to make you a minister and a witness both of the things which you have seen and of the things which I will yet reveal to you. I will deliver you from the *Jewish* people, as well as *from* the Gentiles, to whom I now send you, to open their eyes, *in order* to turn *them* from darkness to light, and *from* the power of Satan to God, that they may receive forgiveness of sins and an inheritance among those who are sanctified by faith in Me" (Acts 26:16–18, NKJV).

The men traveling with him could hear the voice but could see nothing. But Saul got up from the ground, his eyes blinded from the light, and proceeded with the men to Damascus. The Lord told a Christian named Ananias to go pray for Saul and heal his blindness. "Then Ananias answered, 'Lord, I have heard from many about this man, how much harm he has done to Your saints in Jerusalem. And here he has authority from the chief priests to bind all who call on Your name.' But the Lord said to him, 'Go, for he is a chosen vessel of Mine to bear My name before Gentiles, kings, and the children of Israel. For I will show him how many things he must suffer for My name's sake'" (Acts 9:13–16, NKJV).

Very soon after his healing, Saul began to preach in the synagogues that Jesus was the promised Messiah. "Then all who heard were amazed, and said, 'Is this not he who destroyed those who called on this name in Jerusalem, and has come here for that purpose, so that he might bring them bound to the chief priests?' But Saul increased all the more in strength, and confounded the Jews who dwelt in Damascus, proving that this *Jesus* is the Christ" (Acts 9:21–22, NKJV).

Paul had a dramatic change of heart. He preached Jesus to the Gentiles in Israel and to those in many parts of the world. He stood before kings and governors defending the Christian faith. He travelled extensively over the Roman Empire, planting churches wherever he went. Many New Testament books consist of his letters to some of those churches. He was beaten, imprisoned, and stoned for his faith; yet he wrote, "Who shall separate us from the love of Christ? Shall tribulation, or distress, or persecution or famine, or nakedness, or peril or sword? . . . but in all these things we are more than conquerors through Him who loved us . . . nothing shall be able to separate us from the love of God, which is in Christ Jesus our Lord" (Romans 8:35–39).

> From the Jews five times I received forty *stripes* minus one. Three times I was beaten with rods; once I was stoned; three times I was shipwrecked; a night and a day I have been in the deep; *in* journeys often, *in* perils of waters, *in* perils of robbers, *in* perils of *my own* countrymen, *in* perils of the Gentiles, *in* perils in the city, *in* perils in the wilderness, *in* perils in the sea, *in* perils among false brethren; in weariness and toil, in sleeplessness often, in hunger and thirst, in fastings often, in cold and nakedness—besides the other things,

what comes upon me daily: my deep concern for all the churches. Who is weak, and I am not weak? Who is made to stumble, and I do not burn *with indignation?* If I must boast, I will boast in the things which concern my infirmity. The God and Father of our Lord Jesus Christ, who is blessed forever, knows that I am not lying. In Damascus the governor, under Aretas the king, was guarding the city of the Damascenes with a garrison, desiring to arrest me; but I was let down in a basket through a window in the wall, and escaped from his hands. (2 Corinthians 11:24–33, NKJV)

Although I was formerly a blasphemer, a persecutor, and an insolent man; but I obtained mercy because I did *it* ignorantly in unbelief. And the grace of our Lord was exceedingly abundant, with faith and love which are in Christ Jesus. This *is* a faithful saying and worthy of all acceptance, that Christ Jesus came into the world to save sinners, of whom I am chief. However, for this reason I obtained mercy, that in me first Jesus Christ might show all longsuffering, as a pattern to those who are going to believe on Him for everlasting life. Now to the King eternal, immortal, invisible, to God who alone is wise, *be* honor and glory forever and ever. Amen. (1 Timothy 1:13–17)

Remind them to be subject to rulers and authorities, to obey, to be ready for every good work, to speak evil of no one, to be peaceable, gentle, showing all humility to all men. For we ourselves were also once foolish, disobedient, deceived, serving various lusts and pleasures, living in malice and envy, hateful and hating one another. But when the kindness and the love of God our Savior toward man appeared, not by works of righteousness which we have done, but according to His mercy He saved us, through the washing of regeneration and renewing of the Holy Spirit, whom He poured out on us abundantly through Jesus Christ our Savior. (Titus 3:1–6, NKJV)

But you have carefully followed my doctrine, manner of life, purpose, faith, longsuffering, love, perseverance, persecutions, afflictions, which happened to me at Antioch, at Iconium, at Lystra—what persecutions I endured. And out of *them* all the Lord delivered me. Yes, and all who desire to live godly in Christ Jesus will suffer persecution. But evil men and impostors will grow worse and worse, deceiving and being deceived. (2 Timothy 3:10–13, NKJV)

This was Paul's mission in life: to win people to the Lord Jesus by invitation using reasoning and persuasion. This is how the message of Jesus first spread in Paul's day and continues to attract the world's population today despite violent opposition and oppression in many places.

The Twelve Disciples

Jesus chose twelve disciples who followed Him during His life on earth. Other than Judas who betrayed Him and then killed himself, almost all the disciples were martyred except John, the son of Zebedee, and possibly James the Less.

Simon Peter, who denied Christ before the Crucifixion, became a bold and fearless leader of the first-century church and the first pope for Roman Catholics. After preaching his first sermon, three thousand people came to faith in Jesus (Acts 2:41). He spoke for the twelve disciples before the Sanhedrin (Acts 5:27–41). He healed people and raised a woman from the dead (Acts 3:1–10, 9:32–42). He was imprisoned by Herod and released by an angel (Acts 12). He helped the church make important decisions, such as not requiring Gentiles to become cultural Jews before they could become Christians (Acts 15). Peter evangelized in Asia Minor (northern Turkey) with his wife. He wrote two letters included in the New Testament. Some early church fathers said that the gospel of Mark is based on Peter's memoirs. It is thought that he was crucified upside down in Rome by Nero.[348]

Andrew was the brother of Peter. He preached in the Caucasus Mountains, Byzantium, and, finally, in western Greece. It was there that he met his death, where the governor had him tied to a cross with thick ropes. He continued to speak to passersby about Jesus for three days until he died.[349]

James, son of Zebedee, or James the Greater, was killed by Herod Agrippa with a sword (Acts 12:1–19). "The newly-appointed governor of Judea, Herod Agrippa, decided to ingratiate himself with the Romans by persecuting leaders of the new sect. After James was arrested and led to the place of execution, his unnamed accuser was moved by his courage. He not only repented and converted on the spot, but asked to be executed alongside James. The Roman executioners obliged, and both men were beheaded simultaneously."[350]

John, the son of Zebedee, was the youngest disciple. His mother, Salome, is believed to have been a sister of Jesus' mother, Mary. Shortly before the destruction of Jerusalem by the Romans in AD 70, he moved to Ephesus and became a pastor of a church there that had widespread influence. He was the last apostle to die and the only one known to die a peaceful death. He was exiled to Patmos by the Roman emperor Domitian, where he had visions and wrote the book of Revelation. He

---

348. http://www.biblepath.com/peter.html

349. http://www.biblepath.com/andrew.html

350. http://channel.nationalgeographic.com/killing-jesus/articles/how-did-the-apostles-die/

also wrote a gospel account and three letters to the churches, which are included in the New Testament. When he was released from exile, he returned to Ephesus, where "he had to be carried to the church in the arms of his disciples. At these meetings, he was accustomed to say no more than, *'Little children, love one another!'* After a time, the disciples wearied at always hearing the same words, asked, 'Master, why do you always say this?' 'It is the Lord's command,' was his reply. 'And if this alone be done, it is enough!'"[351]

Philip, the first of Jesus' disciples, became a missionary in Scythia (southern Russia). After twenty years there, he moved to Hierapolis, a city in Asia Minor famed for its hot springs. "While in Hierapolis, it is said that the wife of the Roman proconsul was healed by the apostles Philip and Bartholomew, that she became a Christian and that her husband ordered Philip and Bartholomew to be put to death by crucifixion. Philip was crucified, however, Bartholomew escaped martyrdom, when for some special reason, the magistrates caused him to be taken down from the cross and dismissed. Philip's tomb is still to be found in the Turkish city of Hierapolis."[352] Philip was in his eighties when he was martyred.

Bartholomew left Hierapolis and went to India, Armenia, and the south Caspian Sea. It is said that he always carried a copy of Matthew's gospel and was martyred in Azerbaijan.[353]

Thomas preached the gospel in Babylon, Persia, India, and perhaps as far as China. He was killed by a spear in Madras, India, and was said to be fearless.[354]

---

[351] http://www.biblepath.com/john1.html
[352] http://www.biblepath.com/philip.html
[353] http://www.biblepath.com/bartholomew.html
[354] http://www.biblepath.com/thomas.html

Matthew stayed in the Holy Land for fifteen years and preached to the Jewish community.[355] He wrote the important gospel of Matthew, which was used extensively by the early church as the teaching manual of Jesus. Then he went to Persia and possibly Ethiopia. "According to legend, the former tax collector turned missionary was martyred in Ethiopia, where he was stabbed in the back by an swordsman sent by King Hertacus, after he criticized the king's morals."[356]

James, son of Alphaeus, was called James the Less (to distinguish him from James, the son of Zebedee). Nothing specific is known about him.[357] He is not to be confused with James the half brother of Jesus, who was a leader in the Jerusalem church and wrote the book of James.

Thaddaeus, Lebbaeus, Judas, or Jude preached near the Caspian Sea, church tradition holds, and was crucified in Edessa.[358]

Simon the Canaanite, the Zealot, may have been part of a political party that carried out assassinations before following Jesus. "Simon preached in Mauritania on the west coast of Africa, and then went to England, where he was crucified in 74 AD."[359]

The disciples gave their lives so that even their enemies could hear the good news of Jesus.

[355] https://en.wikipedia.org/wiki/Matthew_the_Apostle
[356] http://channel.nationalgeographic.com/killing-jesus/articles/how-did-the-apostles-die/
[357] https://www.thoughtco.com/james-the-less-obscure-apostle-701076
[358] http://www.biblepath.com/jude.html
[359] http://channel.nationalgeographic.com/killing-jesus/articles/how-did-the-apostles-die/

Epilogue

Modern-Day Foundation of Islamism

Growing up in Egypt, many of my neighbors and friends were Muslims. They were friendly, kind, and loyal people. We respected one another's customs and beliefs and often shared in our religious celebrations. In 1962, at age thirty, I left Egypt and came to the USA to start a new life. Egypt had been quite a cosmopolitan country, graciously housing people from many nationalities, many of them successful businesspeople. Europeans, Greeks, Armenians, and Jews lived in Egypt and had their own churches, synagogues, schools, and clubs. They were respected and loved among the Egyptian people. However, in 1952, Gamal Abdel Nasser overturned Egypt from a monarchy to a nationalistic military government with socialist tendencies. The government sequestrated[360] many successful businesses, and life in Egypt changed for all the minorities as well as for many wealthy Egyptians. It was at this time that my family came to the United States as political refugees.

[360.] "Sequestration (in law) is the act of removing, separating, or seizing anything from the possession of its owner under process of law for the benefit of creditors or the state" (*Wikipedia*).

Egypt was changing rapidly when the new president, Nasser, introduced a motto to the working class of Egypt, saying, "Lift up your head, brother. The era of Imperialism is gone." In spite of the fact that this change was not good for my family, I thought in some ways it was fair.

This change, however, was not the only change that was happening. Other leaders were trying to change the world through Islam. In Egypt, Hassan Al-Banna and Sayyid Qutb were also impacting Egypt, promoting a revolution that was different from that of Gamal Abdel Nasser's.

Egypt had been influenced by Western civilization due to colonialism. Nasser wanted social reform, claiming Egypt for the Egyptians without foreign Western rule. President Nasser of Egypt was a moderate Muslim, and his mission was not that of a radical Islamist,[361] nor was his goal that of an "Islamic state."[362]

[361.] A Muslim who holds strictly to the teachings of Muhammad from the Qur'an and Hadith

[362.] A state that follows Islamic law (Sharia)

Sayyid Abul A'la Maududi, Hassan Al-Banna, and Sayyid Qutb

Both Hassan Al-Banna and Sayyid Qutb were born in 1906 and were possibly influenced by Abul A'la Maududi's writings. Maududi was a Pakistani Islamist philosopher, journalist, and imam, born in India in 1903. He wanted to bring Islam back to the teachings of Muhammad through the Qur'an and the Hadith. Maududi knew that what the ulama (religious leaders of Islam) considered to be the teaching of Islam was not in line with the Qur'an but was watered down. He complained that not more than 0.001 percent of Muslims knew what Islam actually was.[363]

[364] **Sayyid Abul A'la Maududi**
Born September 25, 1903, in
Hyderabad, India
Died September 22, 1979, in
Buffalo, New York

Hassan Al-Banna: Founder of the Muslim Brotherhood

Hassan Al-Banna founded the Muslim Brotherhood in the city of Ismailia, Egypt, in March 1928. Like Maududi, Al-Banna believed that the Qur'an and Sunnah[365] (Islamic law and tradition) constitute a perfect way of life and social and political organization that God has set out for man. Islamic governments must be based on this system and eventually unified in a caliphate. He organized the Muslim Brotherhood,

---

[363.] https://en.wikipedia.org/wiki/Abul_A%27la_Maududi
[364.] http://en.wikipedia.org/wiki/File:Abul_ala_maududi.jpg
[365.] http://www.oxfordislamicstudies.com/article/opr/t243/e332. Sunnah is the body of customs and beliefs that make up a tradition.

348

whose goal, according to Al-Banna, was to drive out British colonialism and other Western influences and reclaim Islam's manifest destiny—an empire stretching from Spain to Indonesia.[366] The brotherhood preaches that Islam will bring the eradication of poverty, corruption, and sinful behavior, replacing it with social justice and political freedom to the extent allowed by the laws of Islam.[367]

On the Brothers' green logo is emblazoned a Qur'an, two swords, and the words "and prepare," which is taken from Qur'an sura 8 ("The Spoils of War").

Society of the Muslim Brothers[368]

جماعة الإخوان المسلمين

The Muslim Brotherhood's frequently used slogan is "Islam is the Solution." Their motto is "God is our objective, the prophet is our leader. The Qur'an is our law. Jihad is our way. Dying in the way of Allah is our highest hope."

Al-Banna was assassinated by Egyptian secret police in 1949. His son-in-law emerged as a major leader of the Muslim Brotherhood in the 1950s.[369]

> The *Arabic-language* website [of the Muslim Brotherhood] commemorated the anniversary of the death of their leader Hassan-al-Banna and repeated his

---

[366] Davidson, Lawrence, Islamic Fundamentalism, Greenwood Press, Westport, Connecticut, (1988) ISBN 0-313-29978, pp. 97–98.

[367] "Political freedom" here means the ability to vote for one Islamic candidate versus another Islamic candidate. Social tradition is very defined (for example, extending to which foot you step in the bathroom first, whether you can shake hands with the opposite sex or a non-Muslim with your skin touching, etc.).

[368] https://en.wikipedia.org/wiki/File:Muslim_Brotherhood_Logo.png

[369] John L. Esposito, ed., 2014. Banna, Hassan, *The Oxford Dictionary of Islam*, Oxford: Oxford University Press.

words calling for the teachings of Islam to spread all over the world, to raise the "flag of Jihad," taking their land, "regaining their glory," "including diaspora Muslims," demanding an Islamic State and a Muslim government, a Muslim people, a Muslim house, and Muslim individuals calling for brotherhood between Muslims. The Muslim Brotherhood commemorated Sayyid Qutb and linked to an Arabic-language Al Jazeera video on him.[370]

Sheikh Hassan Ahmed Abdel Rahman Muhammed al-Banna
Born October 14, 1906, in Mahmoudiyah, Egypt
Died February 12, 1949, in Cairo, Egypt
[371]

Sayyid Qutb

Another well-known Islamist author and thinker is Sayyid Qutb. He was born in Upper Egypt in 1906 in a devout Muslim home. He was the eldest of six children. By the age of ten, he had memorized the Qur'an. When he had finished his schooling in his village at the age of thirteen, he went to Cairo and studied at Dar al-Ulum (House of Knowledge) secondary school. During this stage, he was influenced by the Westernizing tendencies prevalent in the school and among Egyptian intellectuals. After graduating from Cairo University, he became a professor, then an inspector of schools. Qutb was impressed with the work of the Muslim Brotherhood, and perhaps to avoid the birth of another radical Islamist, he was sent to the United States. In 1949, he attended Colorado State Teachers College in Greeley, Colorado, now the University of Northern Colorado. His experience in the United States was negative. "He found Western society hopelessly materialistic, corrupt, morally loose, and ridden with injustice."[372] He cut short his stay in the United States when he learned of the death of Hassan Al-Banna and returned to work for the Muslim Brotherhood. Qutb wrote many books, but his most famous and widely read is *Milestones*, which he wrote in prison. It was an immediate best seller and is said to have been published in close to two thousand editions.[373] In *Milestones*, Qutb "lays out a plan and makes a call to action to re-create the Muslim world on strictly Quranic grounds."[374] His other very popular thirty-volume work, where he explains the Qur'an, is *In the Shade of the Qur'an*.

Qutb was imprisoned twice by Gamal Abdel Nasser before he was hanged in 1966. His book *Milestones* was used in his trial as a testimony against him.

Qutb was described by his Arab biographer as "the most famous personality of the Muslim world in the second half of the century . . . Qutb was the most influential advocate in modern times of Jihad, or Islamic holy war, and the chief developer of doctrines that legitimize violent Muslim resistance to regimes that claim to be Muslim, but whose implementation of Islamic precepts is judged to be imperfect . . ."[375]

---

[372] Sayyid Qutb. Encyclopedia.com/people/philosophy-and religious /Islam. Encyclopedia of World Biography, copyright 2004, the Gale Group Inc.

[373] http://www.worldpress.org/europe/0102dagens.htm, review of Lisbeth Lindeborg, *Dagens Nyheter* (liberal), Stockholm, Sweden, October 25, 2001.

[374] https://en.wikipedia.org/wiki/Milestones_(book)

[375] https://www.theguardian.com/world/2001/nov/01/afghanistan.terrorism3,"Is this the man who inspired Bin Laden?" Robert Irwin, *Guardian*, November 1, 2001.

Sayyid Qutb behind bars during his trial in Egypt on charges he was helping an effort to overthrow the government. He was hanged in 1966.[376]

Why I Wrote This Book

Having my background shaped by two cultures, I pondered and researched a lot to reconcile the contradiction between the peaceful Muslim people I grew up with and the atrocities committed in the name of Islam. After searching, I have reached an answer about the subject that satisfies me and can help my fellow Americans. I love both my country of birth and the country that gave me the freedom to be who I choose to be and freely express my views. I love America and the American people, and my heart goes out to them because I believe when it comes to the Middle East, they are uninformed and confused. They hear our presidents say, "Islam is a religion of peace," but they really do not understand the motivation for 9/11. They fail to understand the reasons for hatred expressed by repeated terror in the United States, multiplied many times over in other countries.

I believe that Muslims, for the most part, are peaceful, good people. They follow the example of their peaceful parents, and if they know them, they only quote the Qur'an verses that speak kindly of Christians and Jews. Most do not know much about the sacred writings of their religion, nor do they spend the time learning them. Many do not have access to the full teaching because of the language barrier of Arabic. Most Muslims have been raised in an Islam through a cultural understanding and have not learned nor embraced the stark teachings and commands in their holy texts. On the other hand, the radical Muslims, or Islamists, are intent on embracing the teachings and example of Muhammad in every detail—including the desire for local societal and, ultimately, worldwide domination—and are willing to murder and commit terrorism to move toward that goal. These are the students of Al-Banna, Qutb, Maududi, and others, who have now formed new generations of jihadists who base their lives on Sharia, which does not recognize other governmental systems. They will not stop until they bring back the glory days of Islam and Muhammad. Here are some examples:

1. al-Qaeda: The Base
2. Boko Haram: Western Education is Forbidden
3. ISIS: Islamic State of Iraq and Syria
4. Taliban: Students
5. al-Nusra: The Victor
6. al-Aqsa Martyrs Brigade: The Mosque Martyrs Brigade
7. Al-Shabaab: The Youth
8. Harkat-ul-Mujahideen: The Movement of the Fighters (Jihadists)
9. Quds Force: Extraterritorial Iran Revolutionary Guards
10. Lashkar-e-Islam: Warriors of Islam
11. Jamaat-e-Islami: The Ranks of Islam
12. Jema'ah Islamiyah: Islamic Congregation
13. Jamaiat-e Islami: Islamic Society
14. Haqqani Network: Righteous Network
15. Hezbollah: Party of God

16. Hamas: Zeal
17. al-Ikhwan al-Muslimun: The Muslim Brotherhood

The Muslim Brotherhood's 1991 strategic goals for North America include:[377]

> Enablement of Islam in North America, meaning: establishing an effective and a stable Islamic Movement led by the Muslim Brotherhood which adopts Muslims' causes domestically and globally, and which works to expand the observant Muslim base, aims at unifying and directing Muslims' efforts, presents Islam as a civilization alternative, and supports the global Islamic State wherever it is.

They promote the concept of settlement as cultural jihad, a movement in stages, in which Islam becomes an entrenched part of the homeland it lives in—settlement, establishment, stability, enablement, and rooting.

> The process of settlement is a "Civilization-Jihadist Process" with all [that] the word means. The Ikhwan [Muslim Brotherhood] must understand that their work in America is a kind of grand jihad in eliminating and destroying the Western civilization from within and "sabotaging" its miserable house by their hands and the hands of the believers . . .

> [W]e must possess a mastery of the art of "coalitions," the art of "absorption" and the principles of "cooperation."

[377.] https://clarionproject.org/muslim_brotherhood_explanatory_memorandum/

'Four-Finger Salute' Shows Solidarity With Egypt's Muslim Brotherhood
August 24, 2013 13:30 GMT

Mustafa Varank @varank

Prime Minister Erdoğan shows his support to #**Egypt** #**Anticoup** people by making the resistance sing of #**R4BIA**

Appendix: Prophecies of Jesus Fulfilled
Source: http://christianity.about.com/od/biblefactsandlists/a/Prophecies-Jesus.htm

Although this list is not exhaustive, you'll find 44 messianic predictions clearly fulfilled in Jesus Christ, along with supporting references from the Old and New Testament.

	Prophecies About Jesus	Old Testament Scripture	New Testament Fulfillment
1	Messiah would be born of a woman.	Genesis 3:15	Matthew 1:20 Galatians 4:4
2	Messiah would be born in Bethlehem.	Micah 5:2	Matthew 2:1 Luke 2:4–6
3	Messiah would be born of a virgin.	Isaiah 7:14	Matthew 1:22–23 Luke 1:26–31
4	Messiah would come from the line of Abraham.	Genesis 12:3 Genesis 22:18	Matthew 1:1 Romans 9:5
5	Messiah would be a descendant of Isaac.	Genesis 17:19 Genesis 21:12	Luke 3:34
6	Messiah would be a descendant of Jacob.	Numbers 24:17	Matthew 1:2
7	Messiah would come from the tribe of Judah.	Genesis 49:10	Luke 3:33 Hebrews 7:14
8	Messiah would be heir to King David's throne.	2 Samuel 7:12–13 Isaiah 9:7	Luke 1:32–33 Romans 1:3
9	Messiah's throne will be anointed and eternal.	Psalm 45:6–7 Daniel 2:44	Luke 1:33 Hebrews 1:8–12
10	Messiah would be called Immanuel.	Isaiah 7:14	Matthew 1:23
11	Messiah would spend a season in Egypt.	Hosea 11:1	Matthew 2:14–15
12	A massacre of children would happen at Messiah's birthplace.	Jeremiah 31:15	Matthew 2:16–18
13	A messenger would prepare the way for Messiah	Isaiah 40:3–5	Luke 3:3–6
14	Messiah would be rejected by his own people.	Psalm 69:8 Isaiah 53:3	John 1:11 John 7:5

15	Messiah would be a prophet.	Deuteronomy 18:15	Acts 3:20–22
16	Messiah would be preceded by Elijah.	Malachi 4:5–6	Matthew 11:13–14
17	Messiah would be declared the Son of God.	Psalm 2:7	Matthew 3:16–17
18	Messiah would be called a Nazarene.	Isaiah 11:1	Matthew 2:23
19	Messiah would bring light to Galilee.	Isaiah 9:1–2	Matthew 4:13–16
20	Messiah would speak in parables.	Psalm 78:2–4 Isaiah 6:9–10	Matthew 13:10–15, 34–35
21	Messiah would be sent to heal the brokenhearted.	Isaiah 61:1–2	Luke 4:18–19
22	Messiah would be a priest after the order of Melchizedek.	Psalm 110:4	Hebrews 5:5–6
23	Messiah would be called King.	Psalm 2:6 Zechariah 9:9	Matthew 27:37 Mark 11:7–11
24	Messiah would be praised by little children.	Psalm 8:2	Matthew 21:16
25	Messiah would be betrayed.	Psalm 41:9 Zechariah 11:12–13	Luke 22:47–48 Matthew 26:14–16
26	Messiah's price money would be used to buy a potter's field.	Zechariah 11:12–13	Matthew 27:9–10
27	Messiah would be falsely accused.	Psalm 35:11	Mark 14:57–58
28	Messiah would be silent before his accusers.	Isaiah 53:7	Mark 15:4–5
29	Messiah would be spat upon and struck.	Isaiah 50:6	Matthew 26:67
30	Messiah would be hated without cause.	Psalm 35:19 Psalm 69:4	John 15:24–25
31	Messiah would be crucified with criminals.	Isaiah 53:12	Matthew 27:38 Mark 15:27–28
32	Messiah would be given vinegar to drink.	Psalm 69:21	Matthew 27:34 John 19:28–30
33	Messiah's hands and feet would be pierced.	Psalm 22:16 Zechariah 12:10	John 20:25–27

34	Messiah would be mocked and ridiculed.	Psalm 22:7–8	Luke 23:35
35	Soldiers would gamble for Messiah's garments.	Psalm 22:18	Luke 23:34 Matthew 27:35–36
36	Messiah's bones would not be broken.	Exodus 12:46 Psalm 34:20	John 19:33–36
37	Messiah would be forsaken by God.	Psalm 22:1	Matthew 27:46
38	Messiah would pray for his enemies.	Psalm 109:4	Luke 23:34
39	Soldiers would pierce Messiah's side.	Zechariah 12:10	John 19:34
40	Messiah would be buried with the rich.	Isaiah 53:9	Matthew 27:57–60
41	Messiah would resurrect from the dead.	Psalm 16:10 Psalm 49:15	Matthew 28:2–7 Acts 2:22–32
42	Messiah would ascend to heaven.	Psalm 24:7–10	Mark 16:19 Luke 24:51
43	Messiah would be seated at God's right hand.	Psalm 68:18 Psalm 110:1	Mark 16:19 Matthew 22:44
44	Messiah would be a sacrifice for sin.	Isaiah 53:5–12	Romans 5:6–8

(Sources: *100 Prophecies Fulfilled by Jesus: Messianic Prophecies Made Before the Birth of Christ* by Rose Publishing; *Book of Bible Lists* by H.L. Willmington; NKJV Study Bible; Life Application Study Bible.)